P9-DEJ-652

SMALL STOCKS

BIG PROFITS

Gerald Perritt on Investing in Small Companies

Gerald W. Perritt

Dearborn
Financial Publishing, Inc.

While a great deal of care has been taken to provide accurate and current information, the ideas, suggestions, general principles and conclusions presented in this text are subject to local, state and federal laws and regulations, court cases and any revisions of same. The reader is thus urged to consult legal counsel regarding any points of law—this publication should not be used as a substitute for competent legal advice.

Publisher: Kathleen A. Welton
Associate Editor: Karen A. Christensen
Editorial Assistant: Kristen G. Landreth
Interior Design: Black Dot Graphics
Cover Design: The Publishing Services Group

Published by Dearborn Financial Publishing, Inc.

Printed in the United States of America

93 94 95 10 9 8 7 6 5 4 3 2 1

Library of Congress Cataloging-in-Publication Data

Perritt, Gerald W.
    Small stocks big profits : Gerald Perritt on investing in small companies / Gerald W. Perritt.
        p.   cm.
    Includes bibliographical references and index.
    ISBN 0-79310-635-4
    1. Stocks. 2. Investments. 3. Small business—United States—Finance. 4. Portfolio management. I. Title.
HG4751.P46   1993
332.63'22—dc20   93-18641
                                                      CIP

In memory of Jean Perritt Griggs.
She will be missed but not forgotten.

ACKNOWLEDGMENTS

This was no small effort. Countless hours were spent collecting financial statistics, combing libraries for the latest published academic research, sorting out facts from fiction, and eventually putting pen to paper. I couldn't have completed this task without the assistance of a dedicated staff of analysts who research the small stocks that appear in my investment advisory newsletter, *Investment Horizons*. Michael Corbett, senior analyst, not only assisted in data collection and analyses, but he was also an ever-present sounding board for my ideas. Carol McHugh and Allison Hearst also supplied their expertise in obtaining needed facts. Kathy Welton, my editor, supplied sufficient prodding to turn an idea into reality. To these people, my colleagues and friends, I will forever owe a debt of gratitude.

Gerald W. Perritt
Chicago, Illinois

PREFACE

Investors can be neatly divided into two distinct groups—those who are successful and those who are not. Those who are not repeatedly blame others for their failure. I wish I had a dollar for every time I've heard a disgruntled investor say that he was done in by a mysterious group known as "they" (as in "they" rigged the market against me).

Interestingly, the stock market is in fact "rigged." However, it is rigged in an individual investor's favor. For example, the Standard & Poor's 500 Index (a hypothetical portfolio of 500 blue-chip stocks) has returned an average of 12.4 percent per year since 1926. In other words, investors who held a diversified portfolio of stocks, and watched their trading costs, could have earned double-digit returns on their investments easily without being privy to "inside information" or some other stock market trading secret. With a return of 12 percent per year, you can double your investment nest egg about every six years without a lot of work. Thus, the investment game is not only easy to play; it's easy to win as well. That is, if you can stay in the game over the long run.

In the world of financial markets, investment return is the reward that investors get for taking investment risks. The greater the risks you take, the greater are the potential returns. However, the financial markets also tend to punish the foolhardy. Take extreme risks and you *may* earn extraordinary rewards. However, you also run the risk of losing most if not all of your investment capital. If you want to get the odds of investment success on your side, you must stay in the game over the long run. This means taking only necessary risks and avoiding those that you won't get paid for taking. It also requires that you be able to assess the risk and potential return of each alternative under consideration before taking the plunge.

In the pages that follow, I describe the nature of investment risk and investment return. I show you how to assess investment risk, how to reduce it without decreasing return potential, and how to increase your long-run returns. These are not deep, dark secrets known to only a select few investors. They are tried and true methods of achieving investment success. These relatively few rules are simple to understand, easy to apply, and require little in the way of time or energy. The profits waiting for you in the small-firm segment of the market, for example, can be obtained by all individuals who are willing to assume a little more risk, have the patience to allow their investments to grow in value, and are willing to monitor their investments a few hours a month. These are investments your broker won't tell you about because brokerage firm analysts spend all of their time researching large, blue-chip stocks. You must ferret out these little gems yourself, and I show you exactly how and where to find them.

These stocks, which have provided investors with an average annual return exceeding 17 percent for more than six decades, generally contain no more risk than blue-chip stocks that return far less. Earn 15 to 17 percent per year by investing in small firm stocks and you will double your money in four to five years. Invest $15,000 at these rates of return and you will amass more than $1 million 30 years later. For the record, I am not talking about speculative initial public offerings, penny stocks, or illiquid private placements. These are nationally traded stocks of companies that have proven records of success. They are the Wal-Marts, Home Depots, and Microsofts of the future. Find and invest in these small firm stocks today and earn big profits over your investment lifetime.

CONTENTS

and Investment Risk.   Monitoring Your Investment Holding
Period.   The Overall Investment Portfolio: Case Studies.

The Benefits of Mutual Fund Investing.   The Small Firm
Effect Revisited.   Small Firm Returns: A Rationale.   The
Best Way to Invest in Small Firm Stocks.   Mutual Funds
and the Small Firm Effect.   Mutual Fund Performance
and Market Capitalization.   Small Firm Mutual Fund
Selection.   Small-Cap Funds.   Well-Positioned Small-Cap
Mutual Funds.

Hit 'Em Where They Ain't.   The Crash of 1987: Some
Lessons to Be Learned.   Small Firm Stocks after the
Fall.   Is Conventional Wisdom Still Applicable?   Winning
Made Easy.

CHAPTER 1

SMALL-CAPS: THE DARLINGS OF THE DECADE

Do you want to make a million dollars investing in the stock market? All it takes is a *little* knowledge and a *lot* of time. For example, invest $10,000 today, earn a 12 percent compound annual return, maintain that average return for 49 years and your initial investment will grow to $1,042,000. Invest $10,000 every year, earn an average of 12 percent annually, and 22 years later you will have amassed a total of $1,036,000. While some investors may find it difficult to ante up $10,000 every year, it may come as a surprise to learn that it is relatively easy to earn an average of 12 percent per year on your investment capital. For example, the Standard & Poor's 500 Index of large-cap, blue-chip stocks has returned 11.8 percent per year since the beginning of 1940. Thus, all you need do is invest $10,000 in a highly diversified portfolio of large-cap stocks, hold that portfolio for 49 years, and you will most likely earn your first million dollars.

If you want to amass your fortune in a shorter period of time, you will have to earn a higher rate of return on your investments. For example, invest $10,000 today, earn 16 percent compounded annually and 31 years later your nest egg will have grown a couple of thousand dollars short of $1 million. Invest $10,000 each year, earn 16 percent, and it will take you 19 years to obtain $1,144,000.

Is it possible to earn 16 percent per year by investing in stocks? Yes, if you know the secret. The secret is to invest in small-cap growth stocks. Between 1940 and 1992, small-cap stocks have returned an average of 15.7 percent per year. Pick the right small-cap stocks and you can easily boost the average annual return of your portfolio above 16 percent. Furthermore, for reasons I will outline shortly, small-cap stocks appear to be poised for a lengthy period of overperformance. In fact, it wouldn't surprise me one bit if small-caps returned an average of more than 25 percent per year for the remainder of the decade. Cycles of exceptional small-cap stock performance have occurred with a great deal of frequency during the last half-century. Between 1942 and 1950 small-caps returned an average of 29.9 percent compounded annually. They returned an average of 24.7 percent per year between 1961 and 1968, and between 1975 and 1986 they returned an average of 27.8 percent per year.

Of course, small-cap stocks have had their off years as well. During 1987 their prices declined an average of 9.3 percent and during 1990 their prices tumbled more than 21 percent. In fact, small-cap stocks have, at times, slumped into lengthy cycles of underperformance. Between 1984 and 1990, for example, small-cap stocks returned an average of 2.6 percent per year. During that period, even Treasury bill investors fared better than small-cap investors. However, one of the reasons I believe that small-cap stocks will be stellar performers during the 1990s is the fact that they performed so poorly during the latter half of the 1980s.

WHAT IS A SMALL-CAP STOCK?

Let me first tell you what small-cap stocks are not. They are not unseasoned and highly speculative initial public offerings (IPOs). They are not penny stocks (i.e., those selling below $5 per share). They are not companies with grandiose schemes to extract gold from salt water, mine uranium on the moon, or cure the common cold. The small-caps that I am referring to are companies that provide needed products and services and have attained solid revenue and earnings growth-track records. These are the stocks of companies that are easy to find once you know where to look for them. Moreover, they are the stocks of growth companies that large institutional investors would like to own but can't. They are stocks that are generally reserved for individual investors.

Small-caps are companies with an equity market value below $120 million. Multiply the shares outstanding by the current share price and if the product is less than $120 million, you have found a candidate for your small-cap portfolio. Screen out those companies that haven't demonstrated that they can grow at an above-average rate, those with excessive amounts of debt on their balance sheets, those that haven't been around for three or more years, and those with stocks selling at astronomical price-earnings ratios, and you will have a list of stocks that will provide exceptional returns over the long run.

Of course, each and every one of these stocks will not be an exceptional performer. However, if you maintain a properly diversified portfolio, the losers will be overshadowed by those that perform exceptionally well. In fact, you can count on getting about 80 percent of your long-run return from only 20 percent of the stocks you own. If you hold a diversified portfolio, arithmetic will be on your side. For example, invest in the stocks of two companies. Suppose that one withers and dies, wiping out your entire investment, while the other grows and prospers and the value of your initial investment triples. Despite the one setback, this portfolio will have returned an average of 50 percent. Set your screens properly, invest in 30 to 40 stocks, and you will improve the odds that your portfolio will contain the big winners that will turn mediocre performance into exceptional long-run returns.

THE CASE FOR SMALL-CAPS IN THE 1990s

Although small-cap stocks delivered solid returns during 1991 and 1992, individuals who have regularly invested in this segment of the stock market know the disappointment that small-cap investments can bring. For example, between mid-1983 and the end of 1990, small-cap stocks delivered a dismal 2.6 percent compound annual rate of return. During that same period, the large-cap dominated Standard & Poor's 500 Index returned a whopping 15.6 percent per year.

During the last half-century, however, small-cap stocks have performed best. (See Table 1-1.) A $1,000 investment in small-cap stocks made at the beginning of 1940 would have been worth a whopping $1.96 million by the end of 1991. That's more than six times the value of an equivalent investment made in a portfolio of the stocks of large, well-known companies. In fact, small-cap stocks have been delivering greater returns than anticipated for nearly a century. These extra returns have become known in academic circles as "the small firm effect." According to efficient market theory, investment returns are linked to investment risk and nothing else. If you want to earn a greater rate of return in an efficient market, you must assume additional investment risk. However, this has not been true for small firm stocks. Although the stocks of small firms are riskier than those of large, blue-chip companies, they have been consistently providing larger returns than can be explained by their increased risk. In other words, Wall Street has been serving up a free lunch to small-cap investors for a long time.

Even the authors of the efficient market theory admit that pockets of inefficiencies can exist in the stock market at times. These pockets contain inappropriately priced stocks that represent investment bargains. However, once these pockets of inefficiency are discovered by a large number of investors, according to efficient market theory, their prices will adjust to the point at which future returns will be solely related to their risk (i.e., their non–risk related returns will fall to near zero). Thus, once discovered, bargain-priced stocks become fully priced.

TABLE 1–1
Investment Returns: 1940–1991

Asset Category	Compound Annual Return	Value of $1,000
Small-Cap Stocks	15.7%	$1,965,000
Large-Cap Stocks	11.8	330,300
Corporate Bonds	5.1	13,300
Government Bonds	4.8	11,400
Treasury Bills	4.3	8,900

This is precisely the argument that has been used to sound the death knell of the small firm effect. Efficient market theorists point to the dramatic increase in the popularity of small-cap investing that followed the publication of academic research on small firm stocks in the late 1970s and early 1980s. Less than a dozen years ago, for example, there were only a handful of mutual funds that invested exclusively in small-cap stocks. Today, funds that claim to focus on the small firm sector of the market number more than a hundred. Thus, efficient market theorists were not surprised when small-cap stocks failed to provide excess returns during most of the decade of the 1980s. This was as it was supposed to be—at least according to their theory.

On the other hand, there are solid reasons to believe that the small firm effect is far from dead. First, small-caps have once again begun to deliver exceptional returns. In 1991, they returned 44.5 percent (versus 30.5 percent for large-caps) and during 1992, they tacked on another 16.9 percent return while large-caps barely topped 7.5 percent. Second, the "popularity" argument holds very little water. While a large number of institutional investors claim to invest in small-cap stocks, the truth is that most of these investors have opted for mid-cap rather than small-cap stocks because of the inordinately high trading costs that usually accompany the investment of a large amount of capital in the thinly traded stocks of tiny companies. The domain of small-cap stocks continues to be inhabited primarily by individual investors. If anything, institutional investors have made mid-cap stocks more efficiently priced rather than small-caps.

Third, and more important, the conditions that existed in the stock market during the 1980s have changed dramatically. During that decade, corporate America was engaged in widespread restructuring, which accompanied a rash of leveraged buyouts. (In a leveraged buyout, in order to acquire a company investors borrow capital using the company's assets as collateral for the loan.) Rampant inflation during the 1970s raised the cost of everything, including the cost of doing business. However, large-cap stocks appreciated very little during that decade. Thus, it became much cheaper to buy an existing company during the 1980s than to start one from the ground up. In other words, on the basis of the market value of assets, large-cap stocks were cheap. Pool operators rushed to cash in on a good thing, and the prices of large-cap stocks (which could deliver the largest profits) headed skyward. As a result, large-cap stocks returned an above-average 17.5 percent annual rate of return during the past decade. With inflation now under control and stock prices significantly higher than they were a decade ago, leveraged buyout activity has waned and large-cap stock returns should return to approximately their historical average.

Fourth, small-cap stocks delivered exceptional returns during each year from 1975 through 1983. During that period, small-caps returned 35.3 percent compounded annually, or a total of 1,420 percent, versus a total of 272 percent for large-cap stocks. As a result, small-cap stocks were selling at very high price-earnings ratios relative to their larger cousins. In short, the exceptional small-cap performance cycle had taken small-cap stock prices well into overvalued territory and they began to lose their attractiveness to many investors. It then took several years for small-cap investment fundamentals (i.e., revenues, earnings, and asset values) to catch up with the prices these stocks were commanding.

Fifth, small-cap stocks tend to perform best during the early stages of an economic recovery for two reasons. 1. They tend to be punished during an economic recession. During 1973–74, for example, small-cap stock prices tumbled by slightly more than 44 percent. During the depths of the most recent economic recession, small-cap stocks declined an average of nearly 22 percent. When the economic cycle begins to turn upward, small-cap stock prices rebound sharply merely because they have been severely depressed a year or two earlier. 2. Small firms can be more responsive to economic change than can large firms. During an economic downturn, small firms can streamline their operations much faster than can large firms. When an economic recovery begins, the profits of small firms expand more sharply than those of large companies, and investors eagerly bid up the prices of their stocks.

Finally, small-cap stock returns tend to run in cycles that can last for several years. When they overperform or underperform large-cap stocks, they tend to do so for several years in succession. Cycles of small-cap overperformance have lasted from 5 to 11 years during the last six decades. The last overperformance cycle (1975–1983) persisted for 9 years and the overperformance cycle prior to that (1958–1968) continued for 11 years. The average duration of the small-cap overperformance cycles that have appeared since 1926 is about 8.5 years.

Table 1-2 illustrates the small-cap overperformance cycles that have existed since 1926. During these four cycles, small-cap stocks maintained an average *return advantage* over large-cap stocks of nearly 28 percent per year. Each of these overperformance cycles began after small-cap stocks had taken a severe beating, usually during the midst of an economic downturn. The current, two-year, small-cap overperformance period has also followed on the heels of an economic recession and a severe small-cap bear market. Thus, recent small-cap return behavior has in its causes great similarities to previous overperformance cycles.

Extended small-cap overperformance cycles usually begin when small-cap stocks sell at price-earnings ratio parity (in terms of year-ahead earnings) to the Standard & Poor's 500 Index. This is illustrated in the accompanying chart (Figure 1-1). The overperformance cycles in the 1960s and 1970s began when the price-earnings multiple of small-cap stocks divided by the price-earnings multiple of the Standard & Poor's Index

TABLE 1–2
Small-Cap Stock Overperformance Cycles

Period	Duration	Value of $1,000 Small	Large	Annual Return Small	Large	Small-Cap Advantage
1932–36	5 Years	$ 558,300	$ 175,600	45.8%	22.5%	37.0%
1938–45	8	735,600	157,800	30.4	12.6	27.0
1958–68	11	984,600	272,000	24.4	12.7	21.0
1975–83	9	1,520,000	372,000	35.3	15.7	26.4
Average	8.3	949,500	244,150	34.0	15.9	27.9

(1) The rate of return required to create the difference in the value of $1,000 invested in large-cap stocks relative to $1,000 invested in small-cap stocks.

FIGURE 1–1
Small-Cap P-E/Large-Cap P-E Ratios[1]

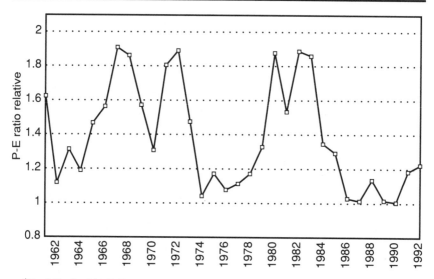

[1]The P-E ratio of the T. Rowe Price New Horizons small-cap mutual fund relative to the P-E ratio of the large-cap dominated Standard & Poor's 500 Index.

approached 1.0. Rarely does this ratio fall below 1.0, and when it does, it doesn't stay there for very long. In late 1990, small-cap P-E ratios reached parity with the P-Es of large-caps for the first time since 1974. That marked the end of the small-cap under-performance cycle that began in mid-1983 and eventually led to the robust 44 percent gain in small-cap stocks the following year. They then went on to score a second year of overperformance during 1992. Even so, small-cap price-earnings ratios are only about 20 percent greater than that of the S&P 500 Index. Generally, the small-cap overperformance cycle does not end until small-cap P-E ratios reach nearly twice those of the S&P 500 Index. Thus, it is still early in the current overperformance cycle.

Although two years is not a lengthy cycle, after two years of overperformance, it becomes much more difficult to argue that the small firm effect has died a natural death. In fact, given the reasons mentioned here, it is easier to make the case that small-cap stocks are about to embark on a lengthy overperformance cycle that could last throughout the remainder of the decade.

While history is rarely a mirror image of the future, clues from history can better guide our actions in the future. And history strongly suggests that small firm stocks will continue to provide greater returns than large firm stocks. Even if the efficient market theorists are correct, small-caps should continue to perform best. Remember, according to the efficient market theory, investment return is tied to investment risk. The greater the risks, in an efficient market, the greater are the potential returns. Since small firm stocks involve more risk than do large firm stocks, they should deliver greater returns, even in an efficient market. On the other hand, if the small firm effect is not dead, small firm stocks should deliver even greater returns. This appears to be a game that you can't lose. It's like playing flip the coin: If the coin falls heads, you win; if it falls tails, you break even. And that's one game I would enjoy playing.

THE ROAD AHEAD

In the pages that follow, I describe the rules of the investment game. I then outline an investment strategy that, if followed consistently, will greatly increase the odds that you will become one of the game's big winners. The small firm effect is examined in great detail, and I explain how to go about making small firm stock selections and how to manage a small firm stock portfolio optimally. For investors who don't want to steer the course alone, I have included a chapter on the use of small-cap mutual funds to capture the small firm effect. The goal is not only to make you a more informed investor, it is to make you a more successful investor as well.

Unlike get-rich schemes that have very little substance, the strategies contained in this book have their roots firmly planted in both academic and professional research. Although these strategies are well known to professional investors, their use is restricted because of the limited size of the small-cap market.

Today there are approximately 2,000 firms that can be properly described as small-cap. The median equity cap of these firms is about $50 million. Thus, the aggregate market value of the small-cap sector of the stock market is about $100 billion. Roughly one third of the outstanding shares of small-cap stocks are in the hands of company founders and their families. Furthermore, another one fifth of small-cap shares are in the hands of other investors who are reluctant to part with them. That leaves only about $50 billion available for individual and institutional investors. (As a point of reference, the market cap of Wal-Mart is $74 billion.) Well-heeled institutional investors with billions of dollars to invest steer clear of the small-cap sector of the market because their buying and selling activities would produce large price swings, with attendant transactions costs that would eliminate the favorable small-cap return differential. Thus, the small-cap sector of the market is best suited for individual investors who possess limited capital and who trade in hundreds rather than tens of thousands of shares. It is the one segment of the stock market where individual investors compete on a level playing field with other investors. In this type of market, the better informed investors usually reap the biggest rewards. This book is dedicated to that end. Read it and reap.

CHAPTER 2

INVESTING SMART FROM THE START

"Will the stock market make me rich?" I must have heard that question a thousand times over the years. The answer, of course, is "Possibly." After all, it's possible to make a fortune at the roulette table as well; it's just not likely. What I hope to do is show you how to become not necessarily rich, but at least richer than you would have been if you hadn't invested. As you'll see, years of small gains can turn into large rewards.

Let's go back to the roulette table. Sit down and place a $1,000 bet on red. You win. You leave your original stake and your winnings placed on red, and it comes up again. If you do this ten times in a row, you'll have $1,024,000.

You can do the same thing with stocks. Every year hundreds of stocks double in price. When you find one of them every year for ten years, you've made your million. Or you can find one or two good growth companies, buy in, and hold on for an investment lifetime. If you had bought 100 shares of Wal-Mart stock in early 1982 and hung on until the end of 1992, thanks to stock dividends and stock splits, you'd have 3,200 shares, and they'd be worth $193,000 (not to mention the cash dividends you'd have pocketed along the way). Not bad for an original investment of $4,000!

The odds of winning at the roulette table on 10 successive bets on red are more than 1,000 to 1. Are the odds that you'll pick stocks perfectly any better? Yes, if you improve your return in the stock market by substituting information for luck and if you use sound planning that recognizes your psychological as well as financial needs. The investment strategies I'll be talking about in this book are well known to professional investors and academic thinkers. These strategies have a particular value to individual investors because institutional investors who know all these strategies can't take advantage of them for reasons that will become clear as we go along. There's no magic to these strategies—they just require careful thought about your own investment needs and some patience.

CHARTING YOUR COURSE

Would you drive from Boston to San Diego without a road map? Most people would plan the trip carefully. They would figure out the distance and the likely cost of gas, maybe call the automobile club to get an idea of highway conditions and places to stay, and factor in contingencies for problems with the car.

The point is to organize your expectations for the trip: how much, how long, how difficult. You need to take the same kind of care for your trip to increased wealth. You know you can't get from Boston to San Diego in a car overnight. You have to be equally realistic about how far you can get in the stock market. However, it's been my experience that hardly anybody is.

Some novice investors expect that by putting a little money in common stocks they'll be rich overnight. Others have more modest expectations—say a return on their capital of 20 to 30 percent a year—so they're willing to wait a little longer. Others don't know what to expect. They're the ones who make the worst mistakes, although the others tend to have a few problems as well. It's possible to aim too low as well as too high, so that your return doesn't even keep up with inflation. Those who aim too high take too many risks; not only do they get poor results, they may even lose their capital. We'll talk about the proper proportion of risk to expected return later; the thing to remember now is simply this: Investment return is your reward for taking investment risks. One purpose of this book is to teach you how to make money without being foolhardy.

History tells us that over the long run, average stock pickers earn from 10 to 12 percent annually on their investments, before accounting for brokerage commissions and income taxes. Slightly more aggressive stock pickers earn from 12 to 14 percent annually. Aggressive stock pickers with exceptional ability may earn annual compound returns up to 18 percent, but this is very unusual. Hardly anyone can earn over 20 percent year after year. For example, over the period 1981–92, out of the hundreds of mutual funds on the market, only six returned more than 18 percent a year. Fidelity's Select Health Care Fund, the top performer, returned only 20.4 percent. (So much for those "conservative" investors with the 30 percent expectations!)

To me, annual returns in the 12 to 18 percent range is a reasonable goal. To expect more is to expect too much. The numbers may look small, but thanks to compounding, small improvements in annual investment returns make big differences in wealth over time. Consider this example: Suppose that Albert Able invests $5,000 each year in a portfolio of common stocks and earns the historical average stock market rate of return—about 10 percent per year. At the end of 15 years, Able's portfolio would be worth $174,745 consisting of $75,000 of capital injections and $99,745 of investment return. On the other hand, suppose that Betty Better also invests $5,000 annually over the same time frame. However, due to slightly better asset selection, Better earns a 14 percent compound annual return. The result is a portfolio valued at $249,900. That's an improvement of $75,000. Furthermore, the wealth differential between Able and Better magnifies as the holding period increases. After 25 years Able's portfolio would be valued at $540,900 while Better's fortune would have grown beyond $1 million! (See Table 2-1.)

When you consider that common stocks in general have given investors a compound annual return of about 12 percent

TABLE 2–1
Investment of $5,000 a Year

Annual Return	Portfolio Value	
	After 15 Years	After 25 Years
10%	$174,745	$ 540,900
14%	249,900	1,036,650

during the last 60 years, you'll see why I'm bullish on stocks. There are a few rules to building wealth through investment in common stocks, but they're so simple they're almost embarrassing:

1. You must add capital to your portfolio regularly.
2. You must invest over a long period of time.[1]
3. You must work hard to make small improvements in your annual returns by reducing transaction costs, watching the tax implications of your investments, and becoming slightly more aggressive. Little by little makes a lot.

WHY INVEST IN COMMON STOCKS?

Because of their opportunities for dividend and capital growth, common stocks provide the best return potential. Table 2-2 gives you a 65-year overview of investment returns for various classes of financial assets. These returns reflect the assumption that all dividend and interest income was reinvested as received.

The most important column in Table 2-2 is the last, Compound Real Return. It represents the actual compound rate adjusted for increases in consumer prices, otherwise known as inflation. This column shows what the instruments earned after inflation.

Real return is the only true measure of wealth expansion. Why? Because it's not how many dollars you have, it's what you can buy with them. You want to be able to buy more than you could have before you began investing, or you simply want the peace of mind that comes from knowing that if you need to buy something you can.

Look at Table 2-2 again. If you don't want to take any risks, the obvious investment is Treasury bills. Unfortunately, although your investment will be safe, it won't make any money

---

[1] It's said that when Albert Einstein was asked what man's greatest discovery was, he replied, "Compound interest!"

TABLE 2-2
Investment Returns: Stocks, Bonds, and Bills, 1926-1991

Investment Category	Percent		
	Compound Annual Return	Average Annual Return	Compound Real Return
Common stocks	10.4%	12.4%	7.3%
Long-term corporate bonds	5.4	5.7	2.3
Long-term government bonds	4.8	5.1	1.6
Treasury bills	3.7	3.8	0.6
Consumer prices	3.1	3.1	—

Source: *Stocks, Bonds, Bills, and Inflation: 1992 Yearbook™*, Ibbotson Associates, Chicago (annually updates work by Roger G. Ibbotson and Rex A. Sinquefield). Used with permission. All rights reserved.

for you—you'll keep ahead of inflation by about 0.5 percent per year.

Let's just look at rates of return for stocks over the last 40 years (because I certainly wasn't investing in 1926, and I doubt that you were). Over the years since January 1, 1953, the average annual compound rate of return on the S&P 500 Index was 12.1 percent. For the same period, inflation averaged 4.3 percent. So the real rate of return from a highly diversified common stock portfolio of average risk, as Table 2-3 shows, was 7.8 percent.

That compound real return of 7.8 percent is not, of course, the real return for the investor, who still has to reduce the return by transaction costs (brokerage fees) and personal taxes. Let's see what happens when we take these into account.

TABLE 2-3
Annual Average Return, S&P Index, 1953-1992

Dividend yield	4.5%
Capital appreciation	+ 7.6
Total compound return	12.1%
Annual inflation rate	− 4.3
Compound real return	7.8%

TABLE 2-4
Return to Investor Compared with Annual Average Return, S&P Index, 1953-1991

	Percent before Taxes	Percent after Taxes and Fees
Dividend yield	4.5%	3.25%
Capital appreciation	+ 7.6	+4.18
Total compound return	12.1%	7.43%
Annual inflation rate	− 4.3	−4.30
Compound real return	7.8%	3.13%

Suppose the investor is paying the statutory maximum tax rate of 28 percent on investment income. This portfolio turns over every three years, so the turnover rate is 33 percent a year. Transaction costs are 3 percent of the round-trip (purchase and sale), and a third of that would be 1.0 percent of the value of the whole portfolio. The effects are spelled out in Table 2-4.

So if you're an average investor with a diversified portfolio of common stocks of average risk and don't turn over your portfolio too often, you can increase your real wealth by about 3 percent a year. Doesn't sound like much, does it? But that 3 percent a year can really add up over time. As you will soon see, by investing in small firm stocks, you'll be able to more than double the net real rate of return.

WHAT DOES ALL THIS MEAN?

What this means is that the stock market will not make you rich overnight. Over the course of a long-term investment program, however, you can enhance your wealth significantly. You can increase your spending power, so you will indeed be richer. Table 2-5 illustrates what can happen to $1 over time. Even at 3 percent, you can buy twice as much. Investment in stocks certainly beats putting the money in a mattress!

Because the stock market will not make you rich, be wary of salespeople who call you each week with a once in a lifetime

TABLE 2–5
Growth in Purchasing Power of $1
over 25 Years

Program	After 25 Years
Uninvested	$0.34
At 3%/year	$2.09
At 8%/year	$6.85

investment opportunity. Tales of investments that double or triple in value in a short time are either accompanied by significant investment risk or are blatantly false. By definition, these strokes of fortune are rare, and you won't hear about them from financial salespeople.

But don't pull your money out of the market yet. The alternatives are no better. Between 1940 and 1990 real estate gave investors a 7.6 percent compound annual rate of return and precious metals returned 4.8 percent before inflation, transaction costs, and taxes. So, they returned far less than common stocks. These investments are burdened with additional costs: precious metals require storage, real estate and collectibles need management, and precious metals never spin off dividends for reinvestment.

So don't be discouraged. You can increase your wealth in the stock market once your expectations are in line with the realities. Something to remember in any investment is that when the rate of turnover increases, your return declines. That's because of heavier transaction costs. If the portfolio in Table 2-4 had been turned over every year instead of every three years, the after-tax, after-cost return would have dropped from 2.9 to 0.8 percent. Active traders who turn over their portfolios two or even three times a year have to more than double the market rate of return to match the returns netted by the passive buy-and-hold investor. In the long run, traders are doomed to failure.

The last thing this analysis should mean to the patient investor is that if there's no risk, there's no return. The closest thing available to a riskless asset is U.S. Treasury bills. As shown in Table 2-2, T-bills earned only 0.6 percent more than inflation over the 66 years from 1926 to 1992; the investor would have had a net loss overall after taxes and transaction costs. So if you want a chance to increase your wealth, you have to take some risks.

The combination of risk and dividend returns must always be kept in mind. Reinvestment of dividends is an important component of return, even though the percentage attributable to dividends is lower in the riskier portfolios because those stocks traditionally pay few, if any dividends.

Table 2-6 shows four hypothetical common stock portfolios with different rates of capital appreciation. The total return percentage is the combination of growth and dividends. For even the most conservative portfolio, total return is 33 percent larger because the dividends were reinvested. And for the most aggressive portfolio earning 16 percent, even though dividend return was only one ninth of total return, it still made a difference of 24 percent in total wealth.

BUILDING WEALTH BY INVESTING IN COMMON STOCKS

If your real wealth is to expand, you have to get a better return than the inflation rate. How much better depends on you.

TABLE 2–6
Dividend Yields, Capital Appreciation, and Terminal Investment Wealth

| | | Ten-Year Investment Returns | | Total Return |
| | | | | Divided by |
Growth Rate	Dividend Yield	Capital Appreciation	Total Return	Capital Appreciation
10%	2%	159%	211%	1.33
12	2	211	271	1.28
14	2	271	341	1.26
16	2	341	423	1.24

Generally, if your investment strategy is to be successful, you must:

1. Set reasonable goals.
2. Diversify your portfolio.
3. Avoid excessive trading.
4. Look to long-run investment returns and ignore day-to-day fluctuations in value.
5. Tailor your strategy to fit your own comfort zone for risk.

I'll discuss the last requirement first, because it affects the others; I'll expand on the first three in later chapters. To set the stage, let's review the historical rates of return on various common stock portfolios. Figure 2-1 compares the compound growth of $1 invested in the S&P 500 with $1 invested in a portfolio of small firm common stocks over the period 1965–91. (Of course, in both cases, the dividends were reinvested!) The computations are pretax, precommission. If $1 had been invested in the S&P 500, it would have grown to $14.33. But if that dollar had been invested in a portfolio of the stocks of small firms, it would have grown to $36.09! Does this mean that the best investment strategy is to invest totally in a diversified portfolio of small firm growth stocks? Some researchers think

FIGURE 2–1
Wealth Indexes, 1965–1991

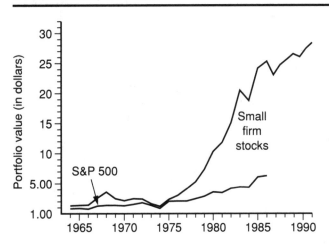

so. In fact, to some degree, I think so, too. This very aggressive investment strategy should yield the greatest increase in real wealth over the long run. And that's the difficulty. Very few investors have the intestinal fortitude to maintain a portfolio fully invested in common stocks through thick and thin. Periods marked by eroding stock prices make investors nervous. When investors get nervous and begin to lose sleep because of their investment posture, they tend to make the greatest blunders. Thus, if you are losing sleep because of your investment position, my prescription is to sell your stock holdings down to the sleeping point.

Table 2-7 lists some quarterly return statistics for portfolios consisting of the S&P Index (large company common stocks), small company stocks, and T-bills over the period 1965–91. Also included are return statistics for three investment strategies. The highly aggressive strategy assumes a 40 percent investment in large firm stocks, 40 percent investment in small firm stocks, and 20 percent invested in T-bills. The neutral strategy consists of equal dollar amounts allocated to investment in large stocks, small stocks, and T-bills (i.e., 33.33 percent allocated to each). The conservative strategy assumes 80 percent investment in T-bills, 10 percent in large firm stocks, and 10 percent in small firm common stocks. Table 2-8 shows the profitability of the various investment strategies.

Over the period 1965–91, all three investment strategies would have shown a profit. (Actually, even a portfolio consisting entirely of T-bills would have bettered the rate of inflation by 1.3 percent annually.) The most profitable strategy would have been to invest 100 percent of your capital in a small company common stock portfolio. However, this portfolio would have declined in value by nearly 30 percent during the crash of 1987 and by more than 50 percent during the bear market of 1968–70. Most likely very few investors could have maintained a 100 percent invested position in small growth company stocks during these two bear markets. Thus, even though this investment posture would have been the most profitable for long-term investors, my guess is that very few would have had the nerve to hang on. In fact, many individual investors finally gave up on common stocks just as the market was about to bottom. The

TABLE 2-7
Investment Returns for Various Portfolio Strategies, 1965–1991

	Small Firm Stocks	S&P Index	Treasury Bills	Portfolio Strategies		
				Aggressive	Neutral	Conservative
Average quarterly return (%)	+ 3.5	+ 2.3	+ 1.7	+ 3.3	+ 3.1	+ 2.0
Largest quarterly return (%)	+44.3	+22.9	+ 3.8	+25.2	+21.2	+ 7.3
Largest quarterly loss (%)	−32.7	−25.2	Gain	−20.2	−16.6	− 4.1
Sustained loss 6/20/68–6/30/70	−51.6	−26.2	+10.3	−29.0	−22.5	+ 0.5
Sustained loss 12/31/72–9/30/74	−43.3	−37.3	+15.5	−29.1	−21.7	+ 4.3
Sustained loss 9/31/87–12/31/87	−28.5	−22.6	+ 1.3	−20.2	−16.6	− 4.1
Sustained loss 6/30/90–9/30/90	−23.2	−13.8	+ 2.0	−14.4	−11.6	− 2.2
Quarters in which a loss occurred	42	39	0	38	35	13

TABLE 2-8
1991 Value of $1 Invested in 1965

	Terminal Amount	Compound Annual Return (percent)
Small firm stocks	$36.09	14.2%
S&P Index stocks	14.33	10.4
Treasury bills	6.25	7.0
Consumer price index	4.41	5.7
Aggressive strategy	23.94	12.7
Neutral strategy	20.51	12.6
Conservative strategy	10.24	9.7

result was catastrophic losses—even though their portfolios could have given them the greatest long-term profit.

However, the three portfolios combining large firm common stocks, small firm common stocks, and T-bills fared a bit better during these two market downturns. During the 1968–70 bear market, for example, the aggressive portfolio would have lost 29 percent of its value, the neutral portfolio would have dropped by 22 percent, while the conservative portfolio would have produced a small gain.

During the 1973–74 bear market, the three mixed investment strategies show even more dramatic results. The conservative strategy gained 4.3 percent even though the S&P Index fell by more than 37 percent. Of course, the conservative strategy produced the least return over the entire 1965–91 period. However, it still produced a compound annual rate of return of 9.7 percent, or a total gain in real (after inflation) wealth of nearly 133 percent, at the end of the 25-year period.

Table 2-8 shows how a dollar grows, and the difference an aggressive strategy can make. Small firm growth stocks clearly made the most money. But how many investors could have held on during the years when these stocks took a beating in the market? Although the value of such a portfolio would have grown significantly between 1965 and early 1974, all the gains would have been wiped out at the end of 1974. Holding on would have been worth it, but who has that kind of intestinal fortitude?

If you have it, more power to you—and, probably, more money as well. Most of us have to ask ourselves how much risk we can tolerate and set our strategies accordingly. We have to find our own comfort zones in relation to investment risk.

Whenever actual portfolio returns can vary above or below expected returns, you have investment risk. The greater the variability, the greater the risk. As returns start to fall below expectations, investors become uncomfortable. When the discomfort becomes too great, the investor abandons the strategy —usually at just the wrong time. Even if it's the wrong time for your portfolio return, however, it's the right time for you. When you're having trouble sleeping because your investments are losing ground, sell off to the sleeping point. That's your comfort zone. Then learn from your reactions and redesign a portfolio strategy you can sleep with.

WHAT LIES AHEAD?

If you invest in the stock market, don't expect to get rich overnight. However, if you invest right and maintain your commitment to common stocks over the long run, you will substantially improve your wealth. Common stocks have been the only financial asset to significantly outpace the rate of inflation during this century. Furthermore, the common stocks of small firms have provided the most generous rewards. However, these rewards are not free of charge—you must pay for them by assuming investment risk. To be successful, you must select the right small firm stocks and you must control investment risks.

In the following chapters, I show you how to select small firm stocks with the greatest return potential. I show you how to recognize, measure, and control investment risk. Successful investing requires more than picking the best stocks. It also requires that you implement sound portfolio management techniques. These are explained in great detail. Although there are no secrets to investing successfully, the few simple rules all successful investors adhere to are spelled out in the pages that follow.

CHAPTER 3

INVESTMENT RISK—NO GUTS, NO GLORY

I have shown you how profitable investing can be. When allowed to compound over many years, even modest sums grow remarkably large. Of course, that's the primary motivation for investing—to increase wealth. But investment return does not come free of charge. You always pay for it by taking risks. Generally, the most potentially rewarding investments contain the greatest risks.

Although most people understand the concept of investment return, their concept of risk is often vague. They know, of course, that if there is a chance that they might lose money it's risky. But how risky? How can risk be measured? How can the risk of two different investments be compared? How much return should you be getting for the risks you're taking? These very important questions must be answered before any investment is made. It has been my experience, however, that most investors avoid these questions. Frequently, they fall for the pitch of a securities salesperson who describes an investment solely by its potential return. They go for the rewards but ignore the concomitant risks. If this describes your behavior, think about changing, because if you haven't lost a bundle yet, chances are you will.

WHAT IS INVESTMENT RISK?

Think about the process of investing for a minute. You give away current dollars for the promise of receiving more dollars some time in the future. But promises can be broken. Thus, investing involves trading sure dollars (a bird in the hand) for future dollars (birds in the bush). Risk exists because the future is uncertain. Some things are more likely to occur than others. Due to the complexity of the world, there is very little certainty about future outcomes. It has been said that the only certain things in this life are death and taxes, yet even here the questions of when and how much are highly uncertain.

Figure 3-1 illustrates the growth of wealth from three different investments. The first is risk free. As time progresses, wealth expands at a predictable rate. The second illustration depicts a moderate risk investment. Although wealth expands over time, it does so in an uneven fashion. In fact, during some short-run periods wealth actually contracts. In the third example, wealth is subject to wide and violent swings. Due to the high degree of uncertainty about the value of wealth from period to period, this investment contains a high degree of risk.

Investment risk is defined by return *variability*. The greater the variability, the greater the risk. Finance practitioners have borrowed a statistical concept called the *standard deviation* to measure variability. The more variable the investment return, the greater the standard deviation.

Figure 3-2 illustrates the standard deviation and distribution of actual returns from a broad range of assets over a number of years. The column labeled "Distribution" gives you a

FIGURE 3–1
Risk and Return Variability

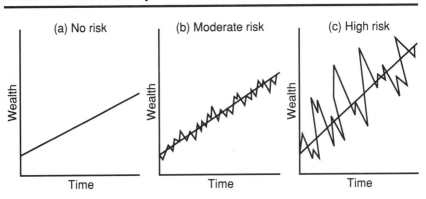

(a) No risk (b) Moderate risk (c) High risk

FIGURE 3–2
Investment Risk by Asset Class

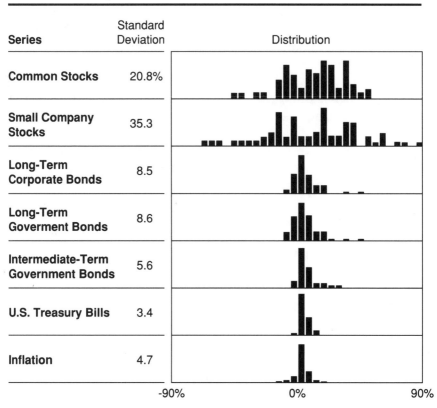

Series	Standard Deviation	Distribution
Common Stocks	20.8%	
Small Company Stocks	35.3	
Long-Term Corporate Bonds	8.5	
Long-Term Goverment Bonds	8.6	
Intermediate-Term Government Bonds	5.6	
U.S. Treasury Bills	3.4	
Inflation	4.7	

Source: *Stocks, Bonds, Bills, and Inflation:* 1992 Yearbook™, Ibbotson Associates, Chicago (annually updates work by Roger G. Ibbotson and Rex A. Sinquefield). Used with permission. All rights reserved.

visual picture of how these investments have fared over the years. The center line in this column represents a zero percent return. Outcomes to the right are gains; those to the left are losses. The "Standard Deviation" column puts a number on the variability of these outcomes.

You should see right away that investments in T-bills had the most certain outcome; that is, the least risk. T-bill returns form a tight pattern in an area of modestly positive return. The low standard deviation reflects the low variability. Investing in T-bills is about as close to a sure thing as we are allowed in this imperfect world. It's analogous to target shooting where you stand up close to the target, lock your rifle in a vise, and use a telescopic sight. Your shots all fall into a tight pattern around the bulls-eye, just like the T-bill returns in Figure 3-2. As with the investment return from riskless T-bills, you don't get big prizes for this kind of easy shooting.

The outcome for stocks—and small stocks in particular—is a different story. Here you see that returns are scattered widely, with some in negative territory and many in highly positive areas. The high variability of stock returns is quantified in a high standard deviation—our measure of risk. By just eye-balling the distributions for stocks, however, you can see that the payoff is much higher than for the low-risk T-bills.

WHICH RISKS DO YOU TAKE WHEN YOU INVEST?

Whenever you invest, you face three general risks—purchasing power risk, interest rate risk, and market risk. Purchasing power risk is the uncertainty surrounding what things will cost in the future. Remember that when investing you part with current dollars in anticipation of earning future dollars. But what will these future dollars buy? During the 1970s and early 1980s many individuals sought the safe havens of insured bank accounts as a repository for their capital. They got the certainty of return they sought, but like the man who stashed his cash in a mattress, the purchasing power of their dollars was severely eroded by inflation. What they thought was a risk-free investment dealt them a great loss in buying power.

All investors faced the same risk during that period. However, real estate investors' returns increased as the cost of the property they owned expanded right along with the price of everything else. And gold investors saw the value of their holdings increase from $200 to well over $700 an ounce. (In this case, an ounce of prevention was really worth much more than a pound of cure.)

Interest rate risk stems from the fact that prevailing interest rates may fluctuate. When these rates go up, the market value of securities that pay a fixed rate of interest, such as bonds, go down (and vice versa). For example, suppose that you bought a bond paying the prevailing market interest rate of 5 percent. You paid $1,000 for a bond yielding $50 in annual interest. A year later, for one reason or another, the market interest rate for a bond like yours pops up to 10 percent. If you tried to sell your bond, no one would pay you $1,000 for it. Because your bond will continue paying only $50 a year, you will have to lower your price to the point where the buyer will get the prevailing 10 percent market return on the investment. Of course, you could wait until the bond matures. At maturity your original investment would be returned. During the intervening years, however, you would have lost the opportunity to earn a higher rate of return—another aspect of interest rate risk.

Market risk is the variability of return caused by changing economic conditions. Whenever you invest, you subject yourself to the vagaries of the market. An economic recession causes corporate sales and earnings to fall. That, in turn, causes stock prices to fall. Even though you may have bought the stocks of good solid companies, their prices erode right along with the economy. When the tide goes out, all the boats go down.

RISK AND COMMON STOCKS

When you buy common stocks you assume company-specific risks in addition to these other risks. Company-specific risks result from the business the firm is in, how it finances its operations, competitive forces, and chance. Some firms are more risky than others merely because of what they do. Oil exploration and development firms are very risky. They spend millions of dollars to sink test holes in the hopes of finding oil. When they succeed, profits skyrocket. When they don't, losses mount. A firm that sinks too many successive dry holes goes bankrupt. On the other hand, public utility companies have a relatively small amount of business risk. They are granted a monopoly and, thus, the market for their products tends to be highly stable and predictable; regulators allow them to price their product so that they are guaranteed a reasonable profit. As a result, sales, earnings, share price, and stockholders' returns also have low variability.

Even though a firm's line of business forms the basis of its risk, its overall risk can be changed through alterations of its capital structure—the way it finances its assets. Firms that borrow money to finance their operations are generally more risky than those that only use owners' (equity) capital. Here's a simple illustration: Suppose that a company believes that it can invest $100 million in assets and produce $20 million in net income. If the firm finances this investment entirely with stockholders' money, the shareholders earn a 20 percent return ($20 million/$100 million). On the other hand, if the firm borrows $50 million at 10 percent interest and finances the balance ($50 million) with common stock, earnings fall to $17 million (after interest expense and taxes) but the return to stockholders rises to 34 percent ($17 million/$50 million). Thus, the rate of return is increased. However, if net income from this investment falls to $2 million, the all-equity firm returns 2 percent while the mixed capital structure firm's shareholders experience a *loss* of 2 percent. As can be seen, the variability of return and risk has been increased because of debt financing.

Finally, common stock investors often face the luck of the draw. Sometimes unexpected events which affect only one company can drive down investment returns even though other firms in the same line of business are doing well.

TOTAL RISK AND ITS COMPONENTS

Common stock investing is risky because investment return is not guaranteed and is subject to wide variations from period to period. The overall variability of return, called *total risk,* is the sum of company-specific risk and market risk. This fact is of more than theoretical interest because the company-specific component of total risk can be virtually eliminated through proper portfolio diversification. That's right. You can eliminate a significant amount of risk just by not putting all of your eggs in one basket.

The risk reduction obtained from proper portfolio diversification is no trivial amount. Nearly two thirds of the total risk, or total return variability, of a single stock is company-specific;

only one third is market related. Thus, well diversified investors take only one third the risks taken by those who hold only one stock. Better still, investment return is unaffected by portfolio diversification.

Figure 3-3 illustrates the risk reduction benefit of diversification. As more and more stocks are added to a portfolio, the variability of return diminishes. According to this figure, adding approximately 12 stocks to your portfolio can create nearly all of the benefits of diversification. Nonetheless, no matter how many stocks you add to your portfolio, some risk remains. This remaining risk, which is entirely market related, is called *systematic risk*. Thus, while investors can avoid the assumption of unnecessary company-specific risk (called *unsystematic risk*), they cannot escape the necessary risk of investing.

FIGURE 3–3
Risk Reduction and Portfolio Diversification

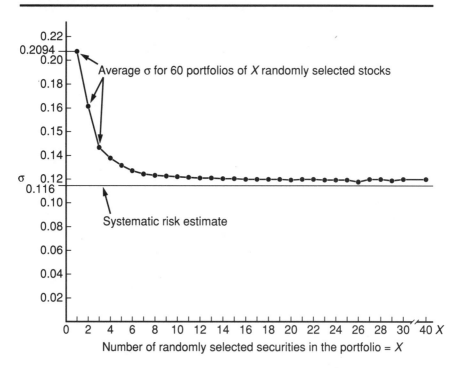

Source: J. L. Evans and S. H. Archer, "Diversification and the Reduction of Dispersion: An Empirical Analysis." *Journal of Finance.* December 1968.

TABLE 3–1
Negative Correlation and Risk Reduction

	Percent		
	Asset A	Asset B	Portfolio ½A + ½B
Economic boom	+30%	−10%	+10%
Moderate growth	+15	+ 5	+10
Recession	− 5	+25	+10

Table 3-1 shows why portfolio diversification reduces investment risk. In this obviously oversimplified illustration we have combined two risky assets in a single portfolio. Although the returns of the individual assets vary considerably over an economic cycle, a portfolio combining these two assets is stable. Table 3-1 also illustrates the secret to reducing risk through diversification. During those periods when the return on asset A is falling, asset B's return is increasing. Thus, diversification works when the returns of the assets held are not in harmony.

Years ago an auto industry tycoon said, "What's good for General Motors is good for America." We know from experience that two different entities often share the same fortunes: both good and bad. If farmers' incomes are down, chances are that local John Deere dealers are in a bad way, too. Their fates are highly correlated. We also know of instances where one person's pill is another person's poison. The buggy whip companies and the auto industries at the turn of the century are a case in point; the good fortune of one signaled the doom of the other.

Investors can measure the relationship between two variables by a statistical construct called the *correlation coefficient*. This number ranges from a high of +1 (the two variables move in perfect harmony) to 0 (there is no relationship between the two variables) to −1 (the two variables are in perfect disharmony). In the example of Table 3-1, the correlation coefficient between the returns of assets A and B is −1. This is an ideal diversification situation because constructing a portfolio of the two assets eliminates all variability. However, this ideal only exists in theory. The returns from most common stocks are positively related to one another. That is, their correlation coefficients are greater than zero. However, by combining assets with less than perfect positive correlation (i.e., a correlation coefficient less than +1) some risk reduction can be obtained. Thus, when diversifying your portfolio, add common stocks that have the lowest correlation of returns with the other stocks in your portfolio.

Even though this sounds very technical, it is easier done than said. Rather than measuring the correlation of returns of all stocks with one another in search of the ideal combination, investors generally select companies from different industries. The notion is that companies in different lines of business are less affected by common factors. High tech companies, for example, are not severely influenced by the same forces that affect the natural resource industries of coal, lumber, and copper. Furthermore, when you hold numerous stocks the chance events that affect one company tend to offset the chance events that affect another. One stock may fall in price because of a product liability suit while another stock may rise because of an unanticipated contract.

Table 3-2 illustrates the correlation of returns for various types of assets. The correlation between the returns of U.S. and foreign stocks is +0.67. Because the correlation is less than +1, common stock investors can lower risk by adding foreign equities to their portfolios. Also, there is a negative correlation of return between gold and both government and corporate bond returns. That is, there is a tendency for gold returns to increase when bond returns decrease. That is understandable because the force that drives the price of gold higher (the fear of impending inflation) also drives interest rates higher and bond prices lower. Thus, risk conscious bond investors can reduce risk by adding gold to their income portfolios.

MEASURING RISK: THERE IS A BETA WAY

Remember that investment return is your reward for taking investment risks. Because all company-specific or unsystematic risk can be eliminated through proper portfolio diversification, the *only* risk that you get paid for taking is systematic or market

TABLE 3-2
Capital Market Security Returns: Correlation Matrix

	U.S. Stocks	Foreign Stocks	Government Bonds	Corporate Bonds	Real Estate	T-Bills	Gold
U.S. stocks	1.000						
Foreign stocks	0.672	1.000					
Government bonds	−0.006	−0.226	1.000				
Corporate bonds	0.323	0.075	0.863	1.000			
Real estate	0.054	0.129	−0.040	−0.123	1.000		
T-bills	−0.070	−0.153	0.325	0.135	0.389	1.000	
Gold	−0.088	0.044	−0.206	−0.323	0.684	0.179	1.000

Source: *Stocks, Bonds, Bills, and Inflation 1992 Yearbook™*, Ibbotson Associates, Chicago (annually updates work by Roger G. Ibbotson and Rex A. Sinquefield). Used with permission. All rights reserved.

33

risk. If you hold only one stock, you are taking three times the risk of a well-diversified investor for the same expected return; you're not being compensated for the extra risk that you are taking. That means common stock returns are only related to the stock's systematic risk.

To determine how much return you should get, assess the systematic risk. This is easily done by examining an index called *beta*. It indicates the relative systematic risk of a particular stock compared to the overall stock market. Beta is a handy device for indicating how much a particular stock will fluctuate in price relative to the entire stock market. For convenience, the beta of the market is set at 1.0. If stock XYZ has a beta of 1.0, its price will go up and down at the same rate as the market. If XYZ had a beta of 1.5, it would rise 50 percent more than a rising market and plunge 50 percent deeper in a falling market. Thus, a stock with a beta greater than 1.0 contains more systematic risk, while one with a beta less than 1.0 contains less systematic risk *when held in a well-diversified portfolio*. This last phrase is most important. A single stock contains about 66 percent unsystematic risk. Thus, when considered in isolation, all stocks are more variable than the market as a whole. It is only when common stocks are contained in well-diversified portfolios, and when all unsystematic risk has been eliminated, that beta becomes a valid indicator of their relative risk.

Beta indicates by how much a common stock can be expected to move relative to a movement in the market. Betas for individual stocks are available from a variety of sources, so it makes no sense to go through the hassle of figuring them out. Still, knowing how they are determined improves your understanding of this important concept and how to use it. Figure 3-4 illustrates a simplified method for determining beta. First obtain the market's return for several time intervals. These returns are then paired with those of a particular common stock during the same intervals. These pairs of returns are plotted on a grid with the market return plotted on the horizontal axis and the stock's return on the vertical axis. Next, draw a straight line which best "fits" the data plot. The slope of this line is the estimate of the stock's beta. To obtain the slope, select two points on the line and determine the horizontal and vertical

FIGURE 3–4
Determining Beta for a Stock

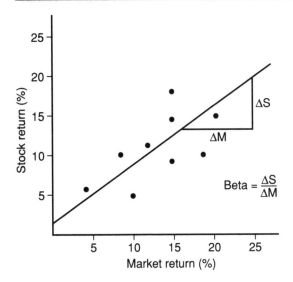

distance between them. The slope is the vertical distance divided by the horizontal distance.[1]

Once you know the betas of individual stocks, you can determine the beta of a portfolio of these stocks. If a portfolio is well diversified, its return is solely a function of its beta. Quite simply, a portfolio's beta is equal to the weighted average of the betas of the stocks in it. The weights are the relative market values of each asset in the portfolio. An example of these calculations appear in Table 3-3. The portfolio contains five common stocks and has a total market value of $100,000. Since asset A has a market value of $10,000, it represents 10 percent of the portfolio. Asset A has a beta of 1.4. Thus, the contribution of this asset to the overall portfolio beta is 10 percent × 1.40 or

---

[1] Most data services that calculate the betas for common stocks use five years of monthly returns with the market taken to be the return on the S&P 500 Composite Index. Instead of drawing the estimation line by hand, these services fit the line using a statistical technique called *least squares regression analysis*.

TABLE 3-3
Determining Portfolio Beta

Asset	Value	Percent of Total		Asset Beta		
A	$ 10,000	10%	×	1.40	=	0.14
B	20,000	20	×	1.00	=	0.20
C	30,000	30	×	0.80	=	0.24
D	15,000	15	×	1.20	=	0.18
E	25,000	25	×	1.60	=	0.40
Total	$100,000	100%		Portfolio Beta		1.16

0.14. Summing the calculations for all five stocks results in a portfolio beta of 1.16.

If we diversify to the point where this portfolio contains no unsystematic risk, its return is solely related to its beta. This relationship is called the *capital market line*. The capital market line, described by the following equation, appears in Figure 3-5.

Portfolio Return = Riskless Return
  + Beta (Market Return − Riskless Return)

All well-diversified portfolios fall somewhere on the capital

FIGURE 3-5
The Capital Market Line

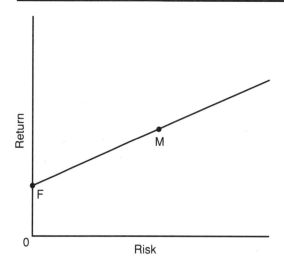

market line. Point M on the line represents the market portfolio. Stocks to the right of M contain more risk and thus should also provide more return. Those to the left of M are less risky and have lower returns than the market portfolio. The least risky point on the line is F. It has no investment risk and its beta is zero. Because T-bills contain very little investment risk, they represent this point on the investment risk continuum. Finally, you can arrive at any point on the capital market line by holding just two securities—a riskless asset and the market portfolio. Points to the left of M can be obtained by investing a portion of your portfolio in T-bills (a riskless asset) and a portion in the S&P Index (the market portfolio). To obtain the risk and return combinations to the right of point M, you must invest all your cash in the market portfolio, and buy on margin to make additional investments in that portfolio.

Although betas for individual stocks are notoriously unstable, betas for highly diversified portfolios are quite stable; thus, they are excellent predictors of investment risk. Beta tends to misstate the relative variability of individual stocks, but accurately depicts the relative variability of well-diversified portfolios.

Given a portfolio with a stable beta, you can use the capital market line to estimate its potential return. For example, suppose that the risk-free (T-bill) rate is expected to be 6 percent while the market is expected to return 15 percent. A well-diversified portfolio whose beta is 1.5 would be expected to return 19.5 percent, determined as follows:

Portfolio return = Riskless rate
+ Beta (Market rate − Riskless rate)
= 6% + 1.5(15% − 6%)
= 6% + 1.5(9%)
= 19.5%

Table 3-4 illustrates the median betas of companies in a sample of industries. Although these industry betas range from 0.75 (electric utilities) to 1.30 (computer software services), most tend to be very close to that of the market (1.00). The reason is that today companies themselves are widely diversified. Among America's largest companies, it is nearly impossible

TABLE 3–4
Representative Industry Betas

Industry	Beta
Air transport	1.15
Auto and truck manufacturing	1.05
Banking	0.90
Computer software and services	1.30
Electric utility	0.75
Financial services	1.20
Machine tool	0.90
Newspaper	1.10
Restaurant	1.05
Steel	1.10
Tobacco	0.85

to find one operating in a single industry. Air transport firms, for example, may own hotels and car rental agencies. Although a travel theme cuts across these segments, each is impacted by unique factors. As a result, risk tends toward the market average.

On the other hand, small firms tend to have very few product lines. Many have only one. Because of this lack of internal diversification, small firms frequently possess betas significantly different from the market average. In addition, these firms possess a much larger percentage of company-specific risk than do large firms. This again results from a lack of diversification. Although chance occurrences do affect the sales, earnings, and share prices of larger firms, the impact of such events is often much less severe for large diversified companies than it is for smaller firms. (Even though the lack of diversification by small firms may appear to be a large negative, as will be seen in Chapter 6 it actually provides small firm investors with a large advantage.)

The absence of diversification by small firms requires that small firm stock investors make up the difference. That is, they must hold a greater number of common stocks to obtain the full benefits of risk reduction. Table 3-5 indicates the betas and systematic and unsystematic risk percentages for a random sample of 10 small firm stocks. The betas range from 0.26 to

TABLE 3–5
Betas and Risks for 10 Small Firm Stocks

Common Stock	Beta	Percentage Systematic Risk	Percentage Unsystematic Risk
S1	1.27	26%	74%
S2	1.02	24	76
S3	1.62	37	63
S4	1.30	16	84
S5	0.26	2	98
S6	1.27	27	73
S7	1.33	32	68
S8	2.37	47	53
S9	0.59	4	96
S10	2.69	46	54
Ten-stock average	1.37	26%	74%

2.69 with an average of 1.37. Rarely do you find a large firm with a beta this extreme. Furthermore, the average percentage of systematic risk is 26 percent, which is lower than the 33 percent average for large companies. In other words, most of the risks in these individual small firms is company-specific, and that risk component is greater than in large company stocks.

We mentioned earlier that large stock investors only need to hold 12 to 15 different issues to achieve adequate diversification. Owing to their greater company-specific risk, small firm investors must hold a larger number of stocks. Our research indicates that it takes from 20 to 30 small firm stocks to achieve the same degree of diversification that can be obtained with as few as 12 large company stocks.

GETTING WHAT YOU PAY FOR . . . MORE OR LESS

We've already seen that the capital market line represents a theoretical continuum of all risk/reward situations. Practitioners generally use short-term T-bills as a proxy for the riskless portfolio, and the Standard & Poor's 500 Stock Index as a substitute for the theoretical market portfolio.

In Figure 3-6, portfolios A and B, which lie on the capital market line, represent portfolios whose investment returns are consistent with the risks taken. Although portfolio A has provided less return than the S&P Index (portfolio M), it has done so while experiencing less volatility of return (less risk). Portfolio B has provided greater investment return than the market portfolio but at the price of greater risk. Portfolios C and D lie off the capital market line and represent abnormal portfolio performance. Portfolios D and D^1 provide an interesting situation. They are equally risky, but D^1 had the greater return. On the other hand, portfolio C has provided returns greater than those dictated by the investment risks taken. Somehow the portfolio manager has obtained a free investment lunch equal to the amount of return represented by the dotted line between C and C^1.

The managers of portfolios A and B have performed as well as can be expected in an efficient market, which we discuss in the next chapter. That is, they have provided investment

FIGURE 3–6
The Capital Market Line

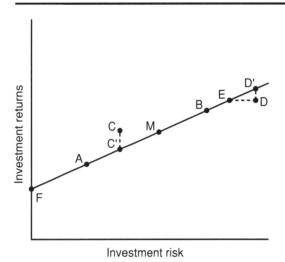

returns consistent with the risks taken. The manager of portfolio D has performed suboptimally because given the risks taken, that portfolio should have earned a return equivalent to D^1. Or at the least, it should have experienced no more risk than portfolio E. The manager of portfolio C would rate the highest of all.

This performance analysis considers risk as well as return. If only return were considered, the manager of portfolio D would get the highest rating while the manager of portfolio C would rank near the bottom. However, when both risk and return are considered, the manager of portfolio C gets the top spot, followed by a tie between the managers of portfolios A and B. The manager of portfolio D, the portfolio that beat the market by the greatest amount, gets tagged with the poorest performance rating. Remember this the next time some ad for a mutual fund or investment advisor touts "80 percent return over the past 12 months." Ask to see the flip side of the coin—how many risks they took to get those returns.

Analysts use several methods to compare investment returns with the risks taken. We know that generally more return means more risk. However, when judging the results of managed portfolios, the appropriate criterion is the amount of return earned per unit of risk taken. Even though an assessment of this kind is essential, the appropriate techniques are somewhat complex and, thus, beyond the scope of this presentation.

STAYING ALIVE

Several years ago while teaching a course in investments, I was pointing out the benefits of portfolio diversification. "The beauty of diversification," I instructed the class, "is that while the price of one stock is going down, the price of another stock is most likely rising. The result is less variability and less risk." Before I could continue, I was interrupted by a student who questioned my wisdom. "Why," she queried, "would anyone want to hold a stock whose price is sinking?" Her contention was that by holding a diversified portfolio of stocks, investment returns would be eroded by the stocks going down in price.

Although I was dumbfounded, I shouldn't have been. Nobody buys stocks that they think will fall in price. You invest to make money, not lose it. In fact, that's how stocks are sold. Brokers, analysts, and other touts are predictably optimistic; they paint glowing pictures of the profit potential of their wares. Has your broker ever told you to buy XYZ stock because it might go up in price? My broker is always upbeat and confident about the outcome. And after I buy a few shares, so am I. The mere fact that I bought shows how optimistic I must have been.

The unhappy fact is that some stocks do fall in price. It makes no difference how optimistic I am, some things just never work out as anticipated. The difference between my student and me is that I am older and wiser. I know that things don't always work out as planned. But when they don't, I stand very little chance of going broke. Diversification keeps me in the game.

And staying in the game is the most important aspect of successful investing. Look at the formula for compound return.

$$\text{Compound value} = P(1 + R)^t$$

The most important variable in that formula is t, the number of periods an investment is allowed to compound. When most investors concern themselves with R (the rate of return), or with P (the amount of money invested), their emphasis is misplaced. This simple example shows why: Suppose that you invest $1,000 and earn 10 percent annually. After 10 years of compounding, your investment will amount to $2,593. Now double the amount invested and repeat the arithmetic. Your initial investment now amounts to $5,186. If you double the rate of return, your initial investment of $1,000 becomes $6,187. Now go back to the original example. Double the length of the investment period and leave the amount invested and rate of return untouched. By doubling the amount of time you stay in the game, your initial investment grows to $6,722. That's the largest increase of all.

This example illustrates the order of importance of the variables affecting investment wealth—time horizon, rate of return, and amount invested. Increasing the rate of return that you earn on your investments leads to greater wealth; however, there is no assurance that you will be able to earn an increased return. If you maintain a well-diversified portfolio whose risk lies within your tolerance zone, you will stay in the game over the long run. That's a virtual certainty. Thus, risk management is one of, if not the most critical factor in achieving long-run investment success—it guarantees that you can increase t.

To properly manage risk, you must be able to measure it. You must also know how to apportion your investment dollars among various assets to eliminate unnecessary risks. In fact, risk management can also assist in obtaining higher rates of return. For example, I stated earlier that the investor holding one stock not only takes three times more risk than the well-diversified investor but also obtains no greater return over the long run. Thus, the well-diversified investor can increase the portfolio risk threefold before butting up against the same degree of risk as the one-stock investor. By taking only necessary risks, however, this well-diversified investor now has the potential to earn three times as much return.

As you will soon see, the stock market is very efficient. Its rewards are closely tied to the risks investors assume. To earn above-average returns, you must usually assume above-average risks. The goal of this book is to give you the tools to increase investment returns while at the same time giving you every opportunity to stay in the investment game over the long run.

CHAPTER 4

EFFICIENT MARKETS, FINANCIAL ANALYSIS, AND STOCK PRICE PREDICTION

When I began to write this book I called my friends and told them to place their orders at their favorite bookstores. One replied: "I have spent so much money buying books on how to get rich, that I'm almost broke." I guess that my friend has been buying the wrong books.

According to Will Rogers it is very easy to make money in the stock market. "You just buy some stocks, and when they go up you sell and make money." When asked what happens if they don't go up, Rogers replied: "It's simple, you just don't buy 'em."

In that spirit I've often had a dream in which my newspaper boy began delivering tomorrow's newspaper today. Armed with today's closing stock prices at 7 A.M., I began placing orders to buy the stocks that would rise the most during the day. The profits rolled in. I sold my old car and bought a very expensive new one. I moved to a new condo overlooking Lake Michigan. I bought new clothes and fancy furniture; then I joined an expensive country club. I also began to buy popularity by giving stock tips to friends. But then something happened. Whenever I placed an order to buy a stock, I had to compete with my friends who were trying to buy the same stock. As a result, my trading profits began to erode. Finally, every time I bought a stock, it was at the high of the day. It's usually at this point that I wake up.

Although I realize when I wake up that the only way to make significant profits in my dream is to not tell my friends, I continue to do so anyway. You see, to make more money than you are supposed to in the stock market, you must know something that few others do, or you must know it before they do. Without this special knowledge, your returns are solely dependent on the risks you take. To earn higher returns you must take more risks. A market in which investment returns are linked to investment risk and nothing else is called an *efficient market*. In a perfectly efficient market, stock prices behave randomly and always equal their underlying values. Although some securities can be overpriced or underpriced in such a market, it is impossible to know which is which.

The implications of an efficient market are clear. Because no investor can obtain an advantage over another, investors need not bother applying either fundamental or technical securities analysis in search of mispriced securities. Instead, investors need only consider the risk and return characteristics of specific securities and then buy and hold well-diversified portfolios of assets meeting their risk and return requirements.

On the other hand, if capital markets are less than perfectly efficient, then some investors may possess the opportunity to gain an advantage over others by acquiring undervalued assets and selling the overvalued. In a less than perfectly efficient market, investors can earn a greater rate of return than that dictated by investment risk. That is, they get something for nothing. In such a market, successful investors must engage in active asset selection rather than take a passive buy-and-hold approach.

WHAT IS AN EFFICIENT MARKET?

Of course, the $64,000 question is: "Is the stock market efficient?" If so, why does it stay that way? According to classical economic theory, efficient, or perfectly competitive, markets must meet five criteria: First, products must be homogenous. That is, the goods and services traded must be direct substitutes for one another. When one good becomes higher priced than a substitute, users shift sources of supply. The producers of the high priced good then lower its price to attract the lost customers. Second, the market must contain numerous buyers and sellers—none of whom can singly affect or control price. In other words, prices cannot be manipulated by either buyers or sellers. Third, there must be an absence of barriers to entry or exit from the market. Everyone can come or go as they please. Fourth, there are no transaction costs. That is, the movement of goods or services from suppliers to demanders is not inhibited by trading costs. Finally, information concerning the nature of the product and of the existing supply and demand conditions is costless and easily accessible to all market participants. When new information appears, it is instantaneously disseminated to all.

How does the stock market stack up against these five requirements? Surprisingly well. First, product homogeneity certainly exists. Investors can readily find numerous securities with similar risk and return characteristics. Any of these securities can serve as a substitute for another. When one stock becomes too high priced given its risk (i.e., its return does not adequately compensate for the risk taken), investors can substitute another more reasonably priced stock.

Second, the stock market is indeed characterized by numerous buyers and sellers. Over 30 million individuals own shares of common stock directly and 200-million-share trading days on the New York Stock Exchange have become commonplace.

Third, no single buyer or seller commands sufficient resources to control stock prices for any appreciable length of time. Furthermore, it is illegal to manipulate stock prices. State and federal regulators keep a constant eye out for unusual stock price behavior. However, in some instances, well-capitalized investors may, over short periods, exert some degree of control over financial asset prices. The Hunt brothers, for example, tried to corner the silver market. Their buying drove the price of the metal from $5 to more than $50 per ounce. In the end the corner failed, silver plunged below $5 per ounce, and the Hunts went broke. Even their legendary fortune proved too small to allow the Hunts to manipulate silver prices for long.

Fourth, it is very easy to enter or exit the stock market with minimal transaction costs. Simply call and ask your broker to buy or sell. The organized exchanges employ hundreds of market makers—called *specialists*—who buy stocks when there are sellers but no other buyers, or sell when there are buyers but no other sellers. Furthermore, competition among brokers for customer business generally ensures minimal commission charges. However, since transaction costs do exist, the stock and bond markets are less than perfectly efficient. Even so, the distortion in market efficiency is minimal.

Most people agree that the stock market conforms quite well to the first four requirements for an efficient market; however, they debate the applicability of the fifth requirement. Namely, that in a perfectly competitive market, monopoly information does not exist and that security prices instantaneously adjust to new information.

On one hand, the existence of more than 12,000 full-time professional securities analysts who actively follow company fortunes and report on developments to their clients, tends to ensure adequate dissemination of financial information. Thus, it is highly unlikely, at least for the stocks of the most actively followed companies, that one investor could possess and profit from unique financial information.

However, corporate insiders such as officers and directors do possess unique information regarding the financial and operating conditions of the firms they manage. Even so, current law requires that when disclosing such information, the company must make it accessible to the investing public and not to only one analyst or investor. In addition, although corporate insiders can buy and sell their company's stock, they must hold purchases for six months and they may not engage in short selling. This reduces the potential to earn extra returns. However, several studies indicate that when numerous officers purchase shares of stock in their own firms, stock prices over subsequent periods tend to outperform the market as a whole. Thus, it does appear that at least one group of investors may possess and act on monopoly information for profit.

The fact that a few investors have a slight edge over others is not proof that the market is inefficient. Even those who believe the stock market to be less than perfectly efficient would concede this. Instead, these detractors have focused on the speed by which security prices adjust to new information. They contend that it takes time for stock prices to fully adjust to new information, and the longer the time it takes for such an adjustment, the greater the market inefficiency.

STOCK MARKET EFFICIENCY—BY DEGREE

Although the earliest studies of stock market efficiency date back to the 1930s, researchers conducted the bulk of efficient market research between mid-1950 and mid-1970. After two decades of theorizing, debating, and investigating, the so-called efficient market hypothesis (EMH) evolved. According to EMH, the stock market, when considered as a whole, is quite sophisticated in the manner in which it processes relevant investment information and arrives at equilibrium security prices. Furthermore, the high degree of sophistication occurs even though many market participants are themselves unsophisticated. (Even though some of us are dumber than others, the market still acts as though we are all smart.) According to EMH, the stock market is efficient because stock prices behave as though they reflect all existing information, and because they adjust nearly instantaneously in unbiased fashion to new information. Let's see how EMH followers came to their beliefs.

Early on, the efficient market debate centered on the issue of whether the stock market was efficient. Later, the issue changed to "how efficient is it?" The degrees of market efficiency appear in Figure 4-1. A completely inefficient market is one in which extensive monopoly information exists. Prices are controlled by manipulators, entry and exit from the market is difficult and costly, and stock prices react with extreme lags to the release of new information.

A weakly efficient stock market is one in which stock prices follow a "random walk." In such a market, stock prices have no memory and successive price changes are independent of one another. That is, past security price changes have no bearing on future price changes. Thus, if the stock market is at least weakly efficient, the various technical approaches to market timing based on perceived price trends are completely without value.

But wait. Isn't this an extreme view? After all, look at any chart of the stock market and you see an upward trending series

FIGURE 4–1
Market Efficiency—by Degrees

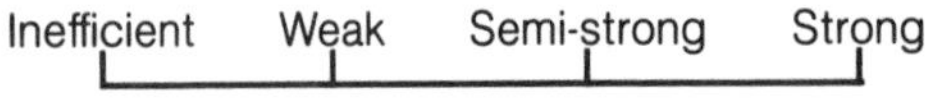

Inefficient	Weak	Semi-strong	Strong

of wave-like patterns with peaks and valleys. Given this stock price behavior, how can one say that prices are generated by a random process? Something must be causing these patterns. If one can find the causes, then prediction is possible.

To illustrate how such patterns can result from random events, I constructed a mathematically "fair game." A fair game is one in which the expected value of an outcome is equal to zero. For example, if you play a game of flip-the-coin in which you receive $1 if the coin falls heads and pay $1 if it falls tails, you are playing a mathematically fair game. (Of course, I'm assuming that you are not flipping a two-headed coin.) Although you may win or lose $1 on any particular flip of the coin, your average winnings after many coin tosses are equal to zero. In this mathematically fair game, it is impossible to tell whether you will win or lose $1 on the next toss. Each outcome is a random event, and even though the last ten tosses may have resulted in ten consecutive heads, there is an equal likelihood that the next toss will produce either a head or a tail.

If the stock market is a fair game, the same holds true. No matter what happened to the price of a stock yesterday, its price today is unaffected and, thus, unpredictable. If the stock market follows a fair game model, it is impossible to continually profit from investment actions taken on the basis of what the market did yesterday, last week, last month, or last year. A fair game stock market is one in which price changes are random and carry an expectation of zero change.

Now, suppose that Jack and Jill decide to play a game of flip the coin. If the coin falls heads, Jack pays Jill $1; if it falls tails, Jill pays Jack $1. Given that there is an equal likelihood that the coin will land heads or tails, the expected winnings for either Jack or Jill, after many coin tosses, is zero. I simulated the outcomes of this game for 10,000 coin flips. (Actually, my personal computer did the flipping and recorded the results.) Figure 4-2 illustrates these outcomes from the viewpoint of Jack's accumulated winnings. Even though I defined a fair game, runs of luck produced wide fluctuations in Jack's accumulated winnings. These runs of luck and the corresponding changes in Jack's wealth occurred even though the expected value of either Jack's or Jill's winnings after many flips is zero.

Historical fluctuations in individual security price levels

FIGURE 4–2
Wave Patterns and Random Events

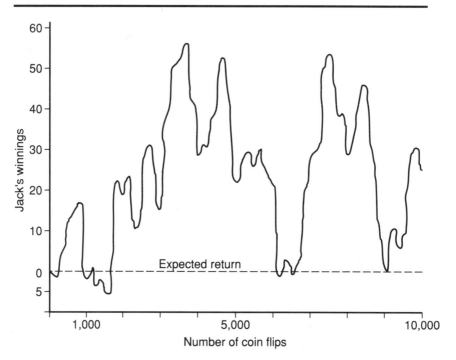

and the levels of stock price averages (e.g., the Dow Jones Industrial Averages) are the result of similar random fluctuations. That is, the random period-to-period stock price changes whose expected value is zero (actually a small positive number reflecting nothing more than long-run growth due to corporate earnings retention and reinvestment) result in a stock price series which gives the appearance of nonrandom fluctuations from peaks to valleys. However, because the stock price changes are themselves random, no one can forecast the peaks and valleys in the series of accumulated changes with any degree of accuracy.

This, of course, is vehemently denied by stock market technicians. These people analyze the price changes for individual stocks and market averages, usually by plotting their prices on graph paper. Either units of time (the bar chart) or units of price change (the point-and-figure chart) are the standards for making entries. Some technicians also include historical trading volume on their charts. From the price and volume patterns depicted on their charts, technicians claim that they are able to forecast future security price movements.

Although market technicians employ several methods to analyze and interpret the numerous patterns on their charts, technical analysis contains some common elements. The theory assumes that:

1. A security's market value is determined solely by supply and demand.
2. Supply and demand are governed by many factors, rational and irrational.
3. The market continually and automatically weighs all of these factors.
4. Security prices tend to move in trends which may persist for an appreciable length of time.
5. Changes in trends result from shifts in supply and demand.
6. These shifts can be detected in the action of the market itself.

In essence, stock market technicians contend that the actions of buyers and sellers recorded each day supply all of the relevant information needed to analyze supply and demand and forecast future market actions. According to this view, the stock market must be less than weakly efficient since the persistence of stock price trends enables the astute analyst, who can interpret such trends, to predict future securities prices.

The semistrong form of market efficiency, on the other hand, depicts the stock market as being one in which stock prices reflect all information contained in historical prices and one in which these prices reflect all publicly available information. According to this view of market efficiency, public information causes stock prices to adjust instantaneously. Because the adjustment process occurs so quickly, no investor can consistently profit by acting on it.

In a semistrong efficient market, nothing can be gained by the analysis of information already in the hands of other investors. Even if a majority of investors are ignorant of these facts, the presence of professional analysts who pass along all new items to paying customers is sufficient to ensure a semistrong efficient market. The only investors who profit from the evaluation of financial information generally know something that nobody else knows. However, the regulatory authorities frown on the use of such information. (If you don't believe me, ask Ivan Boesky and Michael Milkin.)

The strong form of market efficiency requires that security prices not only reflect all publicly available information, but that they reflect all information (public and otherwise). In a perfectly efficient market, monopoly access to information of any kind does not exist.

The degree to which the stock market is efficient or nonefficient dictates appropriate methods to determine which stocks should be bought and sold. A stock market less than weakly efficient warrants a technical analysis approach. On the other hand, if markets are at least weakly efficient, but something less than semistrongly efficient, investors should abandon technical analysis and embrace the fundamental analysis concept. That is, investors can profit by gleaning information from corporate reports, company news releases, and other sources of financial and economic data and using such information to estimate a security's value. If the value estimate differs from current price, they take the appropriate buy or sell action. Finally, if the stock market is at least semistrongly efficient, the investor should give up the search for undervalued or overvalued assets and buy and hold a diversified portfolio of stocks which possess the required risk and return requirements (i.e., investors should follow a passive rather than an active portfolio strategy).

Tests for the Degree of Stock Market Efficiency

As stated earlier, if stock prices behave as though they have no memory, then the stock market is at least weakly efficient. That is, if stock price changes are independent of one another, then the market demonstrates minimal efficiency. Harry Roberts conducted one of the first studies that hinted at such independence. Statistician Roberts illustrated that a series of randomly generated numbers shows patterns highly similar to series of stock prices (i.e., patterns similar to those produced by the Jack and Jill game). Also, a study by M. F. M. Osborne illustrated that stock price changes conform to a pattern highly similar to that of a particle in Brownian motion. That is, security price changes exhibited the same degree of randomness as do dust particles suspended in air. These two studies were a catalyst to a virtual plethora of stock price change investigations.

Acting independently, several researchers correlated price changes of individual securities and market indexes over time. The results uniformly showed little correlation in security price changes. However, skeptics (mostly technical analysts) pointed out that these correlational studies only demonstrated that successive price changes over rigidly defined time periods, such as days, weeks, or months, are uncorrelated. These nonbelievers pointed out that technical analysts are not bound by such rigidities. That is, even though day-to-day price changes might be uncorrelated, it is possible that runs in price change tend to persist. And it is these runs that can be uncovered by charting stock prices.

In response, several researchers tested stock prices for abnormal runs. Generally, they followed the following methodology: If over a defined period a stock's price rose, they assigned a "+"; if it fell in price, they assigned a "−"; a "0" indicated no change. Thus, a pattern such as "+ + + + − − −00 + +" contains four runs. If there is a tendency for price changes to persist, one would find fewer runs over time than could be obtained by chance alone; for example, by flipping a coin. These tests again uniformly indicated an absence of abnormal runs either for individual stocks or for market averages.

Market technicians still remained unconvinced that the market was at least weakly efficient. These analysts emphasized that their methods required an examination of both the direction and magnitude of security price changes. Since correlational studies and runs tests use only the direction of price change, it is possible that noise (small changes in security prices) could account for the finding of independence.

In response, researchers tested every imaginable filter that could eliminate noise. Filter techniques are sets of decision rules calling for the purchase or sale of a security if its price rises or falls by more than a predetermined percentage of its previous price. The percentage rise or fall in price that signals a purchase or sale is called the *filter*. The decision rules are often stated as follows: If the price of a stock rises by X percent, buy and hold until it falls by Y percent, then sell the stock, and go short. When the price rises X percent after reaching bottom, cover the short sale, and go long. For example, if GM stock is trading at $80, you might buy if it rises 5 percent or to $84. You then hold until it falls 5 percent from its interim high; if it continues to rise to $100 then you would sell when it dropped 5 percent or back to $95.

Market timing through the implementation of formula plans is a variant of the filter rule concept. These plans, at least in theory, allow investors to "buy bear markets and sell bull markets" without the requirement of having to forecast the trend of the market. In general, such plans are characterized by the division of an investment portfolio into aggressive (stock) and defensive (money fund) segments. These segments are continually rebalanced depending on the direction of the stock market and the relative values of the segments. For example, begin with $10,000 divided into stocks (60 percent or $6,000) and cash (40 percent or $4,000). If stock prices rise 30 percent, the portfolio will contain $7,800 in stocks, which make up about 66 percent of the portfolio. At this point, a sufficient amount of stocks are sold to bring the ratio back to sixty-forty. Thus, as stock prices rise, investors continually take profits. If stock prices fall, cash is shifted to stocks and, thus, investors buy at lower prices. The goal is to "buy low and sell high."

Again, subsequent tests of nearly every imaginable filter and formula plan failed to produce profits greater than could be obtained by passively buying and holding the market. During the last 25 years, researchers have met every challenge thrown at them by technical analysts. Not even one selection or timing model based on the use of historical security prices has been able to generate investment returns greater than can be obtained by chance selection. To me, the evidence overwhelmingly indicates that the stock market is at least weakly efficient. Use of technical analysis, especially charting techniques, is frivolous.

Nevertheless, technical analysis remains a big business. Numerous technically based stock market advisory services boast large numbers of subscribers. Every brokerage firm of any size has its resident technician. Thousands of individual investors spend countless hours placing X's and O's and lines of all kinds on graph paper. They have made numerous claims of success; the real truth is that most of the rewards from charting stock prices are a result of luck rather than the persistence of stock price patterns.

Tests of the semistrong form of market efficiency involve an analysis of the time that it takes for security prices to adjust to new information. Although stock prices should react to such news, in an efficient market most of the price adjustment would narrowly surround the announcement date. If the market were less than semistrongly efficient, the price change pattern would appear as illustrated in Figure 4-3(a); if it were semistrongly efficient, the pattern would be as illustrated in Figure 4-3(b).

In an efficient market, a security's price would begin to rise before the announcement as market participants anticipate a change in company fortunes. Once the announcement is made, the stock price would rapidly adjust and reach a new equilibrium level. At that time successive price changes again begin to wander randomly. In an inefficient market, the security price would react to the announcement with a lag. That is, some investors obtain and interpret the news. Their buying or selling pressure begins to move the price. As more and more investors become aware of and react to the news, the price continues its trend until the news has been completely digested.

In 1969, the first stock price reaction time study involved an examination of security price changes around the announcement date of stock splits. Although the study identified a price reaction prior to the stock split announcement date, after the announcement stock prices behaved as though the market were semistrongly efficient. That is, investors who purchase shares of stock on the announcement of a stock split cannot earn extraordinary returns because all of the price adjustment occurs prior to the announcement of the split to the public.

Another study examined the price reaction to secondary stock offering announcements. Stock prices tended to decline when the sellers were corporations or corporate officers but remained relatively unchanged when the sellers were banks, insurance companies, or individuals. In addition, all price adjustments occurred within six days of the secondary offering announcement. A study of block trades on security prices

FIGURE 4–3
Stock Market Reaction Time

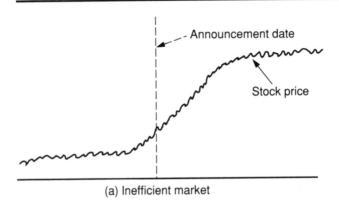

(a) Inefficient market

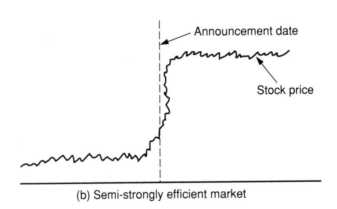

(b) Semi-strongly efficient market

revealed that prices tended to fall when the trades were seller-initiated and tended to rise when they were buyer-initiated. All price changes, however, were complete within the day of the trade.

Evidence regarding the reaction of stock prices to dividend announcements appears to be mixed. Examination of stock prices from 10 days before to 10 days after dividend change announcements indicates that all of the security price adjustment (a fall in stock price due to a reduction or omission of dividends or a rise in price due to announced dividend increases) occurred during both the day of the announcement and the day after. When viewed over a longer time frame of from four months before the announcement to three months after, however, nearly all of the negative adjustments (average price declines of 15 percent or more) to dividend reduction announcements occurred over the four-month period prior to the announcements. For announcements of dividend increases, stock prices rose by nearly 10 percent during the four months prior to the announcement. However, they continued to drift higher (up another 10 percent) during the four-month period after the announcement date.

Several studies of stock price reaction to corporate earnings announcements indicate nearly instantaneous price adjustments occurring during the period immediately following the announcements. Thus, investors have very little opportunity to profit by acting on announcements. For example, Roy Ball and Philip Brown found that when favorable earnings announcements were unanticipated, stock prices gradually adjusted over the 12 months prior to the announcement. However, relatively little price change occurred during the month following the announcements. Professor William Beaver found the absolute level of stock price changes and the volume of trading significantly higher during the week in which the firm's earnings were announced. That is, the duration of investor excitement around news dates appears to be relatively brief. Finally, G. Foster examined the market's reaction to preliminary earnings announcements made by company officials. Foster's study also indicated that investors react quickly. Trading volume increased during the week of the announcement but returned to preannouncement levels by the end of the week.

Given the conclusions of the few studies mentioned here (and more than 100 others), it appears that the stock market is nearly efficient in the semistrong sense. Stocks are generally priced to yield returns based solely on their risk. Excess investment returns (returns beyond that demanded as compensation for taking risk) cannot be obtained.

The belief in market efficiency gained strength during the decade of the 1970s as study after study failed to uncover a strategy that would produce excess investment returns. Several banks and a few mutual funds began to index their portfolios to the market in the belief that if you can't beat it, you might as well join it. However, beginning with the publication of research on the risk and return characteristics of small firm stocks by Rolf Banz in 1978, a few cracks began to appear in the walls of the efficient market hypothesis. In short, Banz found that small firm stocks provide investors with returns greater than can be accounted for by their risk. He found an investment free lunch that should not be on the menu in an efficient market. Since then, researchers have uncovered other puzzles that cannot be explained away by EMH. Such anomalies as the January effect, the low price-earnings ratio effect, the day of the week effect, the holiday effect, and end of the month effect have recently been documented. All indicate that investors can increase their investment returns without increasing investment risk. Thus, it turns out that although the stock market is far from inefficient, it is not nearly as efficient as once thought.

COIN FLIPPING LUCK AND SUCCESSFUL PORTFOLIO MANAGEMENT: HOW WELL DO THE PROS PERFORM?

At this point I am sure that many readers are wondering: If the stock market is so efficient, how can I explain the fact that some portfolio managers have been able to outperform stock market averages by a significant amount over an extended period of time? Warren Buffet and Fred Alger are but two contemporary investment advisors who have been able to earn an average annual rate of return of 20 percent during the last 20 years. During this same period, the annual compound rate of return provided by the S&P index averaged slightly less than 9 percent. Yet these individuals more than doubled the market's rate of return. No doubt some of the excess returns can be attributed to holding portfolios of common stocks which were more risky than the market portfolio. However, it is doubtful that all excess returns could be due to increased portfolio risk. Thus, the exceptional returns of these successful managers must be due to something else. If the "something else" happens to be superior stock picking ability, doesn't this raise a serious question about the degree of stock market efficiency?

The answer to this question can partially be explained by the law of averages and a statistical concept called *gravitation toward the mean*. That is, at any point in time, a random occurrence can be significantly above or below average merely due to chance alone. However, after a time, the average of a series of random events approaches the population mean, or average.

Even though this may sound complicated, I can assure you that it is not. To illustrate these concepts, consider the following game of chance: The game is played by 32 individuals who each toss a coin five times and record the number of heads they obtain. The individual who tosses the most heads in five coin flips wins the game.

As we all know, the likelihood that any one participant will obtain a head on the first toss of the coin is 50 percent. Thus, on average, 16 of the participants will obtain a head after the first toss of the coin. In the second toss, eight of these participants, on average, will toss a second head. Four of these individuals will generally obtain their third head on the third toss of the coin, two get a fourth head on the next toss, and one will usually obtain a fifth consecutive head on the last toss.

Actually, the odds are 32 to 1 that a specific individual can obtain five consecutive heads and about 5 to 2 that exactly 1 of the 32 participants will obtain five heads during any one game. That is, about 40 percent of the time there will be just one winner who has tossed a total of five heads.

At the beginning of the second game, the odds that the same person will be a repeat winner are 32 to 1. On average, a participant will toss a total of five heads during two successive games, or 10 tosses. That means the individual who tossed five consecutive heads during the play of the first game will most likely toss a lesser number during the second game. On the other hand, the individual who failed to obtain a single head during the first game and scored 0 will most likely obtain more heads during the second game. The point is that even though both individuals have recorded results significantly above and below average for the first game, their totals after two games will be closer to the average obtainable for both games, five heads in 10 flips. This phenomenon, gravitation toward the mean, is a result of the law of large numbers.

Although this nonsensical game may have no direct meaning for individual investors, let's change the game slightly to show that there is a great deal to be learned here. Suppose that these 32 players are portfolio managers who must decide whether to invest in stocks or T-bills on January 1, 1987. Since they do not know where the market will be at year-end, they do not know which investment to make. However, each would like to invest in the alternative providing the greatest total return during the year.

For want of a better method, suppose that each manager flips a coin at the beginning of the year. If a head results, the manager invests entirely in common stocks. If the coin falls tails, the portfolio is invested in T-bills. Suppose that the same approach to market timing is also taken at the beginning of 1988, 1989, 1990, and 1991. The probability of making a correct decision at the beginning of each year is 50 percent; that is, a correct decision means investing in the asset yielding the highest total return for the year. Furthermore, like the previously described game, the odds that a specific portfolio manager can make five correct decisions in five successive years are 32 to 1. The odds that only one manager will make five correct decisions are about 5 to 2.

Table 4-1 lists the total annual returns for investment in the S&P Index and short-term T-bills for the years 1987 through 1991. The sequence of correct investment decisions is as follows: 1987 invest in T-bills, 1988 invest in common stocks, 1989 stocks, 1990 T-bills, and 1991 stocks. A manager lucky enough to make five correct investment decisions would have earned a total compound return of 128 percent over this period (an average compound annual rate of return of 18 percent versus a 15 percent average compound annual return for the S&P Index). The poor person who made five successive incorrect decisions would show a total compound return of only 24 percent after five years (an average annual return of approximately 5 percent). A manager who refused to make investments based on the toss of a coin and instead bought only common stocks at the beginning of 1987 and held on to a fully invested position for the entire five-year period would have earned a total return of 104 percent —the total market rate of return—while a T-bill investor would have earned about 38 percent over the five-year period.

TABLE 4-1
Rates of Return: T-Bills and S&P 500 Index

	Percent	
Year	Common Stock Returns	Treasury Bill Returns
1987	5.2%	5.5%
1988	16.8	6.3
1989	31.5	8.4
1990	-3.2	7.8
1991	30.5	5.6

Figure 4-4 illustrates the distribution of total returns for the 32 portfolio managers. The average return for the group is 71 percent and is the same as would have been obtained by a portfolio manager who invested one half of the portfolio in common stocks and one half in T-bills at the beginning of 1987 and maintained these proportions for the duration of the five-year period. One half of the coin flipping portfolio managers beat this average return while the other half underperformed

FIGURE 4-4
Hypothetical Five-Year Returns (32 coin tossers)

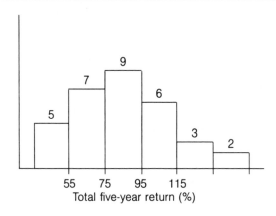

Number of funds

this so-called total market rate of return. (In this case the "market" refers to the market for all securities—stocks and T-bills—and not just the stock market.) Finally, as one moves away from the average rate of return toward either tail of the distribution the number of managers obtaining above- or below-average portfolio returns steadily declines.

So much for games. Let's now look at the returns for some real live mutual fund managers, the professional portfolio managers. I chose this group because their returns are readily available, and because so many individual investors have some of their assets invested in mutual funds. I obtained the total compound returns for the 527 common stock funds in existence from 1987 through 1991 (aggressive growth, growth, and growth and income). I chose this time period to compare actual portfolio returns with those of our coin tossers. These returns do not include the impact of either front-end or back-end sales charges or personal income taxes. (See Figure 4-5.)

Fidelity's Select Health Sciences (up a total of 377 percent) had the best five-year performance record while the 44 Wall Street Fund (which recorded a total loss of 20 percent) had the worst record. The average return for all funds was 81.0 percent. Over the five-year period, 151 funds obtained a total return greater than the total return of the S&P Index while 376 earned less. Furthermore, 181 funds, or 37 percent, failed to outperform the average coin flipping portfolio manager who invested in only common stocks and T-bills. Finally, 37 funds, or seven percent, failed to outperform the investor who maintained a so-called riskless portfolio consisting entirely of short-term T-bills.

What does all of this mean? One of the purposes of this exercise is to show that given a large number of investors, some can be expected to do well by chance alone. The distribution of returns actually earned by professional mutual fund managers shown in Figure 4-5 has a shape quite similar to the distribution of returns obtained by the hypothetical coin flipping portfolio managers illustrated in Figure 4-4. These lucky professional portfolio managers who show exceptional performance during short-run periods find that over the long-run, their over-all portfolio returns tend to reflect the portfolio risk that they have

FIGURE 4–5
Distribution of Five-Year Mutual Fund Returns, 1987–1991

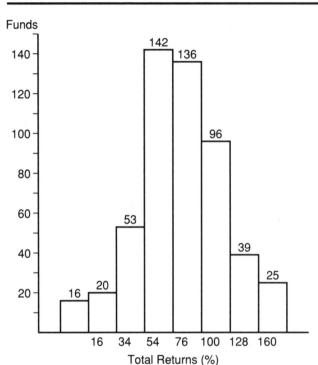

taken. Thus, their long-run performance record eventually falls back in line with the average rate of return available for the level of risk that they have chosen to take.

Of course, one might ask: How long is the long run? Isn't a 5-year, 10-year or 20-year record of exceptional portfolio return long enough to say that skill rather than luck determined the results? Unfortunately, the answer is *no*. One statistician estimated that it would require nearly 70 years of observations to show conclusively that an annual rate of return of 2 percent more than the market rate of return was the result of skill rather than luck. Thus, even the existence of a few seemingly successful portfolio managers may be consistent with the notion that the stock market is indeed a highly efficient mechanism.

BUT WHAT ABOUT MARKET TIMING?

The hottest selling investment newsletters in the country base their recommendations on market timing. Some of these newsletters claim fantastic results. Furthermore, every brokerage house of decent size has its resident technical analysts. If people spend so much money on technical timing services, don't they provide some value?

The goal of technical market timing services is to get investors out of falling markets and to keep them fully invested during periods of rising prices. Even though this is an admirable goal, is it worth pursuing? On the one hand, the potential rewards of being able to sit out prolonged bear markets are nothing short of fantastic. For example, over the period 1945–91 the buy-and-hold investor who owned the S&P index would have earned $233 for every $1 initially invested. During this 47-year period there were eight major bear markets. A market timer who correctly forecasted the onset of these bear markets, and jumped out of the stock market during these declines while remaining fully invested during the bull markets in between, would have earned $1,000 for every dollar initially invested. Even a market timer who escaped only one half of the decline during each bear market, still would have earned $433 for each $1 initially invested.

These returns do not include transaction costs. Thus, the market timer would have earned less than the amounts reported above. However, even after brokerage commissions, the improvement in overall return is still dramatic. Of course, that assumes the market timer has a chance of being successful.

Most timing services advertise fantastic results. That in itself should make you suspicious. Most of the claims made by these services turn out to be highly misleading. All ignore the significant impact of taxation on investment returns. Some services compute their purported investment returns without deducting the fees that they charge for the service. A few even go so far as to report hypothetical rather than actual results. Even if a timing service has a decent record for a few years, does this mean that you will be equally successful if you sign up today? Probably not. Here's why.

Table 4-2 illustrates the total annual rates of return of the Standard & Poor's 500 Stock Index and of Treasury bills during 1971–90. A buy-and-hold approach to investing in this unmanaged index over this period would have produced a compound annual rate of return of 11.5 percent; an investment of $1,000 in the S&P Index at the beginning of 1971 would have grown to $8,727 by the end of 1990, assuming reinvestment of all dividends.

On the other hand, a pure T-bill investment strategy over this 20-year period would have produced a 7.9 percent compound annual rate of return. That is, a $1,000 T-bill investment made in 1971 would have become $4,371 by year-end 1990.

During this period, stock prices fell during five years— 1973, 1974, 1977, 1981, and 1990—and T-bill returns exceeded common stock returns on eight occasions—1973, 1974, 1977, 1978, 1981, 1984, 1987, and 1990. The effective market timer

TABLE 4-2
Annual Rates of Return, 1971-1990

	Percent	
Year	S&P Index	Treasury Bills
1971	14.3%	4.4%
1972	19.0	3.8
1973	−14.7	6.9
1974	−26.5	8.0
1975	37.2	5.8
1976	23.8	5.1
1977	−7.2	5.1
1978	6.6	7.2
1979	18.4	10.4
1980	32.4	11.2
1981	−4.9	14.7
1982	21.4	10.5
1983	22.5	8.8
1984	6.3	9.8
1985	32.2	7.7
1986	18.5	6.2
1987	5.2	5.5
1988	16.8	6.3
1989	31.5	8.4
1990	−3.2	7.8

could have improved on a buy-and-hold approach by being out of stocks and in T-bills during any of these eight years. If market timing were done on an annual basis, the strategy shown in Table 4-3 could have achieved a perfect record and maximum investment returns.

The perfect timing strategy would have produced a 17.3 percent compound annual rate of return over this period. An initial investment of $1,000 would have grown to $23,144 by the end of 1990, assuming reinvestment of all dividends and interest and ignoring transaction costs, management fees, and taxes. Thus, on a before-cost basis, perfect stock market timing would have increased investor wealth by $14,417 for each $1,000 initially invested over a buy-and-hold-the-market investment strategy. This is by no means an insignificant amount. Of course, the results are dependent on the accuracy of the market timer.

Although perfect timing produces superior results, the poor

TABLE 4–3
Rates of Return: T-Bills and
S&P 500 Index

Year	Investment Strategy	Percent Return
1971	Stocks	14.3%
1972	Stocks	19.0
1973	T-bills	6.9
1974	T-bills	8.0
1975	Stocks	37.2
1976	Stocks	23.8
1977	T-bills	5.1
1978	T-bills	7.2
1979	Stocks	18.4
1980	Stocks	32.4
1981	T-bills	14.7
1982	Stocks	21.4
1983	Stocks	22.5
1984	T-bills	9.8
1985	Stocks	32.2
1986	Stocks	18.5
1987	T-bills	5.5
1988	Stocks	16.8
1989	Stocks	31.5
1990	T-bills	7.8

person who made the wrong move each year over the 20-year period would have produced a meager 2.0 percent compound annual rate of return—an initial investment of $1,000 would have grown to $1,497. Of course, over the long run, no market timer is ever 100 percent accurate or 100 percent in error.

Naturally a market timing program that is correct half of the time is probably not worth paying for, because the results could be duplicated by a toss of a fair coin at the beginning of each year. I decided to include the results here, however, merely as a point of reference. The determination of investment results when the accuracy or inaccuracy rate is less than perfect is quite complex because one does not know in which half of the periods the timer will be right. Will the timer err only in those periods when the S&P 500 index is only marginally different from the T-bill return, or will the timer err by investing in T-bills during those years when the market is skyrocketing and be fully invested in stocks when prices are plunging?

This problem can be solved somewhat by examining the returns at both extremes. First, I assumed that for a 50 percent error rate, the timing errors were minimal; for instance, being invested in stocks during 1978 when the market returned 6.6 percent versus a 7.2 percent T-bill return. Next, I assumed that the errors were made at the worst possible times; for instance, being invested in stocks in 1974 and T-bills in 1985.

Given a fifty-fifty market timing record, an initial $1,000 investment in 1971 would have grown to $11,378 by year-end 1990 given minimal timing errors (best case) and to only $3,110 if the timing errors were made at the most inopportune times (worst case). Because a buy-and-hold-the-market strategy results in a terminal portfolio value of $8,727, a timer with a 50 percent accuracy rate runs the risk of producing inferior returns. In fact, in the worst case, the returns produced by market timing fall short of those that could have been obtained by investing in T-bills for the entire 20-year period. Even a timer who is right two thirds of the time could produce returns below both the returns produced from a buy-and-hold strategy and from a riskless T-bill investment strategy.

It is logical at this point to ask: Which accuracy rate would have been necessary to ensure that investment returns would have bettered a buy-and-hold-the-market approach? As it turns out, a market timer would have had to achieve an accuracy rate of at least 80 percent to ensure success. And odds against an 80 percent batting average over these 20 years are more than 30-to-1. In fact, after considering the cost of the service, the brokerage commissions resulting from additional trading, and the erosion in returns due to the premature payment of income taxes, it is highly unlikely that any active market timing strategy will beat a passive buy-and-hold strategy over an investment lifetime.

Remember also, market timing strategies are not infallible. Even a well-designed model can place you in the wrong assets every once in awhile. These timing mistakes can reduce actual portfolio returns by a considerable amount. For example, if a market timer had erred only once during this 20-year period, by keeping investors out of the stock market and in T-bills during 1975 when stocks returned 37.2 percent, the potential annual rate of return would have dropped from 17.3 percent to 15.6 percent before expenses and taxes. After payment of costs totaling 3 percent per year, the investor's actual rate of return would have fallen to 12.6 percent. That is only 1.4 percent higher than the annual market rate of return. Finally, because tax payments have not been considered in this example, it is most likely that this one goof would have reduced an investor's return to that nearly approximating the market rate of return.

WHAT DOES ALL OF THIS MEAN?

I am a professional securities analyst and portfolio manager. I believe that the stock market is reasonably efficient. Does this mean that I also have a split personality? After all, aren't analysts supposed to uncover undervalued stocks? But, in an efficient market, stocks are priced on the basis of publicly available information. Thus, I am either chasing rainbows or cheating my customers. Actually, I am doing neither. First, as you will see in the next chapter, security analysis is an important component of stock selection even if the stock market is efficient. Second, it's because analysts continually digest public information and assess the relative values of securities that the market is so efficient. So if nothing else, analysts help keep the stock market honest (i.e., make it a fair game).

Even though the stock market as a whole is reasonably efficient, there are small pockets of inefficiency. The most notable of these involves the pricing of very small firms. And it is primarily these firms that draw my attention. Few analysts concern themselves with these firms. Most choose or are forced to focus their attention on the real giants of corporate America —IBM, GE, and ITT. That's because large institutional investors generally buy only these stocks. Due to all the attention from analysts and institutional investors, these stocks behave as though that segment of the market were very efficient.

On the other hand, the stocks of small firms lie beyond the grasp of institutional investors. Thus, analysts who devote their attention to small firm stocks have very little to sell. (The way to make money in the analyst and brokerage business these days is to cater to large institutional investors and ignore the individual.) That virtually leaves the small firm segment of the stock market in the hands of the individual investor. Fending for themselves, these investors find not only instances of undervaluation but also opportunities to earn excess returns.

At about 6 percent per year, these excess returns might appear to be small, yet they can accumulate into quite a large pile over a long period. My goal in writing this book and in publishing my *Investment Horizons* small firm stock advisory newsletter is to help individual investors capture what has become known as the small firm effect. In the chapters that follow, I discuss the principles of common stock valuation, the small firm effect, how to capture that effect, and where to look for other excess return potential. I also explain how you can manage a small firm common stock portfolio, and how you can select large firm common stocks by applying the same principles as for small firm stocks. Remember that I am talking about obtaining an investment free lunch—not a seven-course dinner. This is not a scheme to get rich quick. It is, however, a method that can be readily applied by all individuals who want their investment dollars to grow into a larger pile during their investment lifetime.

CHAPTER 5

COMMON STOCK VALUATION

It pays to follow one fundamental rule when buying anything: Never pay more than it's worth. Don't get ripped off. Most people pride themselves on being astute shoppers, able to spot a bargain when one comes along; these very same people tend to get ripped off week after week when buying common stocks. The reason this happens with such regularity is that many people don't know how to place a value on the stocks they purchase.

It is logical to ask at this point: Doesn't the efficient market come to an investor's rescue? In the last chapter I reported that a number of studies indicated the stock market is quite efficient. In an efficient market, the best estimate of the value of a share of common stock is its current price. Thus, investors don't have to work very hard to determine the value of a share of common stock. They merely have to call their brokers and ask for a stock's latest price quote—in an efficient market that's the best estimate of value. If this were so, this would be a very short chapter in a very short book. However, the stock market is not nearly as efficient as it was thought to be a decade ago. Even if the stock market were efficient, stocks are worth different amounts to different people. Thus, when the stock market is efficient and a stock's price is the consensus estimate of its value, you still have to determine what it is worth *to you*.

We discussed investment return in Chapter 2. Chapter 3 examined the nature of investment risk and its relationship to return; namely, greater returns are demanded as compensation for the assumption of greater risks. Thus, in determining the rate of return you require from a common stock, you must first analyze its risk. Once risk has been quantified, you must determine the return necessary to induce you to invest. You can then use this rate of return to determine the price you are willing to pay. If the current price is equal to or less than the price you are willing to pay, you make the investment. Sounds simple enough. Of course, like almost anything else, the process is easier stated than performed. Although many volumes have been written on the analytical methods used in common stock valuation, the various approaches have several common threads. These are examined in this chapter. The object is not to prepare you for a career as a securities analyst, but to arm you with enough knowledge to minimize the chances that you will pay too much when buying stocks.

ELEMENTS OF VALUE

Common stocks have value because they provide future income. Their value is equal to the present worth of the future income they are expected to provide. Present worth depends on the rate of return desired. For example, suppose investors are considering purchasing shares in a company expected to pay a dividend of $1 per share during each of the next two years. Also suppose investors believe that they can sell each of these shares for $10 two years from now. How much should they pay if they require a 20 percent return on the investment?

$$\text{Present worth} = \frac{D_1}{1+R} + \frac{D_2}{(1+R)^2} + \frac{P_2}{(1+R)^3}$$

Where D_1 and D_2 are the first and second year dividends, P_2 is the future selling price, and R is your required rate of return.

$$= \frac{\$1}{1.20} + \frac{\$1}{(1.20)^2} + \frac{\$10}{(1.20)^2}$$
$$= \$0.83 + \$0.69 + \$6.93$$
$$\text{Share value} = \$8.45$$

The concept of present worth applies to the valuation of all assets. Armed with the knowledge of the future cash receipts, the timing of those receipts, and your own required rate of return you can determine an asset's value using elementary mathematics. The difficult part, of course, is predicting the future cash receipts. At least that's how stock valuation works in theory. Even though the theory of value is interesting, theories won't put any groceries on the table. Practical approaches to stock valuation are more financially rewarding. So let's examine a few.

Consider, for example, the valuation of one of Wall Street's favorite stocks, Sara Lee. What is a share of Sara Lee common stock worth to you? In early 1993, Sara Lee common stock was selling for $28 per share. It had just reported 12-month earnings of $1.08 and was paying a $0.58 annual dividend. During the last 10 years revenues grew at an annual rate of 8 percent while earnings grew by 14 percent.

Assuming that Sara Lee stock belongs in your portfolio, it should be bought if you can pay no more than it is worth. Its worth, of course, depends on your required rate of return on investments of this type and the firm's future prospects. For now, let's assume that you would like to earn 15 percent annually on this investment and the firm's future performance will mirror that of the past.

First, let's consider the question of return. When you buy a share of common stock, your return on investment is composed of dividend returns (the stock's dividend yield) and the rate of growth of share price (capital appreciation). This relationship is illustrated in the following simple equation. Dividend yield is merely current cash dividends divided by current share price (D/P). Capital appreciation is the rate of growth (G).

Total return = Dividend yield + Capital appreciation

Thus, $R = D/P + G$ and rearranging terms we have the following:

$$P = D/(R - G)$$

That is, the current price should equal the current dividend divided by the difference between your required rate of return and estimated future growth. Remember that you wanted to earn at least 15 percent annually on an investment in Sara Lee. Assume for the moment that future share price growth will mirror the company's historical earnings and sales growth (about 12% per year). Substituting these values in the preceding equation we have the following:

$$P = \$0.58/(0.15 - 0.12)$$
$$= \$0.58/(0.03)$$
$$= \$19.67$$

If you were to pay $19.67 per share for Sara Lee and the firm grew by 12 percent annually, your annual return would equal 15 percent.

$$R = \$0.58/\$19.67 + 12\%$$
$$R = \quad 3\% \quad +12\%$$
$$\text{Total return} = \text{Dividend yield} + \text{Capital growth}$$

Because Sara Lee is selling for $28, however, a purchase at this price would return less than you require. (Unless, of course, your estimate of future growth is too low.)

Although it is dangerous business to simply extrapolate past growth trends into the future, most analysts begin their forecasts with an analysis of past performance. In addition, when estimating the value of Sara Lee in the previous example, remember that we assumed a 15 percent required rate of return. Thus, the stock may not be overvalued at $28; it may be that our return requirement is too high. Here's a more scientific approach.

In Chapter 3, we reported that the investment return should be related to a stock's systematic risk. Systematic risk is the risk that remains in a well-diversified portfolio. Beta is a commonly used measure of relative systematic risk; we use it here to determine the required rate of return on this investment. Remember that the capital market line relates the market-determined relationship between systematic risk and investment return (see Figure 5-1). A stock with a beta equal to 1.0 (the beta of the market as a whole) should provide a return equal to that of the stock market taken as a whole. The historical return from the S&P Index, a frequently used market proxy, has averaged approximately 12 percent per year over the last 65 years. Thus, stocks with a beta of 1.0 should return 12 percent per year. Stocks with a beta of 1.5 should return 15 percent annually, while those with a beta of 0.5 should return 9 percent. The mathematical relationship between beta and required rate of return is:

$$\text{Required return} = \text{Risk-free return} + \text{Beta (Market return} - \text{Risk-free return)}$$

The risk-free return is usually taken as the return on short maturity T-bills.

The beta of Sara Lee is equal to 1.0. Thus, the market-determined rate of return is 12 percent [6 percent + 1.0(12 percent − 6 percent)] and not the 15 percent rate assumed earlier. A growth rate equal to the required rate of return causes the denominator of our valuation model to equal zero, making share price indeterminant. However, we can use an alternative line of reasoning to learn that, if our estimates are correct, Sara Lee stock is reasonably priced. If you buy the stock at $28, you earn a 2.1 percent dividend yield ($0.59 divided by $28) and obtain 12 percent in capital appreciation. Thus, your total return becomes 14.6 percent. If you require only 12 percent, then the price of this stock represents a bargain.

But what if a stock pays no dividend? Then, of course, you cannot use the dividend-growth model to estimate value. Because many stocks currently pay no dividends, analysts frequently resort to the use of earnings multiplier models to

FIGURE 5–1
Trade-Off between Risk and Return

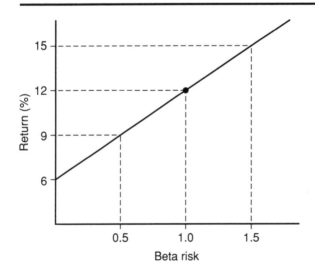

determine value. Nondividend-paying stocks still have value because investors expect to be paid dividends sometime in the future. Nondividend-paying companies plow back all of their earnings. These earnings frequently expand output and result in higher earnings in later years. Such firms are usually called growth companies. Don't confuse the nonpayment of dividends as a causal indicator of a growth company. Some companies pay no dividends because they are so poorly managed they have no earnings to pay to stockholders.

The price-earnings multiplier approach to stock valuation is very simple. First, estimate next year's earnings per share (EPS). Second, determine the stock's appropriate P-E multiplier (M). Third, multiply forecasted EPS by M.

Although this model is arithmetically simple, steps one and two present numerous problems for the individual investor. Estimating EPS is a very tricky business. Even professional analysts' forecasts are frequently in error. I suggest that the nonprofessional analyst estimate next year's EPS for firms with demonstrated records of growth by extrapolating past trends in earnings and sales growth. For example, a firm whose sales and EPS have grown steadily at 15 percent per year for the past four or five years would be expected to grow by that amount over the next year. If the firm's EPS is $1 now, the EPS estimate for next year would be $1.15. Even though this approach is simplistic and prone to error, large errors in forecasting can generally be avoided by first screening firms down to those with a history of stable growth and by leaving EPS estimates for firms in turn-around situations or with highly variable growth rates to professional analysts.[1]

Earnings estimation is, at best, an inexact science; at worst, it's a flat-out guessing game. Determination of an appropriate P-E multiplier for a particular firm is much more straightforward. Three factors interact to determine a firm's P-E ratio: returns on alternative investments, future firm growth, and

---

[1] For companies widely followed by brokerage analysts, investors can obtain earnings estimates from various sources. One of the most complete lists of analysts' earnings forecasts is contained in the *Standard & Poor's Earnings Forecaster*.

risk. All other things equal, the higher the rate of return on alternative investments such as bonds, the lower the P-E multipliers. The greater the anticipated rate of corporate growth, the greater the stock's earnings multiplier. Finally, the greater the degree of risk, the lower the multiplier.

A firm's currently reported earnings multiplier (called the *P-E ratio*) is subject to frequent distortions because it is computed by dividing current price by last year's EPS. Since investors purchase a share of next year's corporate earnings and not those earned last year, the appropriate multiplier is defined as the ratio of current share price to future per share earnings. For example, suppose that a company with a "normal" P-E ratio of eight is currently selling for six times last year's reported EPS. To an inexperienced investor, this situation might be interpreted as a bargain. However, if current share price is $6 and the expectation is that next year's EPS will be $0.75 (down from the $1 reported for the last 12 months), the stock is appropriately priced at eight times next year's EPS estimate and not mispriced at all.

Figure 5-2 illustrates the average annual P-E ratios for the stock market as a whole during the last quarter century. The market sold at an average earnings multiplier of 14 during this period, although as can be seen, it was subject to wide fluctuations. During the late 1960s, the multiplier ranged from 15 to 20 and averaged about 17 times reported earnings. During the 1970s, the multiplier plummeted and in 1979, dipped below seven. The multiplier averaged about 12 during this period. It then grew steadily during the bull market of the 1980s.

One of the biggest factors causing the market's P-E ratio to sag during the 1970s was an upward trend in interest rates. During the 1960s, the yield on high-grade corporate bonds averaged about 5 percent. During the 1970s, the average yield on these bonds rose to more than 8 percent, and during 1979–81, they topped 14 percent! As noted earlier, the earnings multiplier tends to move inversely with the return on alternative investments. The reason is apparent in this simple example: Suppose that a company pays out all of its earnings in dividends. Because it retains no earnings for reinvestment, this

FIGURE 5–2
Stock Market Price-Earnings Ratios: 1965–1992
(S&P 500 Index)

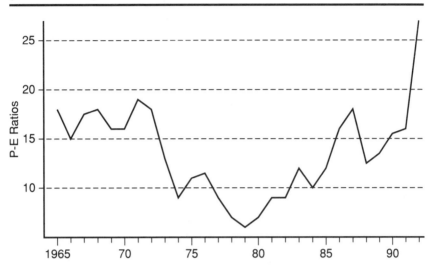

Source: Reprinted by permission of Standard & Poor's Corporation.

company cannot grow. Thus, investors' entire return on investment depends on how much they pay for $1 of earnings. If they pay five times earnings, their return will be 20 percent. This rate is obtained by taking the reciprocal of the P-E ratio; in this case, 1/5 or 20 percent. If they pay ten times earnings, their return will be 10 percent. Now suppose that high-grade bonds yield 5 percent. Since common stocks are more risky, investors demand a higher rate of return, and 10 percent seems reasonable. Thus, the earnings multiplier becomes 10. If rising interest rates drive bond yields up to 12 percent, we have a new ball game. Our investors paying 10 times earnings for common stocks quickly understand that at current prices there is no incentive to hold stocks. As stockholders sell stocks and buy bonds with more attractive yields, stock prices fall and so does the earnings multiple. Of course, since common stocks rarely pay out all of their earnings, this analysis is oversimplified. However, the principle is valid.

A SIMPLE COMMON STOCK VALUATION MODEL

After many years of exhaustive research, Benjamin Graham, a pioneer in investment analysis and a very successful investor, offered investors a simplified common stock valuation model. It states that share price equals next year's per share earnings estimate multiplied by 8.5 plus twice the anticipated five-year annual rate of growth (G). Graham then multiplied the result by the ratio of 4.4 divided by the expected long-term AAA bond yield. Next he divided both sides of the following equation by EPS. Thus, the

$$Price = EPS(8.5 + 2 \times G)(4.4/AAA \text{ bond yield})$$

model can determine the appropriate P-E multiplier for a company or for the stock market as a whole.

$$Price/EPS = (8.5 + 2 \times G)(4.4/AAA \text{ bond yield})$$

For example, suppose that a company is expected to grow at a 10 percent compound annual rate over the next five years, and that long-term AAA-rated bonds are currently yielding 9 percent. The appropriate P-E multiplier for this firm, according to Graham's model, would be determined as follows:

$$P\text{-}E = (8.5 + 2 \times 10)(4.4/9.0)$$
$$P\text{-}E = 28.5 \times 0.49 = 14$$

If the firm is expected to earn $1.20 per share during the next 12 months, then share value would be: 14 × $1.20 or $16.80.

This model has an interesting history. Originally it appeared as P-E = (8.5 + 2 × G). In this version of the model, a zero growth stock should sell for 8.5 times estimated earnings. Thus, zero growth stocks were thought to be correctly valued when they returned (1/8.5) or approximately 12 percent annually. A stock expected to grow by 10 percent annually for the next five years would be correctly valued at 28.5 times expected earnings. This model worked very well throughout the decades of the 1940s, 1950s, and early 1960s. By the late 1960s, however, it began to misfire. It started producing value estimates that were much too high. The culprit, it turned out, was escalating interest rates.

When the model was originally developed and tested, the yield on high-quality long-term bonds averaged about 4.4 percent. Thus, it was reasonable to expect investors to pay as much as 8.5 times next year's earnings for a zero growth stock, that is, to demand a 12 percent rate of return. As bond yields rose and maintained lofty levels, investors increased their required rates of return on stocks and, thus, lowered the earnings multiple. To compensate for extreme changes in the structure of interest rates, Graham added the adjustment factor, 4.4/AAA bond yield. Note, that if AAA bond yields rose to 8.8 percent, the adjustment factor becomes 4.4/8.8 or 0.5. Thus, the model adjusted the multiplier on zero growth stocks from 8.5 to 4.25. The multiple for the average stock, one that grows at a 7 percent annual rate, would decline from 22.5 to 11.2 by applying this adjustment factor. (Refer back to Figure 5-2 and you will see that this is exactly what happened to the stock market's multiplier during the 1970s.)

Before applying this valuation model to a particular firm's common shares, Graham suggested that the universe of common stocks be subjected to a series of four screens that eliminated common stocks of companies with extreme amounts of investment risk from further analysis. The four screens are:

1. Eliminate all firms with negative earnings (losses).
2. Eliminate all firms with debt to total asset ratios greater than 0.60 (i.e., firms with total debt greater than 60 percent of total assets).
3. Eliminate all firms with share prices above net working capital per share (i.e., firms whose current assets minus all debt and divided by the number of shares outstanding is less than current share price).
4. Eliminate all firms with E-P ratios less than twice the existing AAA bond yield.

I have no quarrel with the first two screens. However, the third screen fails to account for differences among industries. For example, rarely does a public utility or bank pass the third screen. Low-risk firms, such as public utilities, can employ more debt in their capital structures than high-risk firms. Furthermore, firms with large amounts of fixed assets are usually large borrowers since such assets serve as loan collateral. Thus, the application of this screen eliminates all firms with a large amount of debt-financed assets.

The fourth screen also fails to account for future firm growth because both high growth and low growth firms are subjected to the same earnings yield screen. For example, if AAA-rated bonds are yielding 10 percent, this screen calls for the elimination of all firms with P-E ratios greater than five times next year's EPS (the reciprocal of twice the current AAA bond yield equals one divided by 20 percent, or 5.0). No matter how fast a firm is expected to grow, application of this screen in this instance would eliminate all firms with P-Es greater than 5.0 from further consideration.

As an alternative, I suggest investors apply the first two screens (i.e., require that all firms possess a positive EPS and a low amount of total debt) to narrow the universe of common stocks and then utilize the following model incorporating risk directly into the valuation process:

$$P\text{-}E = (8.5 + 2 \times G)(4.4/\text{AAA bond yield})(1/\text{Beta})$$

Application of the model is straightforward. For example, suppose that you expect a firm to grow by 10 percent annually for the next five years. Suppose further that its beta is 1.10, and that AAA-rated bond yields are expected to average 8 percent. Simply substitute these values into the model and perform the necessary arithmetic.

$$
\begin{aligned}
P\text{-}E &= (8.5 + 2 \times G)(4.4/\text{AAA bond yield})(1/\text{Beta}) \\
&= [8.5 + 2(10)](4.4/8.0)(1/1.10) \\
&= 28.5 \times 0.55 \times 0.91 \\
P\text{-}E &= 14.3
\end{aligned}
$$

If this firm is expected to earn $1.50 during the next 12 months, the estimated value is 14.3 × $1.50, or $21.45. Finally, an investor need only compare this estimate to current share price to assess the reasonableness of the market's assessment of the stock's worth.

By adding the factor 1/Beta, this model requires that investors buy higher risk stocks at lower P-E multiples than lower-risk stocks. Suppose that the firm in the previous example possessed a beta of 1.20 instead of 1.10. The estimate of the appropriate P-E multiplier would have dropped from 14.3 to 13.1 and its value estimate from $21.45 to $17.65.

$$\text{P-E} = 28.5 \times 0.55 \times 1/1.2 = 13.1$$

Table 5-1 relates the appropriate P-E ratios for firms with betas equal to 1.0 for various estimates of corporate growth and AAA-rated bond yields. For example, if the XYZ Company (whose beta is 1.0) is expected to grow at a 15 percent compound annual rate for the next five years, while AAA-rated bonds are expected to yield 9.5 percent, then XYZ common stock should sell for approximately 17.7 times expected earnings per share. If interest rates rise to 10.5 percent, then the P-E multiplier drops to 16.2 times the expected EPS. As interest rates rise, P-E multipliers fall and as corporate growth accelerates, P-E multipliers increase.

Because the beta of the stock market as a whole is assumed to be 1.0, investors can use Table 5-1 to determine an appropriate market multiplier. For example, if corporate earnings are expected to increase at an annual rate of 8 percent over the next five years while high-grade bonds yield an average of 9.5 percent, the market should sell at approximately 11.3 times the next 12 months' EPS estimate. If interest rates were to rise to 12 percent, the multiplier would be expected to fall to 9.1.

TABLE 5-1
Corporate Growth Rates, Bond Yields, and Price-Earnings Ratios

Growth Rates	AAA Bond Yields								
	7.0	7.5	8.0	8.5	9.0	9.5	10.0	10.5	11.0
5%	11.4	10.9	10.2	9.6	9.1	8.5	8.1	7.8	7.4
6	12.9	12.0	11.3	10.7	10.0	9.4	9.0	8.6	8.2
8	15.4	14.4	13.5	12.7	12.0	11.3	10.8	10.3	9.8
10	17.9	16.7	15.7	14.8	14.0	13.1	12.5	12.0	11.4
12	20.4	19.1	17.9	16.9	15.9	15.0	14.3	13.7	13.0
14	22.9	21.4	20.1	19.0	17.9	16.8	16.1	15.3	14.6
15	24.2	22.6	21.2	20.0	18.9	17.7	16.9	16.2	15.4
16	25.4	23.8	22.3	21.1	19.8	18.6	17.8	17.0	16.2
18	27.9	26.1	24.5	23.1	21.8	20.5	19.6	18.7	17.8
20	30.5	28.5	26.7	25.2	23.8	22.3	21.3	20.4	19.4

TABLE 5-2
Price-Earnings Ratio Risk Adjustment Factors

Beta	1/Beta	Beta	1/Beta
0.65	1.54	1.10	0.91
0.70	1.43	1.15	0.87
0.75	1.33	1.20	0.83
0.80	1.25	1.25	0.80
0.85	1.18	1.30	0.77
0.90	1.11	1.35	0.74
0.95	1.05	1.40	0.71
1.00	1.00	1.45	0.69

Table 5-2 gives the P-E multiple risk-adjustment factors for a wide range of betas. For example, a firm with a beta of 1.4 should possess a price-earnings multiple approximately 0.7 times that of a firm whose beta is 1.0. On the other hand, a firm whose beta is 0.8 should possess a P-E multiplier 1.25 times that of a firm whose beta is 1.0.

For those who are perplexed by mathematical models, Tables 5-1 and 5-2 provide all the necessary calculations for determining appropriate P-E multipliers. For example, suppose you estimate the future growth rate of the ABC Company will be 20 percent annually and AAA-rated bond yields will average 10 percent. Furthermore, suppose that the beta of ABC common stock is 1.2. Table 5-1 indicates that a firm with a growth rate of 20 percent per year when interest rates are 10 percent should sell for 21.3 times expected earnings. Because this firm possesses a beta of 1.2, this P-E multiplier must be adjusted downward. Table 5-2 indicates that the appropriate adjustment factor is 0.83. Thus, the appropriate P-E multiple for this hypothetical firm is 21.3 multiplied by 0.83 or 17.7.

When applying this model, proceed with caution. Estimates of beta can and do change by a significant amount over time. Thus, exercise care when applying the beta risk adjustment factor. Furthermore, beta does not reflect the entire amount of risk contained in a single common stock. (Remember, beta is a measure of relative systematic risk, not total risk.) For example, application of this model to the valuation of highly risky, very low beta gold mining stocks would result in greatly inflated value estimates. Similarly, when a firm possesses an extremely large beta, value estimates are inordinately low. Thus, the model tends to work best when valuing stocks whose betas fall between 0.65 and 1.40.

Although this model is somewhat simplistic and only provides estimates of P-E ratios, it provides a valuable tool for the individual investor. Many investors tend to avoid high P-E ratio stocks, for example, because of perceived risk. By concentrating their investments in the low P-E end of the market, however, investors tend to build highly concentrated portfolios of stocks which possess similar characteristics. This can be a dangerous practice. Widespread portfolio diversification reduces total investment risk by a significant amount; portfolio concentration, however, exposes investors to a significant amount of needless investment risk. Also, by avoiding higher P-E ratio stocks, many long-term oriented investors miss out on numerous growth opportunities. Whether a stock's P-E ratio is high or low does not determine future investment performance. Rather, suboptimal investment returns are earned by investors who purchase common stocks at unreasonable P-E multiples. The model presented here assigns reasonable P-E multiples to common stocks based on their level of risk, future growth prospects, and returns on alternative investments. Finally, since this valuation model requires that investors assess a firm's future prospects to obtain an estimate of fair value, it assists investors in avoiding the frequent disasters which can befall those prone to making their common stock investments based on whim or tips from brokers or other investors. The motto of the Better Business Bureau is "Investigate before you invest." It should also be adopted by all common stock investors.

P-E RATIOS, INFLATION, AND STOCK MARKET VALUATION

Nearly every major bear market since 1949 began only after extreme investor optimism had driven up stock prices beyond any reasonable estimate of value. Table 5-3 illustrates the magnitude of the fall in stock prices during the seven bear markets since 1949. At the beginning of six of the seven bear markets, the P-E ratio of the Standard & Poor's 500 Composite Index was at least 13 times greater than the previous 12 months' per share earnings. During the last half-century the Index P-E ratio has ranged from a high of 22.4 to a low of 5.9. The P-E ratio of this widely followed stock market index has averaged approximately 14 times trailing earnings during the post-World War II period. As was seen earlier, P-E multiples are highly sensitive to the returns on alternative investments. When bond yields rise, P-E ratios and stock prices tend to fall. Because bond yields tend to move in concert with the rate of inflation, one of the fears of growth stock investors is the possibility of a collapse in P-E ratios and share prices during inflationary periods.

Although common stocks are said to be a hedge against inflation, the statement turns out to be more fiction than fact. During periods of modest price expansion, common stocks can provide a measure of protection. When a firm's costs of production rise, the firm can pass along some of these increases by raising the price of its output. Profit margins are maintained, and what shareholders lose on the one hand, they gain on the other. Thus, during periods marked by moderate inflation, common stock prices tend not to be affected.

Although common stocks provide a measure of protection during periods when consumer prices are modestly rising in the 1 to 3 percent range, they fare poorly when faced with a true

TABLE 5-3
Major Bear Markets: 1949-1985

Date Begun	Date Ended	Percent Change S&P Index	P-E Ratio at Beginning
Aug. 1956	Jan. 1958	−18.9%	13.1
Dec. 1961	June 1962	−28.0	22.4
Feb. 1966	Oct. 1966	−22.2	16.7
Nov. 1968	May 1970	−36.1	18.0
Jan. 1973	Oct. 1974	−48.2	18.4
Nov. 1980	Aug. 1982	−27.1	9.2
Aug. 1987	Dec. 1987	−22.6	21.0

TABLE 5-4
Market P-E Multiples and the Rate of Inflation

Inflation Range	Average P-E	P-E Range
0.0%- 2.0%	15.8	21.7-9.8
2.1 - 4.0	14.1	18.5-8.8
4.1 - 6.0	12.1	17.6-7.2
6.1 - 8.0	12.2	16.4-9.3
8.1 - 10.0	10.4	14.2-8.4
Above 10.0	8.2	8.9-7.5

inflationary environment. Table 5-4 illustrates the relationship between the stock market's P-E ratio and the rate of inflation. As can be seen, the higher the rate of inflation, the lower the market's earnings multiple. Correlational analysis indicates that, on average, the market's P-E multiple drops by about 0.7 times EPS for every 100 basis point increase in the rate of inflation. (One basis point equals 0.01 percent.) In general, the relationship between the market's P-E ratio and changes in the consumer price index during the last 38 years is:

$$P\text{-}E = 16.2 - (0.7 \times \text{Change in CPI})$$

This model indicates that at a 0 percent rate of inflation, the S&P Index should sell at 16.2 times the previous 12 months' EPS. With a 4 percent rise in the CPI, the market P-E multiple falls to 13.4. Furthermore, if the rate of inflation were to increase to 10 percent, look for the market P-E multiple to fall to about nine.

INVESTMENT QUALITY, RETURN ON EQUITY, AND CORPORATE GROWTH

One of the most successful approaches to common stock investing is to first identify quality companies and then acquire their common stocks at reasonable prices. This approach distinguishes between a quality company and a quality common stock. Some companies are very well managed, have adequate access to capital, operate in high-growth industries, and are steadily growing at above-average rates. These are quality companies. The quality of their stocks is another question.

High-quality companies often garner such an intense investor following, especially among institutional investors, that their stock prices are bid up beyond any reasonable estimate of value. Fortunately, the valuation model described in the previous section steers you away from these unfavorable situations. Before you can apply this common stock valuation model, you must first identify quality companies. (The next chapter describes quality companies that have yet to become institutional favorites.)

One frequently used measure of quality is a firm's return on stockholders' equity. Simply stated, return on equity (ROE) is the after-tax return earned by the owners of a business expressed as a percentage of their invested capital. You can compute it by dividing net income after taxes by stockholders' equity. (Stockholders' equity is the sum of the book value of common stock and accumulated retained earnings.) ROE is an important variable to consider when analyzing stocks for two reasons: First, ROE indicates how effectively corporate management is using assets to generate earnings. A favorable ROE (sometimes called *earning power)* is one that has been rising over time and is greater than the average ROE for all firms in a given industry. Second, because ROE is directly linked to the future growth rate of the firm, common stockholders' total rate of return is directly affected by ROE.

Three factors directly influence a firm's ROE: net profit margin, total asset turnover, and financial leverage. Net profit margin is the net return earned on each dollar of revenue; it is computed by dividing net income earned during the year by total revenues. A firm's net profit margin is affected by both the degree of competition in the marketplace (i.e., the ability of the firm to control the price of its output) and the overall cost of the firm's operations. The latter, in turn, is influenced by the degree to which the firm is operating efficiently. Remember that when making comparisons of net profit margins, such margins differ widely across industries. For example, grocery chains operate on very thin margins. These days, a highly successful grocery chain is one whose net profit margin exceeds 1 percent. On the other hand, a successful food processing firm's operating margin frequently tops 10 percent. Thus, when evaluating any financial ratio, compare it with other companies in the industry.

To compute total asset turnover, divide total sales by total assets. This ratio indicates how effectively management employs the company's assets. A very low ratio (compared to other companies in the industry) indicates a high degree of inefficiency. In such instances, the company's problems generally stem from a sales slump or overexpansion.

In figuring financial leverage, divide stockholders' equity by total assets. This represents the percentage of invested funds supplied by stockholders. A low percentage indicates that creditors are financing a relatively large portion of the firm's total assets. Financial leverage can increase stockholders' return when the rate of interest on borrowed funds is less than the rate of return on investment. For example, suppose that you purchase 100 shares of common stock at $10 per share. If the share price rises to $12, you have earned $200 on your initial investment of $1,000, or a return on investment (ROE) of 20 percent. If you had used financial leverage in making this purchase (i.e., you purchased 200 shares using $1,000 of your own money and $1,000 borrowed from your broker), the gross return would have been $400. If your broker charged 10 percent interest or $100 for the use of margin, the net return would have been $300 and the ROE would have been $300 divided by $1,000, or 30 percent. The use of financial leverage would have increased ROE because you borrowed money at 10 percent and reinvested it to earn 20 percent. Of course, if you earned less than 10 percent on the reinvested capital, the use of financial leverage would have resulted in a lower ROE than if leverage had not been used at all. Similar to almost everything else in this world, return enhancement comes with its associated cost.

The relationship between return on equity and these three variables is:

ROE =
[(Net profit margin) × (Total asset turnover)] / (Leverage ratio)

This expression indicates that management can enhance the firm's ROE in three ways: It can increase net profit margin (increase revenues or reduce costs), it can increase total asset turnover (increase sales at a rate greater than the rate of increase in total investment), or it can employ a greater percentage of borrowed money in financing its assets (reduce the equity-to-total asset ratio). The last method of increasing ROE increases risk. Thus, it is not always beneficial to seek the firm with the highest return on equity in a given industry. Firms with relatively high ROEs are desirable; yet, it is important that you understand how the firm obtained its high return on equity.

Table 5-5 illustrates condensed versions of a hypothetical firm's financial statements, an income statement and a balance sheet. These two reports provide all the information necessary for an analysis of ROE. During the year, the firm earned $4.12 million on a total investment of $58.87 million with $24.15 million supplied by the firm's stockholders. The firm's ROE of 17.1 percent resulted from dividing $4.12 million of earnings by $24.15 million of owners' equity.

TABLE 5-5
XYZ Corporation Financial Statements

Income Statement
Year Ended December 31, 1991

Revenues	$80,967,000
Cost of goods sold	(60,204,000)
Administrative & selling expense	(11,777,000)
Operating income	8,986,000
Interest expense	(2,816,000)
Income before taxes	6,170,000
Income taxes	(2,055,000)
Net income	$ 4,115,000

Balance Sheet
December 1991

Assets		Liabilities & Equity	
Current assets	$32,327,000	Current liabilities	$11,029,000
Property & equipment	9,529,000	Long term debt	23,690,000
Other assets	17,010,000	Common stock	5,821,000
		Retained earnings	18,326,000
		Shareholder equity	$24,147,000
Total	$58,866,000	Total	$58,866,000

How did this hypothetical firm obtain its 17.1 percent ROE? It earned a 5.1 percent net return on sales, had a total asset turnover of 1.38 times, and financed 41 percent of each dollar of total assets with stockholders' capital.

$$\text{Net profit margin} = \text{Net income/Sales} =$$
$$\$4.12 \text{ million/}\$80.97 \text{ million} = 5.1\%$$
$$\text{Total asset turnover} = \text{Sales/Total assets} = \$80.97/\$58.87$$
$$= 1.38 \text{ times}$$
$$\text{Leverage ratio} = 1 - (\$24.15/\$58.87) = 0.41$$
$$\text{Return on equity} = (5.1\% \times 1.38)/0.41 = 17.1\%$$

Table 5-6 illustrates the ROE and the three component ratios for this firm over a five-year period. The firm's ROE has been on the decline for the past five years. When viewed directly, the downward trend in ROE might cause you to bypass this firm. (Actually this hypothetical firm was a real company that suffered severe losses a year later. Thus, the initial inclination to pass over this firm in search for one with better fundamentals was a good one.) This aside, let's take a closer look at the firm's operations.

This company's net profit margin held firm during the last three years and followed an upward trend during the past five. Furthermore, a rise in the leverage ratio caused most of the erosion in ROE. The firm used a lower percentage of borrowed funds during the current year than it did during each of the

TABLE 5-6
Financial Statistics XYZ Corp.

	1987	1988	1989	1990	1991	Median	Trend
Net Income ($)	1.9	2.6	3.4	3.7	4.1	—	—
Sales ($)	45.3	66.2	68.0	70.3	78.4	—	—
Equity ($)	8.1	13.5	16.9	19.8	24.1	—	—
Total Assets ($)	19.7	29.4	48.0	52.0	58.9	—	—
NI/Sales (%)	4.2	3.9	5.0	5.3	5.2	5.0	Up
Sales/T. Assets	2.30	2.25	1.42	1.35	1.38	1.42	Down
Equity/T. Assets	.41	.46	.35	.38	.41	.41	Up
ROE (%)	23.5	19.3	20.1	18.7	17.1	19.3	Down

prior two years. In fact, had the leverage ratio remained at 0.35 (had it continued to use 65 percent borrowed capital) during its latest year, ROE would have exceeded 20 percent.

The downward trend in total asset turnover is the major cause for concern. Sales continued to expand during each of the last five years, yet total assets grew at a faster rate. As things turned out, this firm anticipated an expansion in demand that did not materialize. As a result, operating costs began to rise and the company suffered severe losses as demand for its products shrank.

Translating ROE analysis into meaningful investment decisions is a difficult task for many investors. It requires a degree of common sense, some knowledge of the practices in various industries, and sometimes a special gut feeling. With some practice, however, even novice investors can benefit from ROE analysis. In addition, ROE is one of the most important determinants of corporate growth which, in turn, is one of the most important factors in valuing common stocks.

Knowledge of a firm's ROE and dividend payout policy makes it possible to estimate the firm's future rate of growth. By payout policy I am referring to the proportion of earnings paid out in cash dividends. A firm which earns $2 per share after taxes and pays an annual dividend of $0.50, for example, is paying out 25 percent of its earnings and is retaining 75 percent (1 − payout ratio) for reinvestment. If this firm earns 20 percent on reinvested capital (its ROE), the future growth rate of the firm will be its ROE multiplied by the retention ratio. In this case, the firm can be expected to grow by 20 percent multiplied by 0.75, or by 15 percent per year.

Return for a moment to the data in Table 5-6. The median ROE for this firm (the middle value when ranked from high to low) over the last five years was 19.3 percent. Over this period, it paid out an average of 20 percent of its earnings in cash dividends. Thus, firm growth is estimated to be 15.4 percent.

$$
\begin{aligned}
\text{Firm growth estimate} &= \text{ROE}(1 - \text{Payout ratio}) \\
&= 19.3\% \, (1 - 0.20) \\
&= 15.4\%
\end{aligned}
$$

Because the firm is growing at a much faster rate than the average company's approximately 7 percent annually, it can be classified as a growth firm.

By analyzing and combining a firm's return on equity with its payout policy, you can reliably estimate future growth. Remember that to use the variant of the Graham common stock valuation model, you must first obtain an estimate of a firm's future long-run growth rate. This is the most critical variable in the model. Small errors in growth estimates can cause extreme distortions in estimated earnings multipliers, and hence, in the value you place on the firm. Thus, the model works best when using reliable estimates of future growth instead of historical trends. Analysis of a firm's ROE provides one of the best insights to a company's future growth prospects.

CONCLUSION

There are two games that you can play in the stock market. One game involves purchasing stocks at any price and unloading them on someone else at a higher price shortly thereafter. The players of this game rarely care how much a particular common stock currently sells for—as long as it can be sold at a higher price later on.

This is an easy game to play. And it can be a lot of fun. First, you follow the daily stock prices of several companies until you find one or two moving up faster than the market as a whole. (The players have given this scenario a fancy name, positive momentum.) You buy these stocks and hold them until the momentum slows. When this happens you quickly sell out. This has been called the "greater fool" theory of investing. You know that you're a fool to buy at these prices, but you expect to find an even greater fool to sell them to later—at higher prices.

If you think about this game, you quickly realize that a lack of scruples helps. After all, according to the rules, you only sell a stock after it becomes overvalued; and, thus, you cheat the next owner out of some hard-earned cash. But in this game, turn-about is fair play; while you are looking for the greater fool, others are looking for you. Similar to a game of musical chairs, playing the game continues to be fun until someone takes your chair away.

A few centuries ago in Holland buyers played this game with tulip bulbs. In the 1920s buyers played with common stocks. During the late 1970s the game involved gold and oil. Like the carnival barker who can tempt even the most skeptical customer with the cry, "hurry, hurry, hurry," tales of easy riches continually lure unsuspecting investors into the stock market at the most inopportune times.

I prefer to play another stock market game. This game is based on investment fundamentals, where success requires careful analysis and a knowledge of the relationship between risk and return. I buy stocks on the basis of their future income potential—the ability of corporate managers to deliver an increasing stream of earnings and dividends. I buy stocks with an eye on their underlying values. That means finding quality companies and buying their common stocks at reasonable prices.

The first five chapters in this book have armed you with the fundamentals of common stock investing. We have examined the concepts of investment return, investment risk, market efficiency, and investment value. In the following chapters, these fundamental concepts are put to work. The goal is to assist you in building and preserving wealth over an investment lifetime. Unlike the carnival barker and some writers of invest-ment books these days, the cry is not "hurry, hurry, hurry." Instead, you are urged to use patience. Rather than teaching you how to become a successful stock market trader, my goal is to assist you in becoming a successful investor.

CHAPTER 6

THE SMALL FIRM EFFECT

If the stock market is highly efficient, the best estimate of the value of a stock is its current price. Although stocks may be overvalued or undervalued at any time, in an efficient market they are quickly repriced at their true value—true, that is, in terms of all publicly available information. Thus, portfolio return is solely determined by the degree of risk assumed. In short, in an efficient market, an investor cannot consistently earn excess returns. To earn greater than average returns in an efficient market, one must take greater than average risks. In an efficient market, the most profitable investment strategy is to buy and hold a well-diversified common stock portfolio containing a level of risk consistent with your needs and goals. Little, if anything, can be gained by active trading.

Many stockbrokers and professional analysts, as well as most individual investors, have always contended that active trading and portfolio management would enhance returns beyond those dictated solely by investment risk. Very few of them could substantiate their contentions with successful, long-term track records. Until recently, academic research had said that it couldn't be done, except by luck. In the late 1970s, however, a University of Chicago researcher discovered a strategy that would have produced superior investment returns for more than 65 years. This discovery, now called the *small firm effect,* has changed the thinking of thousands of individual investors and hundreds of professional portfolio managers.

Simply put, the small firm effect is the tendency of the common stocks of small firms to outperform the common stocks of large firms given the same level of risk. That is, common stock portfolios containing shares of small firms earn rates of return greater than can be accounted for by portfolio risk. Remember, according to modern capital asset pricing theory discussed in Chapter 4, the expected rate of return from any asset is directly related to its nondiversifiable risk. The greater the level of nondiversifiable risk, the greater the expected rate of return. According to this theory, there is no such thing as an invest- ment free lunch: You get what you pay for. Contemporary research, however, indicates that this has not been the case for well-diversified portfolios of small firm common stocks. Highly diversified portfolios consisting of the common stocks of small equity capitalization firms produce larger returns than they should given their underlying systematic risk. Therefore, small firm investors have been helping themselves to a free lunch for more than a half-century.

Many investors have been on the receiving end of the small firm effect without being aware of its existence. These investors usually stumble on the phenomenon inadvertently when buying low-priced or penny stocks, stocks selling at low P-E multiples, or only new issues. When you pursue any of these investment strategies, you usually end up with a large percentage of your portfolio concentrated in smaller firm stocks. For example, a majority of the companies issuing penny stocks are start-up companies and, at least in their early years, are very small. Likewise newer companies are typically small firms. These strategies produce excess returns because they are part and parcel of a small firm investment strategy that is actually responsible for the superior investment results.

The small firm effect was first measured in 1978 by graduate student Rolf Banz. While completing his doctoral dissertation at the University of Chicago—the "most holy" of efficient market shrines—Banz ranked the common stocks listed on the New York Stock Exchange according to size during each year from 1931 to 1974. He defined firm size by the market value of the firm's common stock. Banz multiplied the shares outstanding for each firm listed on the NYSE by its share price at the beginning of the year. He then constructed five common stock portfolios containing stocks ranked according to equity capitalization (i.e., after ranking the firms according to size, Banz cut the list into five equal slices). At the beginning of each succeeding year, he adjusted the NYSE common stock rankings according to their new equity market values and reformed the five portfolios. Banz assumed equal dollar investments in each stock in the revised portfolios at the beginning of each year.

Next he obtained the monthly investment returns for each portfolio. Banz adjusted these returns for the amount of systematic risk contained in each portfolio. He expected portfolios with larger amounts of systematic risk to produce larger investment returns than portfolios with smaller amounts of systematic risk. Thus, before making a meaningful comparison of the investment returns, he adjusted the portfolio returns upward or downward for the effects of investment risk.[1]

Table 6-1 contains a summary of Banz's results. Over the 43-year period studied, the first four portfolios (those containing all but the smallest NYSE firms) provided investors with investment returns dictated by the risk of the portfolio, indicating that these portfolios were efficiently priced. (Actually, these four portfolios provided investors with an average risk-adjusted monthly return of −0.06 percent per month, or −0.72 percent per year—less than they should have, given the amount of systematic risk they contained. These portfolios, if anything, were slightly overvalued by the market during this 43-year period.)

On the other hand, when ranked according to equity market value the portfolio containing the smallest NYSE companies provided investors with a risk-adjusted excess rate of return of 0.44 percent per month, or nearly 6 percent per year. The doctoral student had found an investment free lunch!

The extra, or nonrisk related, yearly return provided by

---

[1] The actual process of adjusting portfolio investment return for risk utilized least squares regression analysis. Portfolio returns were regressed against the returns from a market index which resulted in the following model: $Y = A + BX$. As a result, BX indicates the return that portfolio Y should provide given a specific market return X and portfolio beta B. The value of "A" (known as alpha) is the return to portfolio Y, which cannot be explained by investment risk. A value greater than zero indicates superior or extra investment return, while a value below zero indicates inferior, or a deficiency of, investment return. In a perfectly efficient market, one would expect alpha to equal zero.

TABLE 6-1
Average Monthly Risk-Adjusted Portfolio Returns: 1931-1974

Portfolio	Monthly Risk-Adjusted Portfolio Return	Annualized Risk-Adjusted Portfolio Return
1 (Largest Firms)	−0.11%	−1.30%
2	−0.09	−1.10
3	−0.09	−1.10
4	+0.05	+0.60
5 (Smallest Firms)	+0.44	+5.50

Source: Rolf W. Banz, "Limited Diversification and Market Equilibrium: An Empirical Analysis," Ph.D. dissertation, The University of Chicago, 1978. Reprinted by permission.

small firm common stocks is by no means a trivial amount. The effect of an additional 6 percent annually compounded over many years has a tremendous impact on investment wealth. For example, Table 6-2 illustrates the terminal values of a $10,000 investment made in the S&P 500 Index chiefly comprised of large firm common stocks and in a portfolio of small firm common stocks over various periods.

Look at what would have happened to investment wealth from 1940 to 1991. The $10,000 investment in the 500 stocks in the S&P Index would have grown to $330,350 by the end of 1991, after including the reinvestment of dividends. That's more than a thirty-fold increase. Although impressive, this increase in value is dwarfed by the growth of the same investment in small firm common stocks that, with dividends reinvested, would have multiplied 196 times! That's nearly seven

TABLE 6-2
Common Stock Portfolio Returns
$10,000 Invested in Small Firm Stocks versus the S&P Index

Holding Period	Terminal Portfolio Value	
	S&P Index	Small Firm
1970-1991	$ 11,185	$ 14,714
1960-1991	23,714	62,597
1950-1991	140,734	294,977
1940-1991	330,350	1,965,898

times better. The moral of this tale should be clear: small increments in annual rates of investment return increase wealth by gigantic amounts when earned over a long period of time.

STILL MORE EVIDENCE

According to the methodology employed by Banz, the definition of a small firm by the market value of its equity changed each year. Banz selected stocks for the small firm portfolio based on their relative rankings (the bottom 20 percent of NYSE-listed stocks when ranked according to market value) and not according to a specific dollar value. This raises the question, how small is small? As of September 1992, the smallest 20 percent of firms listed on the NYSE (about 300 firms) had an equity capitalization cutoff point of approximately $120 million, with the average size being about $60 million. By Banz's definition, small firms today are about twice the size they were 20 years ago.

Banz's original study of firm size and common stock returns used only NYSE firms. Thus, the use of his results for portfolio construction are highly restrictive: Investors' portfolios would contain only stocks listed on the Big Board. And, Banz is silent as to whether the small firm anomaly is universal or restricted to NYSE stocks.

More recent research indicates that the small firm effect is indeed universal. Following the lead of Banz, Professors Thomas Cook and Michael Rozeff of the University of Iowa examined the nature of firm size and investment returns, expanding the sample of firms to include 1,436 NYSE-listed stocks, 804 AMEX-listed issues and 890 stocks traded over-the-counter. Their study of the years 1968 through 1978 confirmed the universality of the small firm effect. Table 6-3 describes the monthly risk-adjusted returns for 10 portfolios constructed on the basis of firm size. They ranked 3,130 stocks on the basis of equity market value and divided them into 10 portfolios containing an equal number of stocks. The four portfolios containing the stocks with the lowest market value (less than $50 million) provided monthly returns of 0.14 percent to 0.45

TABLE 6–3
Excess Investment Returns and Firm Size

Portfolio	Monthly Excess Returns (percent)	Market Capitalization ($ million)
1 (Smallest)	0.45%	$ 8
2	0.16	17
3	0.16	28
4	0.14	42
5	−0.01	64
6	−0.04	97
7	−0.11	152
8	−0.08	256
9	−0.31	489
10 (Largest)	−0.35	2,460

Source: T. Cook and M. Rozeff, "Size, Dividend Yield, and Co-Skewness Effects on Stock Returns: Some Empirical Tests," University of Iowa Working Paper 82–20, June 1982.

percent after adjustment for risk. Large firm stocks returned less than they should have given their risk. Thus, the market undervalued small firm stocks during this period and overvalued the large firm stocks. The annualized risk-adjusted returns for the portfolios of the smallest and largest firms revealed a wide distribution, ranging from 5.4 percent to −4.2 percent.

Table 6-4 illustrates the recent total returns provided by small and large firm common stocks. During the last 18 years, small firm stocks have returned an average of 20.7 percent per year versus an average of 14.5 percent for the S&P Index. Although small firm stocks provided 6.2 percent per year more than large firm stocks, small firm stocks did not outperform the S&P Index each year. In fact, they outperformed the S&P Index during 12 out of 18 years, or about 67 percent of the time. (During the last 55 years, the track record of small firm stocks was a bit better, as they outperformed the S&P 500 Composite Index during 37 years, or 67 percent of the time.) Small firm stock returns tend to be more variable than large firm stock returns. They tend to perform better than the S&P 500 Index during up markets and poorer during down markets.

TABLE 6–4
Total Rates of Return: Small Firms versus Large

Year	Small Firm Stocks	S&P 500 Index	Difference Favoring Small Firms
1974	−19.9	−26.5	6.6
1975	52.8	37.2	15.6
1976	54.7	23.8	30.9
1977	25.4	− 7.2	32.6
1978	23.5	6.6	16.9
1979	43.5	18.4	25.1
1980	39.9	32.4	7.5
1981	13.9	− 4.9	18.8
1982	28.0	21.4	6.6
1983	39.7	22.5	17.2
1984	− 6.7	6.3	−13.0
1985	24.7	32.2	− 7.5
1986	6.9	18.5	−11.6
1987	− 9.3	5.2	−14.5
1988	22.9	16.8	6.1
1989	10.2	31.5	−21.3
1990	−21.6	− 3.2	−18.4
1991	44.6	30.5	14.1
Average	20.7%	14.5%	6.2%

Source: *Stock, Bonds, Bills, and Inflation: 1992 Yearbook*™, Ibbotson Associates, Chicago (annually updates work by Roger G. Ibbotson and Rex A. Sinquefield). Used with permission. All rights reserved.

In the last two decades, many researchers who doubted the existence of a small firm effect have subjected stocks of small and large firms to numerous tests using various statistical techniques. All confirm its existence, although its explanation appears to be a subject of current debate.

THE SMALL FIRM EFFECT: A RATIONALE

From the outset, numerous efficient market theorists doubted the findings of this research. After all, if small firm stocks actually provide an investment free lunch, then a big hole had been blown into their theory. Thus, it is not surprising to find that much of the research following Banz's seminal study focused on the reliability of his statistical techniques and sampling methods.

To obtain a measure of risk-adjusted returns for small firm stocks, researchers first had to obtain an estimate of portfolio risk (i.e., beta). Perhaps, the efficient market theorists reasoned, there is something unique about beta measurements taken for small firm stocks. Suppose, for example, that while beta adequately measures portfolio risk for large firm stocks, it systematically underestimates the risk of small firm stock portfolios. Thus, small firm returns would not be excess rates of return at all, but errors in estimating beta. Then, their old theory could be patched up and flying again in no time!

Although this was solid reasoning, tests for systematic biases in beta measures for small firm stock portfolios revealed that betas of small firm portfolios tended to be slightly understated; therefore, the small firm effect remained after correcting for errors in risk measurement. Even after removing some selection biases—notably those which resulted from the selection of common stocks traded infrequently—the excess small firm stock returns remained. Like a friendly but unwanted stray cat, the small firm effect wouldn't go away. It remains one of the great cracks in an otherwise solidly constructed efficient market hypothesis.

Whatever the explanation of the small firm effect, it is not because firms are small. Firm size is most likely just a proxy for one or more true, but unknown, factors which highly correlate with firm size. For example, David Dreman in his book *Contrarian Investment Strategy* (Random House, 1979) popularized the notion that lower priced common stock issues tend to outperform higher priced issues. It could be that firm size is actually a proxy for the low P-E ratio effect. (Two firms with the same number of shares outstanding and the same earnings per share have differing equity market values if their stocks have different P-E multiples. The smaller firm has the lower P-E multiplier.) However, recent research indicates the reverse—that the P-E anomaly is actually a proxy for the small firm effect. We discuss this research in detail in Chapter 8. Other research indicates that neither stock price nor book value are acceptable proxies for the small firm effect. However, numerous other factors proxied by the small firm effect, such as debt-to-equity ratio or lopsidedness of return distributions, have yet to be tested.

BULLS IN THE CHINA SHOP

An examination of the characteristics of small versus large firms reveals striking differences. One of the most apparent is the lack of significant small firm ownership by institutional investors. These investors control vast amounts of wealth. Nearly 50 percent of all common stocks are held by institutional investors; for example, mutual funds, bank trust funds, pension funds, and insurance companies. These days, they account for more than 80 percent of the daily trading volume in domestic stocks. Their absence from the small firm market segment has a significant effect on the values of small firm stocks.

Nearly everyone knows that supply and demand determine price. Reduce supply while keeping demand constant and prices rise. Conversely, reduce demand while keeping supply constant and prices fall. Now suppose that, based on its ability to produce growing earnings and dividends, a small firm is worth $10 per share. The interaction of buyers and sellers, each given the same information regarding future earnings and dividends, should ultimately produce a share price that reflects its value. Expand this scenario across the universe of thousands of small firms. Now, remove a large portion of the potential buyers, such as institutional investors. The result is a reduction in price and the creation of a set of securities selling at bargain prices.

If these bargains are available for the taking, why don't institutional investors come in and gobble up every bit of the free lunch on the table? After all, these people are the pros. Although there is no doubt that institutional investors would like to enter this market segment, there are several real barriers to their entry. Primarily, most institutions simply have too much money. Spreading it among thousands of small firm stocks is too much of a nuisance. For example, suppose that a mutual fund manager has $10 billion to invest. Given that the typical small firm has an average equity market value of about $50 million, and the fact that mutual funds are barred from owning more than 10 percent of a firm's outstanding common stock, this fund manager would have to spread the cash across at least 2,000 different companies to invest the entire amount. It is doubtful that the fund manager would take a 10 percent position in each company; therefore, the number of different issues required for complete investment would probably number more than 4,000 or 5,000! And that's too many stocks to watch. On the other hand, if the fund manager invests in companies with equity market value measured in the billions of dollars, far fewer issues are needed to fill the portfolio. These people are big players and they need big pastures in which to roam.

Even if institutional money managers could somehow solve the administrative problems associated with investment in thousands of different companies, they would bump up against an even more formidable barrier to small firm investment— excessive transactions costs.

A study of common stock trading costs in the May/June 1983 issue of the *Financial Analysts Journal* vividly illustrates the trading barrier that all but prohibits institutional investment in small firms. Figure 6-1 illustrates the components of common stock trading costs. Included are both the inside costs (the market maker's bid-ask spread) and outside costs (brokerage commissions). Round-trip inside costs for an individual

FIGURE 6–1
Trading Costs and Large Block Trades

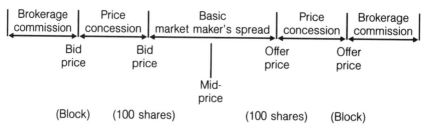

Source: Thomas Loeb, "Trading Cost: The Critical Link between Investment Information and Results," *Financial Analysts Journal,* May-June 1983, p. 41.

seeking in a round lot (100 shares) are far less than for an institutional investor who must purchase larger blocks of stock. The difference is the amount over and above the current bid-ask quote that a large block trader must offer the market maker to affect the trade. Therefore, the inside trading costs are much larger for institutions than for individuals. Of course, the heftier inside costs are offset to some extent by the lower brokerage commissions that institutions pay compared to individual investors.

Tables 6-5 and 6-6 outline the extent of these inside and outside trading costs for the individual and institutional investor. Table 6-5 presents stock price and inside trading cost data for a round-trip (initial purchase and subsequent sale) 100 share trade for various equity capitalization classes. For the common stocks of firms with equity capitalizations between $25 million and $100 million (a total of 1,177 issues representing 4.46 percent of the U.S. equity market), the average price per share was $17.27. The average bid-ask spread per share was $0.40, which represented 2.32 percent of the average share price. That is, an investor buying and selling one round lot of a stock priced at approximately $17 per share would lose 2.32 percent of the investment due to the bid-ask spread. To find the total trading costs, brokerage commissions must be added to

TABLE 6–5
Stock Price and Inside Trading Costs

Capitalization Sector ($ million)	Issues	Percentage of U.S. Market	Average Price	Average Spread	Spread/Price Cost*
0–25	1,763	1.25%	$ 7.04	$0.35	4.97%
25–100	1,177	4.46	17.27	0.40	2.32
100–500	956	15.65	28.31	0.32	1.13
500–1,000	238	12.29	35.43	0.27	0.76
Over 1,000	282	66.35	49.50	0.28	0.57

*Spread/Price = Round-trip trading cost for 100 shares excluding brokerage commissions.

Source: Thomas Loeb, "Trading Cost: The Critical Link between Investment Information and Results," *Financial Analysts Journal*, May-June 1983, p. 41.

TABLE 6-6
Institutional Round-Trip Trading Costs

Capitalization Sector ($ million)	Percentage		
	Block Size ($ thousand)		
	$250	$500	$1,000
$25–$50	18.8%	25.9%	30.0%
50–75	9.6	16.9	25.4
75–100	5.9	8.1	11.5
500–1,000	3.1	4.0	5.6

this percentage. I called several brokerage houses in 1986 and found that the round-trip commission to trade 100 shares of stock trading at $17 averaged 5.3 percent at full-service brokerage firms and 2.8 percent at discount firms. Thus, the full round-trip trading cost to an individual trading in small equity capitalization firms averages approximately 7.62 percent at a full-service brokerage house and 5.12 percent at a discount firm.

Table 6-6 outlines the full round-trip trading costs by equity capitalization class for large stock purchases. For example, suppose that an institutional investor wishes to acquire 50,000 shares of stock in a firm whose equity capitalization is approximately $57 million. If the stock is currently trading at about $19 per share, the total value of the purchase would be $950,000 before trading costs. According to this study, the full round-trip trading cost for this large block investor would average 25.4 percent! For a firm in the $25 million to $50 million equity class, the percentage trading cost jumps to 30 percent. The same dollar value round-trip trade made in the stock of a firm whose equity market value is greater than $500 million results in a 5.6 percent round-trip trading cost. It is little wonder that institutional investors generally avoid small equity capitalization stocks. Transaction costs are just too high in this market segment. So, the Wall Street behemoths conduct the bulk of their business in the shares of the corporate giants. This is the market segment where trading costs are acceptable to the large block trader.

THE REWARDS OF BEING UNLOVED

Because institutional investors shy away from small equity capitalization firms, it is not surprising that few analysts keep tabs on their activities. Financial analysts at brokerage firms generally serve institutional masters; they research companies that interest their patrons. Fees for stock analysis performed by these individuals are usually charged on a "soft dollar" basis; the institution directs its stock trades or commissions to the brokerage firms supplying free advice. Thus, if institutions don't buy small firm common stocks, brokerage house analysts generally don't follow them.[2]

The first study focusing on common stock returns and their degree of popularity appeared in *Financial Analysts Journal* in 1964. Professor Scott Bauman sought to examine two alternative investment selection concepts. One concept is that investing in the widely owned stocks of the large, well-entrenched companies in major industries maximizes long-term profits. The other concept is that investors obtain better returns from stocks of smaller, lesser-known companies. These Bauman dubbed "less popular stocks." He mentioned their degree of popularity by the frequency with which stocks appeared in the portfolios of investment companies with open-end and closed-end funds. Each year the popular stock group consisted of the 30 stocks most widely held by the funds, and the least popular group consisted of stocks held by only one or two different funds. Although this may not appear to be a wide range of popularity, during this study of 1954 to 1961, only an average of 80 funds had assets totaling more than $15 million and possessed diversified portfolios of industrial stocks.

Table 6-7 summarizes Professor Bauman's results. During this eight-year period, the average annual returns of the least popular stocks exceeded both those of the most popular group of

---

[2] In fact, many of the companies recommended for purchase in my small firm investment advisory newsletter, *Investment Horizons,* have asked permission to reprint our write-up of their companies for distribution to shareholders. Frequently, our advisory firm is the only one actively following the company.

TABLE 6-7
Investment Returns and Investment Popularity

Year	Least Popular Group	S&P Index	Most Popular Group
1954	58.2%	56.1%	56.3%
1955	17.4	34.6	27.4
1956	8.8	7.1	10.7
1957	−11.0	−10.7	−14.5
1958	52.2	41.8	42.6
1959	17.9	12.6	7.3
1960	4.0	− 1.6	− 6.1
1961	26.2	26.5	23.1
Average	19.8%	18.9%	16.2%

Source: Scott Bauman, "Investment Experience with Less Popular Common Stocks," *Financial Analysts Journal*, March-April 1964, p. 85.

stocks and the Standard & Poor's 500 Stock Average. The average return differential between the most and least popular stock groups may not appear to be substantial. Remember, however, that all stocks were held by at least one mutual fund, so no stock was truly neglected.

Although Bauman's study hinted at the gains possible by selecting stocks of unloved and unfollowed companies, it took nearly 20 years before another comprehensive study of analyst interest and stock returns appeared. This study was prompted by the discovery of the small firm effect. In a 1982 article entitled "The Neglected and Small Firm Effects," in *The Financial Review* Professors Avner Arbel and Paul Strebel addressed the question of whether the differential attention companies receive affects the capital asset pricing process. They measured the degree of attention by research concentration rankings based on the number of analysts regularly following the firm's securities. Arbel and Strebel hypothesized that after adjusting for risk, less researched companies would provide excess rates of return. They also hypothesized that such excess returns would remain even after adjusting returns for firm size.

Their study focused on the 500 companies included in the S&P Index. Although they admitted that the sample would be biased toward larger firms, they found the companies adequately diverse in analyst attention, which they defined by the number of analysts making earnings forecasts. They divided the stocks into three groups, the 30 percent with the greatest analyst attention, the next 40 percent, and the 30 percent which received the least attention. Over the five-year period from 1972 to 1976, they found that about 30 percent of the S&P 500 companies were intensively researched, while about 25 percent received either no attention at all or coverage by just one forecaster. Table 6-8 illustrates risk and return measures for these three groups of stocks.

As Table 6-8 shows, the annual returns increased as analyst interest decreased, ranging from 6.6 percent for the most researched firms to 17.7 percent for the least researched. After adjusting the portfolio returns for risk, the least researched group of stocks provided a 12.6 percent annual average return greater than they were supposed to given their level of risk. Even though these results are impressive in and of themselves, they are even more startling considering the fact that the so-called "neglected" firms were in the S&P 500 Index.

Because the sizes of firms in the S&P 500 Index vary considerably, Arbel and Strebel investigated the extent to which size and not neglect could have accounted for the return differences. They wondered if, based on what was said earlier regarding institutional interest and analyst attention, it could have been that the smaller the firm, the less the attention. Therefore, Arbel and Strebel divided each of the three research concentration groups into 10 subgroups based on equity capitalization.

TABLE 6-8
Average Risk and Annual Return by Research Concentration Group

		Annual Percent	
Group	Beta	Return	Excess Return
1 (Most Researched)	0.98	6.6%	1.7%
2	1.03	9.8	4.8
3 (Least Researched)	1.00	17.7	12.6

Source: Avner Arbel and Paul Strebel, "The Neglected and Small Firm Effects," *The Financial Review*, November 1982, p. 209.

TABLE 6-9

Average Annual Excess Returns by Firm Size and Research Concentration

Research Concentration	Firm Size (1 = smallest, 10 = largest)										Average
	1	2	3	4	5	6	7	8	9	10	
1 (Most)	1.6	-9.6	-4.5	10.5	4.2	5.8	8.8	4.8	5.6	6.5	5.1
2	0.9	14.0	8.7	7.1	11.6	5.4	8.0	8.4	9.3	4.1	8.2
3 (Least)	13.2	20.9	15.6	16.6	21.0	14.7	14.8	4.0	8.5	4.6	15.0
Average	10.2	12.1	10.3	12.1	12.5	7.7	9.2	6.1	6.7	6.2	

Source: A. Arbel and P. Strebel, "The Neglected and Small Firm Effects," *The Financial Review*, November 1982, p. 213.

Table 6-9 illustrates the returns from each of the 30 portfolios. The average excess returns indicate a small firm effect in the bottom row, as the returns ranged from 10 percent to 12 percent for the two portfolios containing the smallest firms to only about 6 percent for the two portfolios containing the large firms. Although the data suggest that analyst neglect is the dominant variable (rather than firm size), the portfolios containing both the smallest and least researched firms provided much larger annual returns than did the portfolios containing the largest and most researched firms. (These comparisons are marked in Table 6-9.)

In another study of neglect (defined by the number of institutional investors holding a stock), Arbel, Carvell, and Strebel focused on 510 companies drawn equally from the NYSE, AMEX, and the OTC market. They divided these firms into three portfolios depending on their institutional concentration rankings (ICR). They found that about one third of the companies in their sample were institutionally neglected—held by either no institution at all, or just one.

Then they ranked the firms in each institutional concentration category by their market capitalizations and divided them into three size groups. They rebalanced the resulting nine portfolios annually for changes in institutional holdings and market capitalization.

The data in Table 6-10 suggest a strong neglected firm effect. For the 10-year period, the (20.8 percent) average annual return for the institutionally neglected securities was twice that of the stocks most widely held by institutional investors (10.4

TABLE 6-10
Risk, Return, and Institutional Concentration

Institutional Concentration	Percent Return	Beta	Percent Excess Return
Intensively held (ICR1)	10.36%	0.99	−5.80%
Moderately held (ICR2)	16.89	0.92	1.11
Neglected (ICR3)	20.84	0.90	5.64

Source: A. Arbel, et al., "Giraffes, Institutions, and Neglected Firms," *Financial Analysts Journal*, May-June 1983, p. 59.

TABLE 6-11
Returns by Institutional Holding and Company
Size: 1971-1980

Institutional Concentration	Company Size		
	Small	Medium	Large
ICR 1	*	8.6%	10.9%
ICR 2	14.7	17.3	23.2
ICR 3	20.1	26.0	*
Average	18.4	16.3	12.2

*Meaningless because of the small number of cases in this category.

percent). Furthermore, on a risk adjusted basis, it appears that institutional investors tend to bid up the prices of the stocks they buy to the point where they remain consistently overvalued. Of the three portfolios, only the one most intensively held by institutions yields a risk-adjusted return less than zero.

The data in Table 6-11 also indicate the presence of a size effect in the bottom row. However, for firms preferred by institutions, the larger firms tended to outperform the smaller firms. This suggests that the small firm effect may be a reflection of the neglected firm effect, rather than the other way around. Neglect, both on the part of institutional investors and securities analysts, may be a proxy for the small firm effect. Neglect may also account for differential returns among large companies. That is, investors looking to add large company stocks to their investment portfolios should begin their search among those large companies not followed by more than one analyst or whose shares are held by relatively few institutional investors.

HOW LIQUID ARE SMALL FIRM COMMON STOCKS?

Market makers are securities dealers who act as middlemen—similar to an investor's Sears, Roebuck and Company, they buy wholesale and sell retail. As noted earlier, the costs of trading large blocks of small firm stocks are excessive. Market makers in stocks increase their bid-ask spread on large orders (increasing the ask on purchase orders and decreasing the bid on sell orders). The bid-ask spread is the difference between the prices quoted by a dealer who makes a market in a stock and bridges the time gaps between public buy and sell orders. The ask (offer) price quoted for a stock includes a premium for immediate buying. The bid price reflects a price concession for immediate sale. The bid-ask spread is the price the dealer demands for providing liquidity and immediacy of execution.

The reason that market makers widen the spread between the bid and ask prices for large blocks of small firm stocks is that small firms have relatively few shares outstanding. Furthermore, of those outstanding, very few change hands during relatively short periods of time. Thus, market makers face an additional risk. If they purchase a large block of stock, they may not be able to resell the shares for some time, exposing themselves to the day-to-day variations in price due to market or company-specific factors.

The fact that small firm stocks trade infrequently also exposes investors in general to the risk of not being able to turn their investments into cash within a short period of time. Thus, the additional return being offered by small firm stocks might, at least in part, be a liquidity premium demanded by investors to compensate them for the additional risk they are taking.

A recent study by two finance professors, Yakov Amihud of New York University and Halm Mendelson of the University of Rochester, investigated the payoff that investors receive by holding low liquidity stocks. They hypothesized that stock returns would increase as the size of the dealer's bid-ask spread increased. For example, if all stocks were held for one year, a stock with a 2 percent spread between the bid and ask prices would be expected to yield 1.5 percent more than a stock with a 0.5 percent spread. Variations in investors' holding periods, as well as uncertainty about their liquidation needs, complicate the return spread relation. That is, investors with different holding periods require different gross rates of return from the same security. Investors with shorter holding periods are willing to pay more to acquire the low-spread securities than investors with longer holding periods because the latter can amortize the spread over a longer time.

To test this hypothesis, the researchers examined bid-ask spreads for NYSE stocks over the 1961–80 period. Initially, they ranked securities by their bid-ask spread in each year and divided them into seven equal portfolios. (The average spread for the seven portfolios ranged from 0.49 to 3.21 percent.) They then estimated the beta risk of each portfolio and calculated the excess return (alpha) for the next year.

Over the 20 years covered by this study, the least-liquid stock group which had the largest bid-ask spread, provided an 8.5 period average annual return—more than the most-liquid group. Thus, the loss of liquidity and the attendant increase in total investment risk are rewarded with additional investment return. As was mentioned earlier, some investors can tolerate the additional risk of holding low liquidity securities and, thus, receive these additional returns without the assumption of any investment pain. Furthermore, it is arguable whether or not the investor who holds one round lot of a thinly traded issue obtains any significant increase in investment risk. Thus, for individual investors who hold only a few round lots of thinly traded small firm stocks, or for those with very long investment horizons, the extra return promised by less liquid securities is delivered virtually free of cost.

WHAT ABOUT MANAGEMENT?

Most fundamental security analysts place a great deal of emphasis on the quality of management. Undoubtedly, management quality is an important ingredient in corporate success. Frequently, the talent and dedication of management determine how profitable a company becomes. Even though the quality of management is obviously important, how to judge management abilities is not so clear. Some analysts judge management quality by corporate results. Managers who articulate their goals and achieve them are given high marks. Top quality managers have companies ranking near the top of their industry group in sales and earnings growth and with respect to operating margin and return on equity. Finally, managers of firms that have demonstrated a high degree of consistency in financial and operating results year after year receive high quality ratings.

Many analysts give the impression that rating the quality of management is highly scientific; the truth is that judging management's capabilities is more art than science. Thus, it is not too surprising to find one analyst giving high marks to a firm's management while other analysts are downplaying its abilities.

I, too, believe that management is an important ingredient in corporate success. But I have a completely different method of rating management. Managers who own a large stake in the corporations they run receive high marks from me. If a corporate president owns 25 percent or more of the firm's outstanding stock, as a shareholder, I have to believe that his interest is the same as mine—increased share price. After all, this manager has the bulk of his personal wealth tied to the fortunes of the company. If it and the common stock perform well, his wealth increases. If the company and its common stock perform poorly, his wealth suffers dramatically. Managers whose ties to a company are limited to salary and benefits lack a commonality of interest with the shareholders. Owner/managers don't have to protect themselves with golden parachutes should they lose their jobs because of a takeover. Neither do they have to inflate their incomes with large bonuses during a particularly good year. Remember, a large bonus negatively affects earnings and share price, and whatever the owner/manager gains on the one hand is lost on the other. (In fact, owners lose more than they gain by bleeding their companies with large bonuses because such bonuses are taxed when paid. Increases in share price go untaxed until the shares are sold.)

So what does all of this have to do with small firm common stocks? Plenty. One researcher has found that the smallest firms listed on the New York Stock Exchange—the bottom 20 percent when ranked according to size—have about 30 percent of their shares held by operating management. When the researcher moved up to the next 20 percent of the firms listed on that exchange, he found less than 5 percent of the shares were held by management. As the size of the firms increased, the percentage of stock held by management continued to decline. The largest companies in America, on average, have less than 1 percent of their shares in the hands of management, and quite a few chief executives own none of their company's common stock! Is it any wonder that the managers of these firms are widely criticized for being unresponsive to shareholders' wishes?

One possible explanation for the small firm effect is that the managers of small firms care about share price performance over the longer term because they are such large shareholders themselves. Of course, some large companies also have a high degree of management ownership. And these companies also tend to be good performers.

DIVERSIFY THYSELF

Another possible explanation of the small firm effect lies in the nature of risk. As was seen in Chapter 3, total investment risk has two components—systematic or market-related risk and unsystematic or company-specific risk. Although investment return is the reward obtained for taking investment risk, such rewards are generally tied to systematic risk and not total risk because all unsystematic risk can be eliminated through portfolio diversification.

Consider the manager of a small firm who owns a significant portion of the company's outstanding stock. This individual has the greatest portion of his or her wealth tied to the company. This manager does not, and cannot, possess a well-diversified portfolio; the investment return he or she demands is based on the firm's total risk, not just systematic risk. Because the total risk of the typical small firm stock exceeds that of the typical large firm stock by approximately 50 percent, the manager demands greater rewards. Individual investors, however, can diversify their portfolios of small firm stocks and receive the same high return while taking far less risk. Because this extra return is obtained risk free, the risk-adjusted returns from small firm stocks tend to be greater than those of large companies whose management owns very little common stock.

In addition, small firms themselves tend to be underdiversified. Most large firms offer multiple lines of products or services —often everything from asphalt to zippers. During the 1970s, it became fashionable management practice among America's larger corporations to restructure themselves into diversified portfolios of minibusinesses. Corporate strategists bought and sold divisions and subsidiaries with gusto as they put together the equivalent of corporate mutual funds. Small firms, on the other hand, tend to provide a single product line—often a single product. Thus, the small firm tends to contain more unsystematic risk than the large firm. The typical small firm stock contains about 75 percent unsystematic risk compared to the 60 percent in the typical large firm stock. If the sales of its single product tumble, earnings and share price take a major hit. On the other hand, if the sales of one of the products of a large, well-diversified company suffer, chances are that sales increases of another product can buoy up earnings and the share price remains on an even keel. Thus, the sales, earnings, and share prices of large firms tend to be more stable than those of their small firm counterparts.

Even though some investors might view large firm diversification as a benefit, it is a benefit that comes at great cost. Corporate mergers are expensive. One firm seeking to acquire another firm must frequently pay a premium to acquire all of the firm's stock, much more than it would have to pay for just a few shares. Furthermore, mergers go hand-in-hand with golden parachutes and investment banking fees that outrage common sense. Thus, the reduction in risk is partially offset by lower investment returns.

As an investor, you can effect the same diversification and resultant risk reduction at a very low cost. Just call your broker and buy a few shares of several companies. You'll get all the risk reduction benefits of diversification for only a fraction of the cost—the payment of minimal brokerage fees. It may well be that the superfluous diversification practiced by almost all large companies reduces investment returns more than investment risk. The result is a lower risk-adjusted return. On the other hand, the increased risk of small firms can be offset by personal portfolio diversification that does not reduce investment returns. The result is greater risk-adjusted returns for small firm stocks.

SMALL FIRM COMMON STOCKS
AND THE INDIVIDUAL INVESTOR

Although the empirical evidence concerning small equity capitalization firms overwhelmingly indicates that, taken as a whole, their common stocks provide significant excess rates of return, practical suggestions on taking advantage of this free lunch have been few. How can the individual investor reap the rewards of the small firm effect? Some researchers suggest that you buy shares in all publicly traded small firms. Because more than 2,000 small firms trade in the national markets, this is far from a practical suggestion. But it is possible to capture most, if not all, of the small firm effect with a properly selected sampling of small firm stocks.

Table 6-12 illustrates small firm portfolio returns obtained from the application of two different portfolio management strategies: buying them all and buying a sample. It compares the returns from the Dimensional Fund Advisors (DFA) Small Firm mutual fund with the returns from purchase recommendations given in my small firm advisory newsletter, *Investment Horizons*. DFA believes that to capture the small firm effect they must buy them all, and they attempt to do this.[3] On the other hand, since 1984 the *Investment Horizons* portfolio has contained only 45 to 58 common stocks at any particular point in time. The returns from this portfolio have been adjusted to account for management fees and transaction costs; thus, they are directly comparable to DFA's buy-them-all strategy. The returns are highly similar from year to year. Also, the correlation

---

[3] The Dimensional Fund Advisors Small Firm Fund is not sold in all states.

TABLE 6-12
Small Firm Stocks: All versus a Sample

Year	Portfolio Returns	
	DFA Small Company	Investment Horizons
1984	−7.1%	−6.4%
1985	24.4	26.9
1986	6.8	6.4
1987	−9.3	−7.7
1988	22.9	36.0
1989	10.2	2.7
1990	−21.6	−14.0
1991	44.6	32.4
Total	71.9%	80.6%

between the month-to-month price changes of both portfolios is exceptionally high (0.95). As both portfolios contain about the same amount of risk, it appears that individual investors do not have to buy them all to capture the full small firm effect.

Even though later chapters detail stock selection and portfolio management techniques enabling you to capture the small firm effect, we can draw several preliminary observations from the literature review presented in this chapter. First, it appears that small firms do not provide greater returns merely because they are small. Firm size is a proxy for a set of other variables that produce the excess returns. Current research indicates that small firm common stocks produce superior investment returns because:

They are underresearched by brokerage analysts.

They are neglected by institutional investors.

They are less liquid than large firm stocks.

They possess a greater concentration of management ownership.

Their product lines are not overly diversified.

If size is merely a proxy for these variables, then you should look for companies possessing these characteristics rather than concentrating on size alone. By doing so, investors can construct a portfolio with a reasonable number of small firms and still be assured that they can capture the excess returns offered by small firm stocks.

A famous baseball player was once asked: "To what do you attribute your great batting success?" He responded: "I hit 'em where they ain't." This is good, practical advice for investors, who should select stocks from that segment of the market where institutional investors and security analysts ain't.

Second, because small firm stocks tend to possess company-specific risk which cannot be effectively diversified away, you should include both small and large firm stocks in your investment portfolio. Some scant evidence indicates that the equity returns from small firms possess a relatively low correlation with the equity returns from large firms (S&P Index stocks, for example). Thus, proper diversification requires that both classes of stocks be held. Although small firm stocks provide greater investment returns than their larger brethren, the small firm stock portfolio is not a substitute for a well-balanced portfolio. Recent research suggests that additional returns can be earned from investment in large firm stocks as long as investors use the same selection criteria as for small firm stocks.

Third, you need to hold a greater number of small firm stocks in a portfolio if you want adequate diversification. Although investors can obtain most of the risk reduction benefit of a portfolio of large firm stocks with as few as 10 issues selected from unrelated industries, my own research indicates that they cannot obtain the optimal benefit of small firm portfolio diversification until they hold from 20 to 30 stocks. If these stocks are bought in round lots to minimize brokerage commissions, this strategy implies a dollar commitment of at least $30,000. If you don't have resources of that magnitude, invest in a small firm mutual fund. Don't limit your portfolio to only one or two small firm stocks. We discuss small firm mutual funds in Chapter 11.

Finally, concentrate your attention on those small firms with demonstrated growth in both sales and earnings. The growing, small firm soon becomes a large firm, and large firms draw a following by institutional investors. Thus, you may be able to capitalize on abnormal common stock price increases which tend to occur when institutions follow one another onto the company's future bandwagon.

At present, there are over 2,000 publicly traded firms with equity capitalizations of less than $120 million. Of that large universe, you will want to own only a select few. The next chapter helps you to identify them.

CHAPTER 7

HOW TO CAPTURE THE SMALL FIRM EFFECT

The small firm effect may be the largest free lunch served up by an otherwise efficient stock market. Well-managed small firm stock portfolios have provided investors with a 50 percent greater return than the market as a whole. That's a lot. But how do you build a solid portfolio of small firm stocks? How small is small? Which small firms should you select? Where can you obtain data needed to evaluate small firm stocks? How many stocks do you need to capture the full effect? What are the financial characteristics of a small firm portfolio? When should you sell? Answers to these questions are crucial to investment success.

HOW SMALL IS SMALL?

When assessing company size, analysts use either total sales or equity capitalization, the total market value of a firm's outstanding stock. Although many financial publications use sales or revenues to measure size, equity capitalization is the correct measure. Remember, firms in different industries possess varying sales margins depending on the nature of their businesses. Thus, sales volume may not adequately reflect a firm's true size. Consider, for example, the two firms whose income statements appear in Table 7-1. Company A is a supermarket chain and company B is an electronics manufacturer. Supermarket chains operate on very narrow sales margins, while electronics manufacturers' margins are generous. Because grocery chains turn

120

TABLE 7-1
Firm Size: Revenues versus Equity Capitalization

	Company A *Supermarket Chain*	Company B *Electronics Manufacturer*
Sales	$500 million	$ 60 million
Cost of sales	440	20
Sales margin	60	40
Other costs	50	20
Income	10	20
Taxes	3	6
Net income	7	14
Shares	5 million	10 million
Earnings per share	$1.40	$1.40
P-E ratio	10	15
Equity cap	$ 70 million	$210 million

over their inventory frequently, even though they might only keep one or two cents of every sales dollar, an inventory turnover eight to ten times a year produces handsome profits. On the other hand, an electronics manufacturer may turn over its inventory only once a year. Thus, while the sales of one firm might be greater than those of another in a different line of business, its profit may actually be smaller. That is exactly the case in this example. The supermarket chain has nearly nine times the sales of the electronics manufacturer, but the electronics firm earned twice the profit of the supermarket chain. The electronics firm, in this instance, is the larger firm because the owners' income and wealth (value of the firm) is greater.

In the original study of firm size and investment returns, Rolf Banz defined a small firm by relative equity capitalization. Banz ranked all NYSE-listed stocks by equity market value and focused on the slice containing the smallest 20 percent. In 1992, a small firm, according to Banz's definition, would be one whose equity capitalization is less than $120 million.

Obviously, the definition of "small" is stated in relative terms. As market conditions change, the definition of small also changes. During a bull market the market value cutoff point increases; in a bear market it declines. Therefore, when looking for small firms, you must continually rank NYSE-listed issues according to equity capitalization and revise the cutoff point. Although this sounds like a monumental task, it is not. Furthermore, since the definition of a small firm is somewhat arbitrary, it is not necessary to revise it daily, weekly, or even monthly. I rank NYSE stocks only twice each year, and set my cutoff at 80 percent of the equity capitalization of the marginal firm. For example, if the threshold firm has an equity capitalization of $120 million, I set the size screen at $96 million. Thus, even though the equity capitalization separating large firms from small grows over time, I avoid the task of continuous ranking, and err on the conservative side.

SEPARATING THE WHEAT
FROM THE CHAFF

Once the definition of a small firm is set, you can begin screening publicly traded common stocks. The first screen to apply, of course, is firm size. In the following examples, I use the *S&P Investors Stock Guide* as my primary data source. (Figure 7-1 illustrates two pages from this guide.) Most business libraries are subscribers, and your broker will most likely give you a copy of the latest issue free of charge. To determine a firm's size, multiply the closing monthly stock price by the number of shares outstanding. If the result is less than your cutoff point, you have found a small firm. Cross all other firms above that point off the list. This will generally reduce the 5,300 stock list to approximately 2,000.

Next, compute the percentage of shares outstanding held by institutions and eliminate those with a high degree of institutional ownership. Again the *Stock Guide* provides the data. (Standard & Poor's continually surveys the stock holdings of about 2,700 institutions and lists the number of institutions that have invested in the company along with the total shares held at the end of the month.)

Similar to the definition of size, the degree of institutional holdings is also relative. Investors looking for truly neglected stocks may wish to screen out all stocks with any institutional following whatsoever. However, I believe that this screen is too restrictive. Frequently, the trust department of one or two local banks will invest in the stocks of local companies. The same might be true for a couple of pension fund managers who have local knowledge regarding a small firm's potential.

Large firm stocks have about 50 percent of their outstanding stock in the hands of institutional investors. The typical small firm, on the other hand, has only about 20 percent of its shares in institutional hands. Lacking any hard rule, I arbitrarily use this percentage in my initial screen.

The application of this screen reduces the number of potential small-cap stocks to approximately 800 stocks. At this point, I contact these remaining firms and obtain their annual reports, 10-K reports, proxy statements, and the latest quarterly reports. Then I examine the proxy statement to obtain the percentage of shares held by management. (As an alternative, you can also obtain this data from the *S&P Stock Reports*.) On average, small firms have about 33 percent of their shares held by operating management. Believing a high degree of management ownership is a large plus, I screen out those firms whose management holds less than 25 percent of the outstanding shares. If they don't have much interest in the company, why should you? The application of this screen generally eliminates about half of the 800 or so companies still on your list.

At this point you have identified about 400 to 500 companies which are small, have only a few shares in institutional hands, and have a high percentage of stock in the hands of management. The application of these three screens will probably take a few hours, but the result is well worth the effort. You will have a modest list of small firms neglected by analysts and institutional investors, and possessing the potential to deliver above-average returns.

At this point, the real work begins. The object is to locate those firms possessing above-average growth potential but not extreme risk. Begin by focusing on growth potential. This, of course, means attempting to predict the future. The future for small firms can be highly uncertain; this makes achieving a high degree of accuracy when making predictions of future growth a Herculean task. One might interview management, assess industry prospects, or analyze financial ratios (net

FIGURE 7–1

6 A&W-ADV

¶ S&P 500 · # MidCap 400 · • Options

Index	Ticker Symbol	Name of Issue (Call Price of Pfd. Stocks)	Market	Com. Rank. & Pfd. Rating	Par Val.	Inst. Hold Cos	Inst. Hold Shs. (000)	Principal Business	Price Range 1971-90 High	1971-90 Low	1991 High	1991 Low	1992 High	1992 Low	Dec. Sales in 100s	December, 1992 Last Sale Or Bid High	Low	Last	%Div Yield	P-E Ratio
#1	SODA	✓A & W Brands	NMS	NR	1¢	143	7169	Mfr soft drink concentrate	34¾	6¼	39¾	26½	40½	30¾	18037	35	31¼	31⅞	1.4	19
2	AAMS	Aames Financial	NMS	NR	.001	9	507	Mortgage brokerage, California	....	....	10	8	11¾	5¾	4695	11¼	8¾	10½	3.8	9
3•[1]	AIR	✓AAR Corp	NY,M,Ph	A–	1	81	9493	Mkts aviation parts/service	37½	1¼	16⅞	9¼	15⅞	10¾	14514	12¼	10¾	11¾	4.1	22
4	ABAX	✓Abaxis Inc	NMS	NR	No	15	1367	Dvlp stge:blood analyzer sys	....	....	....	....	17½	3½	2653	6¾	5¼	6	...	d
5	ABBY	Abbey Healthcare Grp	NMS	NR	0.001	24	3538	Home hlth care svcs/products	....	....	....	....	24½	9½	45576	24½	15⅝	24	...	...
¶6•[2]	ABT	✓Abbott Laboratories	NY,B,C,M,P,Ph	A+	No	910	432011	Diversified health care prod	23¼	½	34⅞	19⅝	34¼	26⅛	219574	33	30¼	30⅝	2.0	21
7	ABE	❖Abex Inc	NY	NR	1¢	48	3863	Mfr aerospace/defense subsys	....	....	....	....	9⅞	4⅜	12620	5¾	4⅝	5¾	...	..
8	ABMD	✓ABIOMED, Inc	NMS	NR	1¢	11	645	Medical equip/cardiac sys	16⅞	4¾	22¾	5¼	18⅝	8¾	3561	13¼	10	10¾	...	d
9•[3]	ABY	Abitibi-Price[53]	NY,Mo,To,P,Vc	B–	No	38	2277	Newsprint,paper prods	28⅝	2 5/16	14⅝	9⅞	13⅞	10⅜	1586	11½	10⅞	11⅜	◆3.5	d
10	ABRI	❖Abrams Industries	NMS	B	1	9	435	Construct'n/mfg, real estate	5⅝	¾	4¼	2¾	4¾	3¾	268	4½	4	4⅜	1.8	21
11	ACCC	**ACC Corp**	**NMS**	**B**	**0.015**	**27**	**2035**	**Full-svc telecommun'n co**	**14⅞**	**1⅛**	**15**	**7¼**	**22¾**	**12¼**	**7261**	**22¼**	**19¼**	**20¼**	**0.9**	**55**
12	ACLE	✓Accel Int'l	NMS	B	10¢	16	1016	Insurance:credit life/disab	14⅜	1 11/16	13	6⅜	10	2¾	2791	4⅜	2¾	3⅛	...	d
13	AIF	✓Acceptance Insur Cos[54]	NY,B,M,P,Ph	C	40¢	16	656	Hldg co:citrus operations	54⅝	10⅜	22½	9	15	6	1213	15	9⅝	9⅝	...	d
14	ACCS	✓Access Health Marketing	NMS	NR	0.001	7	606	Healthcare ind market'g svcs	....	....	....	....	7½	2⅞	4132	5⅝	4¾	5⅜	...	22
15•[4]	AKLM	✓Acclaim Entertainment	NMS	NR	2¢	59	8702	Dvlp video game cartridges	16	3⅛	6⅜	2⅞	18⅜	4½	94328	18⅜	14⅞	18⅛	...	33
16	ACET	❖Aceto Corp	NMS	B+	1¢	33	1687	Mfrs & dstr chemicals	11⅜	⅜	10¼	7¾	17½	9⅜	9519	17½	14¼	17¼	1.6	15
17	AK	❖Ackerley Communications	AS	NR	1¢	13	955	Brdcstg:pro basketball:adv	12	2⅜	4⅛	1¼	3	1¼	1987	2⅝	2⅛	2⅝	...	d
18	ACG	ACM Govt Income Fund	NY,M	NR	1¢	25	446	Closed-end investment co	12⅛	8¾	11⅝	10⅜	11⅝	10⅛	13472	11	10¾	11	8.7	..
19	AOF	ACM Gvt Opportunity Fd	NY,Ph	NR	1¢	4	33	Closed-end investment co	10⅛	7¾	9¾	8¾	10⅜	9	3921	9⅝	9	9⅜	(·)8.5	..
20	GSF	ACM Gvt Securities	NY,P	NR	1¢	25	1189	Closed-end investment co	12⅛	8⅝	11	9⅜	11⅞	9⅞	28433	11	9⅞	10⅝	9.0	..
21	SI	ACM Gvt Spectrum Fund	NY,M	NR	1¢	16	228	Closed-end investment co	10⅛	7¼	9½	8¼	9¾	8⅜	11639	9	8⅝	9	9.4	..
22	AMF	ACM Managed Income Fund	NY,M	NR	1¢	8	140	Closed-end investment co	10⅛	6½	9⅛	7⅝	10⅝	8⅝	7980	10⅛	9⅞	10⅛	10.7	..
23	MMF	ACM Managed Multi-Mkt	NY,M,Ph	NR	1¢	3	10	Closed-end investment co	12⅛	10	12⅞	11½	12⅞	8⅝	10389	9⅜	8⅝	8¾	8.9	..
24	AMT	✓Acme-Cleveland	NY,M,Ph	B–	1	63	3229	Mfr indus & telecom prod	35⅝	4½	7½	4¾	11¾	4¾	2365	9⅛	7¾	8¼	4.8	16
25	ACE	❖Acme Electric	NY	B–	1	19	1279	Pwr conv eq: transformers	10¾	⅜	6	3⅜	7⅛	3¾	2451	7⅛	4¾	7⅛	...	..
26	ACME	✓Acme Metals	NMS	NR	1	38	1765	Producer steel/steel prod	26½	8	15¾	10¾	19¾	11	1861	13¼	11¾	13¼	...	d
27	ACU	❖Acme United	AS,M	B–	2½	12	1217	Medic eq:shears,scissors	19½	1⅜	7⅜	4¼	8⅜	5¼	250	6¼	5½	5¾	3.5	34
28	CCS.EC	ACOI Inc	ECM	NR	3¢	3	8	Retail non-standard auto insur	9½	1	2½	¾	1⅜	⅜	198	13/16	9/16	9/16	...	19
29	ACO	✓Acordia Inc	NY	NR	1	..	...	Hldg co:insurance brokerage	....	....	....	....	22¼	14½	3407	22¼	19⅛	21½	1.7	14
30	ACX	✓Action Indus	AS,B	B–	10¢	18	1769	Merchandising programs	18¼	½	7⅛	2⅝	7⅛	2¼	3887	4	2 7/16	3½	...	d
31	APII	❖Action Products Intl	NSC	NR	.001	..	...	Mfr space,nature&custom prod	8½	11/16	5½	1⅝	5½	1 5/16	902	1 11/16	1 7/16	1 11/16	...	42
32	ATN	✓Acton Corp	AS,B,M,Ph	C	33⅓¢	10	176	RE mgmt,devlp:prop,cslty ins	94¾	1 7/16	6¾	3½	6¾	4⅛	301	6	5⅛	5½	...	d
#33•[5]	ACN	✓Acuson Corp	NY	B	.01¢	119	12430	Medical ultrasound imaging	32¾	5	40	22¾	33⅜	14⅜	25943	17½	15¼	15¾	...	14
34	ACXM	Acxiom Corp	NMS	B+	10¢	31	4556	Computer-based mkting svcs	12	4	11	5	19¼	7	12545	19¼	15¼	18¼	...	37
35	ADAC	✓ADAC Laboratories	NMS	B–	No	37	8280	Nuclear medicine comput sys	27⅜	½	2⅝	1	5¼	1 11/16	104777	5¼	4⅜	5	3.2	19
36	ADX	Adams Express	NY,B,M,P,Ph	NR	1	36	312	Closed-end investment co	23⅞	7	20¼	14¼	21⅛	18⅛	2585	20⅛	19⅜	20	2.3	..
37	AE	❖Adams Res & Energy	AS,B,M,Ph	B–	10¢	8	388	Oil&gas explor,dev,prod'n	70½	1¾	4	2¼	6½	3	555	5¾	4⅞	5⅛	...	8
38•[6]	ADPT	✓Adaptec Inc	NMS	NR	0.001¢	131	20215	Mfr computer data flow sys	12⅛	2 3/16	9¾	4¼	31	8⅝	121093	26⅝	22½	26	...	19
#39•[7]	ADCT	✓ADC Telecommunications	NMS	B	20¢	99	9532	Telecommunications equip	26	⅛	43¼	20½	48½	22¾	17426	48½	44¼	46¼	...	30
40	ADDR	✓Addington Resources	NMS	B–	1	40	3618	Mining,mkt bituminous coal	23	7	13⅝	6	16	7⅜	11666	16	13½	15	...	21
41	SOLD	ADESA Corp	NMS	NR	No	12	550	Auctions autos to auto dealers	....	....	....	....	12⅛	4⅞	4111	8¼	6⅜	7	...	16
42	ADIA	✓Adia Services	NMS	NR	25¢	27	1838	Temporary personnel service	32¼	6¼	25¾	17¾	22¾	11¼	1717	18½	16	16¾	1.0	21
#43•[5]	ADBE	✓Adobe Systems	NMS,M	NR	No	156	19511	Print,graphic software sys	50¾	2⅞	67¾	26¾	68½	25¼	83915	35½	29	31½	1.0	15
44•[3]	ADT	ADT Limited	NY,M,Ph	NR	10¢	81	40217	Security svcs/auctions	....	....	9½	5	9½	6	43678	8⅛	7¼	7¾	...	7
45	WS	Wrrt(Pur 1 com at $10)	NY,Ph	....	..	36	3956		....	....	....	....	2½	15/16	6212	1½	1	1⅛	...	..
46	AVCR	AdvaCare Inc	NMS	NR	1¢	43	5771	Provides medical mgmt svcs	....	....	....	....	16½	3⅝	32188	6	3⅞	4¾	...	d
47	ADVC	Advance Circuits	NMS	B–	10¢	31	2385	Mfr printed circuit boards	8⅞	1/16	8¼	3½	11	5⅜	27680	11	8¼	10¾	...	13
48	AROS	❖Advance Ross	NMS	B	10¢	13	239	Metal fabric'n,envirmt'l use	15½	⅝	12	8¼	16⅜	8¾	3617	16⅜	11	15¾	...	61

Uniform Footnote Explanations-See Page 1. Other: [1]Ph:Cycle 1. [2]Ph:Cycle 2. [3]To:Cycle 1. [4]CBOE:Cycle 1. [5]P:Cycle 1. [6]ASE:Cycle 1. [7]P:Cycle 2. [8]CBOE,NY:Cycle 3. [51]©$0.95. [52]Incl redemption of stk purch rt. [53]1986 & prior prices in Canadian. [54]Formerly Stoneridge Resources. [55]Fiscal Aug'89 & prior. [56]12 Mo Dec'90,Aug'90 earned $d0.78. [57]®$1.14,'92. [58]©$0.414. [59]©$0.04,'92. [60]©$0.95,'93. [61]Pfd in $M. [62]Redemption of stk purch rt. [63]In cash or stk:©$1.12,'92. [64]$1.26 in cash or stk:©$1.16,'92. [65]®$2.15,'90. [66]Stk dstr of Help/38 Systems.

❖ See Directory of Company Investor Contacts on page 254.

Common and Convertible Preferred Stocks

Index	Cash Divs Ex Yr Since	Period $	Date	Ex Div	Total $ So Far 1992	Ind Rate	Paid 1991	Cash & Equiv	Curr Assets	Curr Liab	Balance Sheet Date	Lg Trm Debt Mil-$	Shs Pfd	Shs Com	Yrs End	1988	1989	1990	1991	1992	Last 12 Mos	Period	1991	1992	Index
1	1991	Q0.11	1-15-93	12-28	0.43	0.44	0.30	3.96	28.7	20.1	9-30-92	1.13		9362	Dc	0.81	□1.14	□1.39	1.53		1.66	9 Mo Sep	1.05	1.18	1
2	1992	¹¹Q0.10	11-24-92	11-5	0.25	0.40		Equity per shr $3.95					3304	Je		1.56	1.60	0.93	1.01	1.17	3 Mo Sep	p0.21	0.37	2
3	1973	Q0.12	12-3-92	10-27	0.48	0.48	0.48	3.65	292	93.4	8-31-92	66.7		15842	My	1.34		0.91	d1.46	0.63	0.54	6 Mo Nov	0.39	0.30	3
4	None Since Public	Nil						8.59	8.95	2.06	9-30-92	0.19		6190	Mr		d0.91	p0.64	d1.39		d1.39	9 Mo Sep	d0.65	d0.58	4
5	None Since Public	Nil						2.43	68.6	43.5	9-26-92	★133		p4953	Dc							9 Mo Sep	n/a	0.94	5
6	1926	Q0.15	2-15-93	1-11	¹²0.57⅔	0.60	0.48	198	3295	2684	9-30-92	95.2		836924	Dc	0.83	0.96	1.11	△□1.27	E1.47	1.42	9 Mo Sep	△□0.90	1.05	6
7	None Since Public	Nil						64.0	369	212	p3-31-92	369		19758	Dc				p□17.66			9 Mo Sep	□0.55	pd0.05	7
8	None Since Public				g0.50	0.50		15.9	17.5	0.95	9-30-92	8.49		+6438	Mr	d0.48	d0.36	d1.08	d0.79		d0.80	6 Mo Sep	±d0.35	td0.36	8
9	1949	g0.12½	1-29-93	1-11	g0.50	0.50	g0.50		541	420	12-31-91	371	1831	69267	Dc	△2.60	0.70	d0.68	d1.12		jd2.90	9 Mo Sep	d0.42	d2.20	9
10	1960	Q0.02	1-4-93	12-8	0.17	0.08	0.20	4.55	17.0	14.5	10-31-92	46.6		2978	Ap	0.36	0.48	0.51	0.34	0.34	0.21	6 Mo Oct	0.28	0.15	10
11	1989	Q0.04½	2-4-93	12-28	0.16	0.18	0.16	0.30	15.2	19.8	9-30-92	12.6		4465	Dc	0.10	*0.93	0.43	0.53		0.37	9 Mo Sep	0.20	0.34	11
12	1990	0.07	5-1-92	3-26	0.13	Nil	0.13	Equity per shr $7.43			9-30-92	21.8	.1	4446	Sp	*0.93	*1.02	1.50	0.23		d5.02	9 Mo Sep	0.94	d4.31	12
13	5%Stk	12-17-84	11-26		Nil			Equity per shr $4.172			12-24-92	21.0		3468	Sp	d4.00	%d2.00	%d1.76	△d12.76		d11.76	9 Mo Sep	△d1.52	d0.52	13
14	None Since Public	Nil						11.8	15.5		8-31-92	0.95		5961	Sp	0.05	0.11	0.77	d0.31	P0.24	0.24				14
15	None Since Public	Nil						112	112	60.8	8-31-92	2.07		23600	Au	0.29	0.54	0.77	d0.31	0.55	0.55				15
16	1985	S0.14	1-1-93	12-14	0.222	0.28	0.212	20.4	62.3	14.4	9-30-92	2.75	383	4951	Je	0.83	0.88	0.90	0.97	$1.15	1.19	3 Mo Sep	0.11	0.15	16
17	None Paid	Nil						13.8	61.1	70.2	9-30-92	214		+15419	Au	±d0.48	±d0.48	±d0.44	±d2.54		d1.63	9 Mo Sep	±d0.96	±d0.05	17
18		0.03	1-22-93	1-5	0.98½	0.96	1.26	Net Asset Val $10.53			12-24-92			18084		10.55	9.59	9.01	10.59						18
19		S0.48	1-22-93	12-22	90.853	0.80	1.058	Net Asset Val $9.11			12-24-92			11742		9.19	9.59	9.01	9.00						19
20		0.13	1-8-93	12-21	1.01	0.96	1.27½	Net Asset Val $10.49			12-24-92			67037		10.48	10.60	10.16	10.55						20
21		¹0.116	1-15-93	12-22	0.832	0.85	1.014	Net Asset $8.91			12-24-92			31531	Je	$8.76	$9.13	$8.76	$9.15			3 Mo Sep	0.11	△0.03	21
22		¹0.18½	1-22-93	12-22	1.008	1.08	1.008	Net Asset $9.07			12-24-92		⁶195	p17673	Au	$9.40	$9.39	$8.39							22
23		¹0.06½	1-22-93	11-2	1.04	0.78	1.50	Net Asset Val $9.58			12-18-92	3.40		9903	Nv	$11.53	$11.22	$10.52	d1.60			9 Mo Sep		0.36	23
24		0.10	1-20-92	11-2	0.40	0.40	0.40	28.6	77.8	39.8	9-30-92	20.8	161	6291	Sp	△0.44	△0.78	d0.52	d1.60						24
25		0.08	12-3-90	11-5		Nil		0.21	33.3	7.91	10-02-92			4818	Je	△0.75									25
26		²0.02	4-6-92	3-10	²⁰0.02	Nil	²⁰0.02	41.5	142	56.2	9-27-92	56.0		5358	Dc	*3.22	3.00	1.05	d0.43		d0.75	9 Mo Sep	d0.26	d0.58	26
27		0.05	12-4-92	11-9	0.20	0.20	0.17	0.44	35.4	9.75	9-30-92	15.1		3338	Dc	0.01	△0.46	0.40	0.41		0.17	9 Mo Sep	0.37	*0.13	27
28		None Since Public	Nil					Equity per shr $0.25			9-30-92	1.51		10317	Dc		0.10	0.09	0.04		0.03	9 Mo Sep	1.05	*0.04	28
29		0.09	12-17-92	11-27	0.09	0.36		21.4	85.4	119	9-30-92	6.49		13373	Jl		1.01	1.26	0.44	0.44	1.53		1.05	1.13	29
30		0.06	6-15-87	5-26		Nil		0.14	55.3	34.6	6-28-92	9.33		5539	Dc	△0.66	0.33	d3.08	0.44	0.44	d0.23	9 Mo Sep	0.43	d0.24	30
31		Wrrt	12-1-88	10-26		Nil		0.14	2.01	0.41	12-24-92	0.40		993	Dc	*0.11	d0.19	0.12	*0.15		0.04	9 Mo Sep	0.23	0.12	31
32		5%Stk	7-15-82	6-25		Nil		Net Asset Val $10.23			12-31-91	p72.8		p1256	Dc	d1.08	△3.77	d5.10	d8.16	d5.97	d5.97	9 Mo Sep	d2.92	d0.73	32
33		0.09	12-17-92	11-27		Nil		67.4	214	67.7	9-26-92			30354	Mr	0.78	1.07	1.33	1.59	E1.15	1.31	6 Mo Sep	1.17	0.89	33
34	1992	0.04	1-4-93	12-18	0.12	0.16		1.19	37.0	17.4	9-30-92	31.3		10303	Mr	0.42	0.58	0.39	0.22	P0.27	0.50	6 Mo Sep	d0.01	0.27	34
35								8.49	50.1	27.2	6-28-92			44894	Je	0.27	0.39	0.08	0.02		0.27				35
36	1936	³1.26	12-27-92	11-17	⁴1.62	0.46	1.63	Net Asset Val $20.49			12-24-92			32747	Dc	$16.11	$18.35	$16.82	$20.21			9 Mo Sep	0.26	0.46	36
37		8-15-78	7-10		Nil			2.58	52.9	49.4	9-30-92	3.60		4163	Mr	0.56	0.44	0.46	0.45		0.65	6 Mo Sep	0.24	0.91	37
38		None Since Public	Nil					124	198	25.6	10-02-92	16.3		24691	Mr	0.09	0.75	0.59	0.70	P1.55	1.37		1.37		38
39		None Since Public	Nil					20.7	114	40.3	7-31-92	129		13583	Dc	1.30	1.25	1.73	1.65	E0.70	1.55		1.55		39
40		None Since Public	Nil					37.8	107	73.3	9-30-92			15236	Dc	□1.19	0.67	0.93	0.41		0.10	9 Mo Sep	□0.09	0.60	40
41		None Since Public	Nil					9.73	37.5	21.4	12-24-92	31.0		9112	Dc				p0.38		0.44	9 Mo Sep	p0.29	*p0.35	41
42	1984	0.04	12-18-92	12-3	0.16	0.16		22.3	124	59.7	9-30-92	2.04		p12548	Dc	1.50	±△1.63	±1.41	±0.67	E2.05	0.80	9 Mo Sep	±0.48	±0.61	42
43	1988	0.08	10-14-92	9-24	0.32	0.32	0.30	152	213	47.2	8-28-92	881	p436	22592	Nv	0.98	1.55	1.83	2.25		2.07	9 Mo Aug	1.68	1.50	43
44		Wrrt	4-24-92	4-27	Wrrt			162	538	459	12-31-91			p10968	Dc	3.07	3.32	△²2.17	□1.04		1.16	9 Mo Sep	□0.73	0.85	44
45		Terms&trad basis should be checked in detail						Wrrts expire 6-30-94						18275											45
46		None Since Public	Nil					11.7	52.5	24.0	6-30-92	24.9		11439	Sp	0.02	d0.15	Nil	Nil	P□d0.53	d0.53	3 Mo Nov	0.14	0.26	46
47		h..	6-17-88	6-20		Nil		4.21	23.2	10.8	11-28-92	0.07		6805	Au	d1.23	0.72	1.19	d0.81	0.70	0.82	9 Mo Sep	3.69	0.01	47
48		h..	11-27-64					20.8	21.9	1.24	9-30-92	1743		1743	Dc	d0.04	0.26	1.37	3.94		0.26				48

◆Stock Splits & Divs By Line Reference Index ¹²2-for-1,'90. ¹²To split 3-for-1,ex Feb 5. ¹²Adj to 5%,'90. ¹⁵3-for-5 REVERSE,'92. ¹³1-for-2 REVERSE,'88.¹-for-2 REVERSE:'89
¹Adj to 4%,Jun,'90.¹⁰%,'91.6-for-5,'92. ²⁵Adj for 5%,'88. ¹¹To split 3-for-2,ex Feb 5. ¹²Adj for-1,'92. ³⁷1-for-2 REVERSE,'92. ³⁸2-for-1,'92. ⁴²2-for-1,'89. ⁴³2-for-1,'88.
⁴¹1-for-10 REVERSE,'91. ⁴⁷5-for-4,'90,'92.

Source: Reprinted by permission of Standard & Poor's Corporation.

income margin, payout ratios, or return on equity) when making a prediction. In fact, I use all of these methods. Before undertaking this effort, however, I first look to the past. The real proof of the pudding is in the eating. Similarly, the best method of assessing future growth prospects for a firm is to look for firms that have demonstrated they are capable of growing at above-average rates. Such a history does not imply that future growth will mirror the past. However, if a firm has not been able to grow at a high sustained rate in the past, this is a clear signal of its inability to do so in the future.

When assessing historical growth rates, analysts look at several variables—sales, earnings, dividends, and book value. I believe the most dependable to be sales growth. Earnings and book value suffer from what I call creative accounting. Although a firm's financial statements must be prepared according to "generally accepted accounting principles and practices," these practices vary widely from company to company. One company might value its inventory using a "last-in-first-out" basis while another might use the "first-in-first-out" method. One might depreciate, or write off its assets faster than another. All of these accounting choices impact a firm's reported earnings. Furthermore, management can actually "manage earnings." For example, if it looks as though the year's earnings may decline, management might sell some assets at a profit to boost earnings. If the period's earnings appear to be particularly strong, management can write off obsolete equipment or sell assets at a loss. Finally, because many small firms do not pay any dividends or only a small fraction of earnings, dividend growth generally does not adequately reflect a firm's future growth prospects.

When assessing historical sales growth, use sales reported during the last six years. Compute the percentage sales growth from year to year. Look for firms with steady year to year sales growth percentages and those with an average annual growth rate at least 10 percent greater than the rate of inflation over the previous six years. The object is to measure real growth or growth in output. During inflationary periods, some firms can give the appearance of growing by increasing their selling prices when, in fact, the firms are not growing at all. A 10 percent real growth rate is approximately twice the rate of growth of the average common stock. It is also twice the target real growth rate of the economy as a whole. Remember, you are seeking small companies that can grow into large ones. As these firms grow they attract the attention of Wall Street analysts and institutional investors. And their buying pressure tends to propel the firm's share price.

High growth firms almost always sell at higher P-E multiples than do slow growth firms. Thus, the companies remaining after applying a growth screen generally possess higher than average P-E multiples. Later on I present a method for determining how much you should pay for a growth stock. The object, of course, is to avoid paying too much. At this point, however, you would probably not want to evaluate the specific P-E ratio of every company still on your list. You can omit those with extremely high P-E ratios without the danger of missing out on an exceptional investment opportunity. How high is extreme? My rule of thumb at this point is to screen out any firm whose P-E ratio exceeds 40 times trailing earnings. Although this is a very high multiple and I would not likely include such a company in my small firm portfolio, I do retain these firms for further observation. Remember, I apply this series of screens only twice a year. Setting a very restrictive P-E screen at this point frequently eliminates a number of potentially profitable investments whose P-E ratios may be temporarily high.

Next, I examine the balance sheets of all firms still on the list, giving particular attention to the firm's capital structure. I discard those with a relatively large amount of debt. Note that I used the term *relatively*. Some firms naturally use more debt financing than others. Retail chains that own rather than rent their outlets have more debt than oil exploration and development firms. Exceptions aside, my general rule of thumb is to exclude firms with debt to total asset ratios greater than 25 percent.

The reason for applying a debt screen, is to control for risk. Small growth oriented companies frequently stumble and fall. Since they tend to have narrow product lines, a temporary industry sales slump can cause sales, earnings, and share price to plummet. Furthermore, many small companies have only a few customers. The loss of a single customer can cause a swift and severe profit reversal. Many times these setbacks result in periods of negative cash flow. A firm that is strapped with a lot of debt, and huge interest payments, can find itself in serious financial trouble. Although its problems may be only temporary, the large debt burden can result in irreparable financial damage—and may cause the firm to cease operations.

Generally, the application of these screens results in a list of about 100 small growth-poised companies. Final selections can be made from this list. This process requires a lot of work—perhaps there's no such thing as a free lunch after all. Just remember, you are seeking small companies that are not followed by the crowd. Even though it would be much easier to ask your broker which stocks the firm is recommending, chances are these recommendations will not be the stocks for which you're looking. Thus, there is no easy way out. But be assured that your efforts will be well rewarded.

SOURCES OF SMALL FIRM DATA

Of course, to apply the screens outlined above you need financial data for a large number of companies. There are several excellent sources of data available at modest cost. In fact, most business libraries subscribe to the publications with the data you need, and it's free of charge. Computerized data bases are available, although expensive. In addition, using computerized screens can be highly nonproductive. If you program your computer to apply all of the previously mentioned screens and run the program, all you would get is a list of stocks. You would have no idea what happened to the missing companies. And sometimes very good companies are omitted because they failed to pass only one of the screens by a very small margin. For example, a company that passes all screens yet has a debt-to-total-asset ratio of 26 percent, instead of the required 25 percent, is most likely not significantly different from the 100 or so remaining companies. In addition, this company might possess higher sales growth and a lower P-E ratio than any other company on your final list. Yet, because it failed to pass the last screen, you may never know of its existence.

Before you accuse me of living in the Dark Ages, I must tell you that I like to use computers. They make things around my office a lot easier. Our newsletters are written and typeset on a computer. Our firm's accounting system is computerized. Our list of 12,000 subscribers is maintained on a computer. God bless computers. But I don't use a computer to make stock selections. Successful stock selection involves a whole set of decisions that can only be made on a subjective basis. That is a task best left to humans.

Here are some of the better sources of small firm financial data. For each publication I have included a checklist which indicates the availability of the data needed to conduct the aforementioned screens.

Standard & Poor's OTC Profiles
Standard & Poor's Corporation
25 Broadway, New York, New York 10004
Three times a year; annual subscription $75
Contains profiles of 600 OTC listed companies with market caps below $200 million.

Recent share price	YES
Shares outstanding	YES
Institutional holdings	NO
Insider holdings	NO
Annual sales	YES
Recent P-E ratio	YES
Total debt	YES
Total assets	NO

Standard & Poor's Stock Guide
Standard & Poor's Corporation
25 Broadway, New York, New York 10004
Monthly; annual subscription $118
Financial data, in compact form, on more than 5,300 common and preferred stocks. Also contains return data for 450 mutual funds.

Recent share price	YES

Shares outstanding	YES
Institutional holdings	YES
Insider holdings	NO
Annual sales	NO
Recent P-E ratio	YES
Total debt	YES
Total assets	NO

S&P Stock Reports
Standard & Poor's Corporation
Updated weekly; annual subscription $2,855. (It can also be found in most public library business sections.)
Service contains one page reports for about 4,500 companies. Three volumes: NYSE, AMEX, and OTC. Also publishes a supplement to OTC Stock Reports covering actively traded small OTC securities.

Recent share price	YES	
Shares outstanding	YES	
Institutional holdings	YES	
Insider holdings	YES	
Annual sales	YES	(last 10 years)
Recent P-E ratio	YES	
Total debt	YES	
Total assets	YES	

Value Line Investment Survey
Value Line, Inc., 711 Third Avenue, New York, New York 10017
Annual subscription $525
One page reports and analysis for 1,700 companies. Industries updated weekly—all reports updated once every 13 weeks.

Recent share price	YES	
Shares outstanding	YES	
Institutional holdings	YES	
Insider holdings	YES	
Annual sales	YES	(last 15 years)
Recent P-E ratio	YES	
Total debt	YES	
Total assets	YES	

WHAT DOES A SMALL FIRM LOOK LIKE?

In July 1992, I applied the previously described screens to an initial list of 6,000 nationally traded companies. As a result, I obtained a list of 175 firms after also excluding public utilities and stocks selling under $5 per share. A summary of the financial statistics of these firms appears in Table 7-2.

As you can see, these are not penny stocks although share price was far less than the approximately $50 average for NYSE-listed firms in late 1992. Furthermore, even though these companies are small relative to America's industrial giants, they are by no means tiny. Their annual sales averaged slightly more than $65 million. The most striking feature, however, is their five-year growth rates. The typical company in the S&P Index grew at an annual rate of less than 7 percent over this period. These small firms, on the other hand, averaged a 14 percent annual increase in sales and a 12 percent annual increase in earnings. On average, their management held more shares than institutions (29 percent versus 26 percent). Remember, the 1,000 largest firms in America have fewer than 2 percent of their shares in the hands of management and more than 50 percent in the hands of absentee landlords—institutional investors. In July 1992, these small firms were priced at about 14 times trailing earnings. Even though this may appear

TABLE 7-2
Small Firm Stocks: Financial Characteristics

Annual sales	$66 million
Return on equity	14%
Shares outstanding	3.8 million
Share price	$12.00
Equity cap	$42 million
Five-year annual sales growth	14.0%
Five-year annual earnings growth	12.0%
Management ownership	29%
Institutional ownership	26%
Dividend yield	1.1%
Percent paying cash dividends	43%
P-E ratio	13.7

to be abnormally high, the average large company stock was selling for more than 25 times trailing earnings at that time. Thus, small firm investors obtained twice the growth potential of large firm stocks but paid almost 50 percent less!

The Appendix to this chapter contains a list of 175 small firm stocks. Included with the list is the company's stock trading location, ticker symbol and industry group. For those of you who wish to do a little preliminary scouting before you begin a formal search for small firm stocks, I have provided a pasture in which to roam.

HOW MANY IS ENOUGH?

Your small firm stock portfolio should contain enough issues to ensure that you are properly diversified and that you have eliminated most unsystematic, or company-specific, risk. It should also contain a sufficient number of issues to ensure that you are capturing all of the small firm effect. Of course, one way of doing this is to buy only stocks with equity capitalizations below $120 million. However, that would mean buying approximately 2,000 stocks and investing at least $4 million. This clearly is beyond the reach of most individual investors. On the other hand, you could buy 100 shares of each of the 100 or so companies that pass all screens. While this greatly reduces the number of companies, it would still require the investment of approximately $200,000.

During the ten years that I have been publishing my small firm advisory newsletter, I have maintained a recommended list of about 50 firms. The returns for that portfolio correlate almost perfectly with an index containing all small firm stocks. Thus, investors can be assured of capturing the entire small firm effect by holding no more than 50 stocks. In fact, the required number of stocks is far less if the selections are made from a large number of industries.

As to the minimum number of stocks needed to ensure adequate diversification, our research indicates that nearly all company-specific risk can be eliminated by holding from 20 to 30 stocks. Figure 7-2 illustrates the reduction in risk that occurs

FIGURE 7–2
Risk Reduction and Small Firm Portfolio Diversification

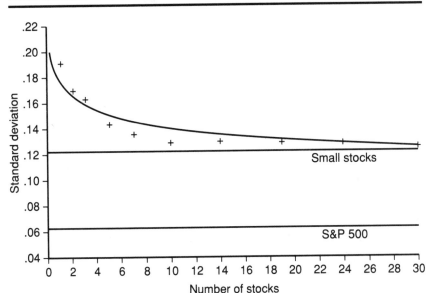

by increasing the number of stocks in a small firm portfolio. The data consisted of the quarterly returns of 214 stocks with equity capitalizations below $100 million, institutional holdings of less than 20 percent, management holdings greater than 20 percent, and those with reasonable P-E ratios and above-average earnings and sales growth. I then constructed random portfolios comprised of the following number of stocks: 1, 2, 3, 5, 7, 10, 14, 19, 24, and 30. I constructed 20 different random portfolios for each portfolio size resulting in a total of 200 hypothetical portfolios. I obtained the standard deviation of return for each portfolio size and graphed it as illustrated.

As Figure 7-2 shows, increasing portfolio size to 20 stocks eliminates nearly 90 percent of the company-specific risk. When the number of stocks was increased to 30, less than 5 percent of the average company-specific risk remained. The same degree of risk reduction for a large firm stock portfolio can be obtained with from 12 to 15 stocks. To be properly diversified, therefore, small stock investors must hold nearly twice the number of issues. However, small firm stocks sell at less than half the price of their large brethren. Thus, although more small firm stocks are needed to ensure proper diversification, the dollar requirement is actually less.

WHEN SHOULD YOU SELL?

Chapter 10 details the general conditions under which stocks should be sold, so I won't give away the entire plot here. However, one obvious reason for selling a small firm stock is that it has ceased to be small. If a small firm stock was defined as one with an equity capitalization below $110 million in 1992, is a large firm stock one with an equity capitalization above $120? Technically, the answer is yes. However, there is little profit in buying a stock whose equity capitalization is $100 million and selling it when the equity capitalization reaches $120 million. That's only a 20 percent gain; most of that can be erased by brokerage commissions. Thus, you must either buy only tiny companies or hold until firms become much larger than the $120 million equity capitalization. I recommend doing both.

First, as I suggested earlier, consider setting your equity capitalization screen 20 or 30 percent below the small-cap threshold. That way you have some room left for small firms to grow before you are required to sell. Second, set your growth sights higher than the initial cutoff point. After all, if one of your selections ascends beyond the initial cutoff point, it must be growing and providing investment profits. You have found a winner. It doesn't make sense to cut your profits short by selling merely because stock price is rising.

I recommend setting a second cutoff point that can be used to trigger a sale. Set this equity cap at the point which divides the largest 70 percent of the NYSE firms from the smallest 30 percent. In 1992 that firm had an equity capitalization of about $300 million. Once a firm passes this equity capitalization threshold, it is definitely a large firm and should no longer be held in a small firm portfolio. Table 7-3 illustrates the equity capitalizations defining the four smallest deciles of NYSE stocks as of December 1992.

TABLE 7-3
NYSE Equity Cap: Smallest Listed Firms

Smallest 40%	$500 million
Smallest 30%	300 million
Smallest 20%	120 million
Smallest 10%	60 million

Some good small firm stocks may also be good large firm stocks. As mentioned previously, due to the relatively low correlation of returns between large and small firm stock portfolios, investors may obtain additional risk reduction by holding both large and small firm stocks in their portfolios. In short, the object is to select large firm stocks the same way you select small firm stocks. Look for those with a low degree of institutional interest, those with a relatively high degree of management ownership, and those that have demonstrated they are capable of growing at above-average rates. Frequently a firm which grows from small to large still has all of the characteristics of a small firm. If so, rather than selling it, you may merely move it from the small firm segment of your portfolio to the large firm segment.

CONCLUSION

In Chapter 6, I described the reasons why small firms provide extra investment returns. These included neglect by institutions and analysts, low degree of liquidity, and a large percentage of ownership by management. Small firms do not provide extra returns merely because they are small but because of other causal factors. These causal factors are of more than academic interest—they indicate the characteristics to be examined when making stock selections. In this chapter, I have illustrated how you can use these characteristics in the selection-decision process. They are quite simple to apply and the needed data is readily available.

Although proper stock selection is a requisite to investment success, it does not ensure it. To be a successful investor, you must select the right stocks and practice proper portfolio management. In the chapters that follow, I outline these proper portfolio management techniques.

APPENDIX

The following list of small firms was developed in mid-1992 by applying some of the screens outlined in this chapter. All of the firms on the list are small, have a low percentage of shares held by institutions, and have a large percentage of their shares in the hands of management.

Company	Exchange	Ticker Symbol	Industry
AEP Industries	OTC	AEPI	Mfr. plastic products
Aaron Rents	OTC	ARON	Rents & leases equipment
Aceto	OTC	ACET	Mfr./distr. specialty chemicals
Advanced Logic Research	OTC	AALR	Mfr. microcomputers
Advanced Marketing Service	OTC	ADMS	Book club
AEL Industries	OTC	AELNA	Mfr. defense electronics
Aileen	NYSE	AEE	Mfr. women's apparel
Allen Organ	OTC	AORGB	Mfr. electronic organs
Altron	OTC	ALRN	Mfr. circuit boards
American Biltrite	AMEX	ABL	Mfr. floor covering
American Ecology	OTC	ECOL	Waste management
American Filtrona	OTC	AFIL	Mfr. tobacco & ind. filters
American Precision Instruments	NYSE	APR	Mfr. industrial equipment
Analysts International	OTC	ANLY	Computer software applications
Applied Extrusion Technology	OTC	AETC	Mfr. thermoplastic nets
Arrow Automotive Industries	AMEX	AI	Mfr. automobile parts
Artistic Greetings	OTC	ARTG	Distr. stationery products
Astro Med	OTC	ALOT	Mfr. high-speed printers
Aydin	NYSE	AYD	Elect. & Communication equip.
Badger Meter	AMEX	BMI	Mfr. fluid meters
Badger Paper Mills	OTC	BPMI	Mfr. paper products

Company	Exchange	Ticker Symbol	Industry
Baldwin Piano & Organ	OTC	BPAO	Mfr. pianos and electric organs
BEI Electronics	OTC	BEII	Defense contractor
Belding Hemingway	NYSE	BHY	Fabrics and home sewing products
Benchmark Electronics	AMEX	BHE	Circuit board manufacturer
Big B	OTC	BIGB	Discount retail drug stores
Bio-Rad Laboratories	AMEX	BIOA	Mfr. health care products
Blessings	AMEX	BCO	Mfr. plastic/geriatric products
Boston Acoustics	OTC	BOSA	Mfr. loudspeaker systems
Brandon Systems	OTC	BRDN	Temp. computer personnel
Cagle	AMEX	CGLA	Poultry and food producer
CEM	OTC	CEMX	Mfr. microwave test equipment
Central Sprinkler	OTC	CNSP	Mfr. residential sprinkler systems
CIMCO	OTC	CIMC	Mfr. plastic components
Computer Data Systems	OTC	CPTD	Data processing services
Concord Camera	OTC	LENS	Mfr. camera/photo equipment
CONMED	OTC	CNMD	Mfr. health care products
Cosmetic Center	OTC	COSCA	Discount retail cosmetics
CPAC	OTC	CPAK	Photographic equipment
Crown Books	OTC	CRWN	Discount bookstore chain
Dataram	AMEX	DTM	Mfr. minicomputer products
Datron Systems	OTC	DTSI	Mfr. radar systems
Del Electronics	AMEX	DEL	Mfr. high voltage power supplies
Detection Systems	OTC	DETC	Mfr. intruder detectors
Ecology & Environment	AMEX	EEI	Environmental remediation
EKCO	NYSE	EKO	Mfr. household products
EMCON Associates	OTC	MCON	Environmental remediation
Engraph	OTC	ENGH	Printing/packaging materials
Espey Mfg. & Electronics	AMEX	ESP	Mfr. elect. power supply systems

Company	Exchange	Ticker Symbol	Industry
Esquire Radio & Electronics	AMEX	EE	Mfr. private band radios
Esterline Technologies	NYSE	ESL	Mfr. instruments
Federal Screw Works	OTC	FSCR	Mfr. auto parts
Flexsteel Industries	OTC	FLXS	Mfr. business furniture
Franklin Electronic Publishers	OTC	FPUB	Computer and elect. products
Fredericks of Hollywood	NYSE	FHO	Specialty retailer
Frozen Food Express	AMEX	JIT	Trucking/transportation
Genovese Drug Stores	AMEX	GDXA	Retail drug store chain
Geraghty & Miller	OTC	GMGW	Environmental remediation
Giga-tronics	OTC	GIGA	Mfr. measuring instruments
Gish Biomedical	OTC	GISH	Mfr. health care products
GoodMark Foods	OTC	GDMK	Mfr. snack foods
Graham Field Health Products	NYSE	GFI	Mfr. surgical equipment
Grist Mill	OTC	GRST	Mfr. snack foods & cereals
Halsey Drugs	AMEX	HDG	Generic drug manufacturer
Handex Environmental	OTC	HAND	Groundwater pollution control
Hastings Manufacturing	AMEX	HMF	Mfr. auto replacement parts
Health-Mor	AMEX	HMI	Vacuum cleaners/metal tubing
Helix Technology	OTC	HELX	Mfr. cryogenic equipment
Hexcel	NYSE	HXL	Honeycomb cores/ plastics
Hipotronics	AMEX	HIP	Hi-volt test/pwr. supply equip.
Hologic	OTC	HOLX	Dvl./mfr. X-ray systems
Horizon Industries	OTC	HRZN	Mfr. residential carpets
Hospital Staffing Services	NYSE	HSS	Recruitment serv./ healthcare ind.
ILC Technology	OTC	ILCT	Mfr. light sources & sensors
Industrial Acoustics	OTC	IACI	Mfr. noise suppressant products
Insteel Industries	AMEX	III	Mfr. welded wire fabric
Instron	AMEX	ISN	Material testing equipment
Intermagnetics General	OTC	INMA	Mfr. superconductive metals

Company	Exchange	Ticker Symbol	Industry
International Shipholding	NYSE	ISH	Ocean freight transportation
Iomega	OTC	IOMG	Mfr. computer disc drives
Jaclyn	AMEX	JLN	Popular-priced handbags
J&J Snack Foods	OTC	JJSF	Mfr. snack foods
Johnson Products	AMEX	JPC	Personal grooming aids
Johnston Industries	NYSE	JII	Mfrs. ind'l/apparel textiles
Keane	AMEX	KEA	Computer software/consulting
Keithly Instruments	AMEX	KEI	Mfr. electronic test equipment
Kenan Transport	OTC	KTCO	Transports bulk commod.
Kewaunee Scientific	OTC	KEQU	Furniture & equipment for labs
Keystone Consolidated	NYSE	KES	Mfr. steel & wire products
Kiddie Products	OTC	KIDD	Mfr. infant products
Kirchner Medical	OTC	KMDC	Mfr. orthopedic products
Lancer Corp. Texas	AMEX	LAN	Mfr. beverage dispensing systems
Leslie S Poolmart	OTC	LESL	Retail swimming pools/products
Lindal Cedar Homes	OTC	LNDL	Pre-cut home packages
Lindsay Manufacturing	OTC	LINZ	Mfr. agric. sprinkling systems
Lumex	AMEX	LUM	Mfr. hospital furniture/equip.
Macdermid	OTC	MACD	Industrial metal finishing chemicals
Mark Controls	OTC	MRCC	Mfr./sell industrial valves
Marten Transport	OTC	MRTN	Long haul refrigerated carrier
MATEC	AMEX	MXC	Steel & cable coatings
Max & Erma S Restaurants	OTC	MAXE	Family style restaurants
Maxwell Laboratories	OTC	MXWL	Defense/commercial electronic systems
Medex	OTC	MDEX	Mfr. health care products
Medical Graphics-Minn.	OTC	MGCC	Computerized diagnostic systems
Merrimac Industries	AMEX	MRM	Mfr./design signal componants
Mestek	NYSE	MCC	Climate control equipment
Met-Pro	AMEX	MPR	Mfr. pump and water systems

Company	Exchange	Ticker Symbol	Industry
Microage	OTC	MICA	Franchises computer stores
Midwesco Filter Resources	OTC	MFRI	Mfr. air pollution filter bags
Mobley Env. Services	OTC	MBLYA	Waste mgmt./oilfield services
Moore Medical	AMEX	MMD	Dstr. drugs, med., beauty products
MOSCOM	OTC	MSCM	Telecommunications mgmt. systems
Newcor	OTC	NEWC	Specialized industrial machine
Norstan	OTC	NRRD	Digital comm./infor. processing
NSC	OTC	NSCC	Asbestos abatement services
Nuclear Metals	OTC	NUCM	Mfr. depleted uranium parts
O'Charley's	OTC	CHUX	Full service restaurants
Oglebay Norton	OTC	OGLE	Lake shipping, mining, mfr.
Ohio Art	AMEX	OAR	Mfr. toys/plastic products
Oneita Industries	AMEX	ONA	Mfr. T-shirts for printing
Orange	NYSE	OJ	Citrus groves/juice products
Osmonics	OTC	OSMO	Mfr. water purification systems
Patlex	OTC	PTLX	Patent enforcement
Paul Mueller	OTC	MUEL	Mfr. steel equipment
Penn Engineering & Mfg.	AMEX	PNN	Captive fasteners/DC Motors
Perini	AMEX	PCR	Construction & development
Photronics	OTC	PLAB	Mfr./mkt. photo masks
Pitt Des Moines	AMEX	PDM	Steel fabricating
Plasti Line	OTC	SIGN	Mfr. illuminated outdoor signs
Powell Industries	OTC	POWL	Electrical equipment & controls
Pronet	OTC	PNET	Radio/telephone communication
PSICOR	OTC	PCOR	Perfusion services to hospitals
Pulse Engineering	OTC	PLSE	Mfr. elec. computer components
Rainbow Technologies	OTC	RNBO	Mfr./dev. computer security programs

Company	Exchange	Ticker Symbol	Industry
Raven Industries	AMEX	RAV	Balloons/plastics/ sportswear
Recoton	OTC	RCOT	Home entertainment accessories
Rexon	OTC	REXN	Mfr. computer tape drives
Roto Rooter	OTC	ROTO	Sewer/drain cleaning services
SafetyTek	OTC	SAFE	Mfr./mkt. pressure sensors
Salem	AMEX	SBS	Equipment for coal/metal industries
Sands Regent	OTC	SNDS	Casino-hotel Reno, Nev.
Sandwich Chef	OTC	SHEF	Delicatessan style restaurants
SBE	OTC	SBEI	Mfr. semiconductors
Schult Homes	AMEX	SHC	Mobile home mfr.
Schultz Sav O Stores	OTC	SAVO	Food wholesalers/ supermarkets
Selas Corp. of America	AMEX	SLS	Heat processing equipment
Sierra Tucson	OTC	STSN	Alcohol/drug rehabilitation centers
Sifco Industries	AMEX	SIF	International metalworking
S&K Famous Brands	OTC	SKFB	Mens clothing retailer
Southwest Cafes	OTC	TXMX	Mexican restaurants
Span America Medical System	OTC	SPAN	Foam pads for health care industry
Stage II Apparel	AMEX	SA	Mkt. sport/casual apparel
Stanford Telecommunications	OTC	STII	Mfr. systems for earth stations
State O Maine	OTC	SOME	Design/mfr. clothing
Sun Sportswear	OTC	SSPW	Mkt. casual sportswear
Tech Ops Sevcon	AMEX	TO	Mfr. vehicle speed controllers
Technalysis	OTC	TECN	Systems analysis, programming
Technical Communications	OTC	TCCO	Communications equipment
Technitrol	AMEX	TNL	Electronic/mechanical products
Tekelec	OTC	TKLC	Telecommunications test equipment
Thomaston Mills	OTC	TMSTA	Mfr. textiles, fabrics, yarns
Trak Auto	OTC	TRKA	Retail auto parts store

Company	Exchange	Ticker Symbol	Industry
Tranzonic	AMEX	TNZA	Personal care disposable products
Tuesday Morning	OTC	TUES	Specialty discount retailer chain
United States Banknote	NYSE	UBK	Printer of currency and stamps
Uno Restaurant	NYSE	UNO	Pizza restaurants
Valley Forge	AMEX	VF	Marine products & mfr. industrial products
Varitronic Systems	OTC	VRSY	Print on tape lettering
Vertex Communications	OTC	VTEX	Mfr. communications equipment
Video Display	OTC	VIDE	Mfr./dstr. new & rebuilt CRTs
Vulcan International	AMEX	VUL	Shoe laces, heels, bow pins
Wellington Leisure Products	OTC	WLPI	Mfr. cordage/leisure products
Zeos International	OTC	ZEOS	Mfr. IBM compatible PCs
Zitel	OTC	ZITL	Mfr. semiconductor memory systems
Zygo	OTC	ZIGO	Mfr. measuring instruments

CHAPTER 8

OTHER INVESTMENT RETURN ANOMALIES

As discussed in Chapter 6, small firm common stock investors are treated to an investment free lunch. These stocks have been providing investors with nearly 6 percent per year in excess investment returns. According to efficient market theory, these excess returns are not supposed to exist. Nonetheless, these excess returns have been documented over the last 67 years, and they have probably existed for much longer. Because a free lunch exists in one sector of the market, it is logical to ask whether or not additional free morsels exist elsewhere.

During the 1970s—the high water decade of the efficient market theory—it was not fashionable to ask such a question. However, ever since Rolf Banz uncovered the small firm effect, academics have been asking, and answering, this question. While probing the underbelly of the efficient market, they have uncovered the existence of a number of puzzling anomalies that challenge the extent of stock market efficiency. The evidence from a large body of research now indicates that the stock market, while generally efficient, may not be as efficient as once thought. Academics are now inclined to admit what practitioners have known intuitively: Pockets of inefficiency similar to the small firm effect exist and hold promise for the astute investor. During the past 15 years, investigators have uncovered seasonal anomalies, such as the January effect, the day-of-the-week effect, the holiday effect, and the intramonth effect. They have also noted pricing inefficiencies, primarily the low P-E ratio effect.

Like the medieval alchemists parlaying their supposed knowledge of turning lead into gold, nearly every stockbroker and investment analyst has created a personal model for generating excess investment returns. Unfortunately, few of these models have been subjected to either scientific scrutiny or the test of time. Most of these models are founded on spurious correlations, more coincidental than causal. For example, a rising stock market correlates very positively with an old NFL team winning the Superbowl. It also correlates strongly with women's rising hemlines. But there is no causal relationship with a rising stock market, and no predictive value in those events. In this chapter we'll look at those market anomalies that have stood the test of rigorous scientific investigation.

STOCK MARKET LORE AND INVESTMENT FACTS

I am always amazed at the inclination of investors to accept myths regarding the predictability of stock prices. Perhaps I should not be surprised. Most investors want to believe and, of course, their stockbrokers want them to believe. After all, the more one believes that future stock prices are predictable, the more inclined one is to trade. And the more one trades, the greater are the commission revenues collected by stockbrokers. Thus, it's of little wonder that Wall Street is built more on myth than fact. Here's but one example:

Every winter, tales of the so-called January market barometer begin to surface. According to the wizards of Wall Street, the direction taken by stock prices during the month of January will be continued through the remainder of the year. The wise investor, then, is supposed to watch the market very carefully during January and assume a portfolio position dictated by the market's tone during that month. If stock prices increase in January, investors are supposed to become fully invested for the remainder of the year. If prices fall during this month, investors are to flee the stock market and park their money elsewhere.

In an attempt to investigate the accuracy of this market "truism," I computed the price changes of the Standard & Poor's 500 Stock Average for each January from 1926 through 1991. I then computed the price changes for the remaining 11 months of each year and compared the results. Here's what I found.

The January barometer correctly forecast the direction of stock market prices during 48 of the 66 years examined, or 72.7 percent of the time. For the 25 Januarys during which stock prices fell, the market continued downward during the remainder of the year on 14 occasions. That is, during down-market Januarys, the barometer incorrectly forecast the direction of market prices on 11 occasions, or 44 percent of the time. For the 41 Januarys in which stock prices increased, the market continued upward during 34 years. The forecasting accuracy for up-market Januarys was 78.4 percent. This gives an overall accuracy rate of 72.7 percent—48 correct predictions during 66 years.

So, is the January barometer a good forecasting tool? I don't think so. Remember that because corporations retain some of each year's earnings for reinvestment in additional productive assets, the long-run direction of stock market prices is biased upward. Thus, if each January 31 (regardless of the direction taken by stock prices during the month) you guessed that stock prices would be higher 11 months later, you would have been correct 45 times during the last 66 years. Your accuracy rate would have been 68.2 percent. That's almost the same forecasting accuracy as if you'd used the so-called January barometer!

WILL THE REAL JANUARY EFFECT PLEASE STAND UP?

Mark Twain warned us, "October, this is one of the particularly dangerous months to speculate in stocks." He then went on to name all the other months of the year as equally dangerous. Even though Twain was a notoriously ill-starred investor, and the January barometer appears to be more folklore than fact, investors should consider the common stock returns during January when constructing or revising their small firm common stock portfolios. January, it turns out, is a very important month for small firm stock investors.

The existence of a seasonal pattern for returns from small equity capitalization stocks was initially discovered by Donald

Keim in research at the University of Chicago in 1980. In a paper published in the June 1983 issue of the *Journal of Financial Economics,* Professor Keim reported, "nearly 50 percent of the average magnitude of the (firm) size effect over the period 1963–1979 is due to January abnormal returns."

The study utilized data for firms listed on the NYSE or the AMEX. At the beginning of each year, Keim ranked all firms by the market value of their common equity. He then divided these stocks into 10 portfolios on the basis of size. Each portfolio was updated annually and, on average, contained approximately 200 stocks.

Table 8-1 illustrates the risk-adjusted annual rates of return for each of the 10 portfolios. The portfolio containing the smallest equity capitalization stocks (average equity market value of $4.4 million) provided a 20.7 percent annual rate of return above that dictated by portfolio risk. On the other hand, the portfolio of the largest equity capitalization stocks (average size $1.09 billion) earned 9.6 percent per year less than it should have, given its risk. The annual return difference between the portfolios comprised of the stocks of the smallest and largest firms averaged a whopping 30.3 percent. Thus, this study adds additional support to the small firm effect thesis reported in Chapter 6.

TABLE 8-1
Average Excess Annual Returns and Equity Capitalization: 1963–1979

Portfolio	Average Excess Annual Return (percent)	Equity Market Value ($millions)
1 (Smallest)	20.7	$ 4.4
2	7.6	10.5
3	3.8	18.9
4	0.8	30.3
5	− 1.8	46.7
6	− 3.5	73.4
7	− 5.0	118.1
8	− 6.0	210.2
9	− 7.3	433.0
10 (Largest)	− 9.6	1,092.1

Table 8-2 illustrates the average daily and monthly excess return differences between the portfolios containing the stocks of the smallest and largest firms. Note that both the mean daily and monthly data are excess return differences. For example, during the month of January, the portfolio containing the stocks of the smallest firms provided a 15.4 percent greater rate of return than the portfolio of large firm stocks after adjusting the portfolio returns for investment risk. During this time period nearly one half of the total difference between the excess investment returns earned by the small firm portfolio and the large firm portfolio (15.4 percent out of a total difference of 30.3 percent) were earned during the month of January.

On closer examination of these abnormal January returns, Keim found that a large portion of the size effect occurred during the first five trading days of the year. Table 8-3 illustrates these excess daily returns. The difference in abnormal returns between the smallest and largest market value portfolios totaled more than 8 percent over the first five trading days in January. Thus, approximately 10 percent (3.2 percent divided by 30.3 percent) of the size effect for an average year during 1963–79 can be attributed to the first trading day of the year, and more than 25 percent (8.2 percent divided by 30.3 percent) can be attributed to the first five trading days. On the other hand, if the small firm return premium were spread uniformly throughout the year, then only 0.4 percent of the annual premium would be expected to occur each day and about 2 percent during the first five trading days of the year.

Although the January small firm effect is certainly a puzzle, even more puzzling is the reason for its existence. Professor Keim suggested tax loss selling as a possibility. That is, during late December investors sell stocks that have declined in value to realize losses offseting investment income earned during the year and, thus, lessen the tax bite. Because a decline in stock price causes the equity capitalization of a firm to decrease, the portfolio consisting of the stocks of the smallest firms may contain an abnormally large number of stocks whose prices are temporarily depressed at year-end due to an abnormally large amount of selling pressure. These stocks quickly rebound once a new tax year begins and, thus, exhibit unusually

TABLE 8–2

Average Differences between Daily and Monthly Excess Returns of Portfolios Constructed from the Stocks of Firms in the Top and Bottom Decile of Size (Measures by Market Value of Equity) on the NYSE and AMEX over the Period 1963–1979

Month	January	February	March	April	May	June	July
Average daily excess return (percent)	0.714	0.223	0.136	0.042	0.072	0.028	0.105
Average monthly excess return (percent)	15.0	4.5	2.9	0.9	1.5	0.6	2.2

	August	September	October	November	December	All Months
Average daily excess return (percent)	0.063	0.092	−0.070	0.006	0.420	01.21
Average monthly excess return (percent)	1.3	1.9	−1.5	0.1	8.8	2.5

TABLE 8-3
Differences in Average Daily Excess Returns between Portfolios
of Smallest and Largest Firms on the NYSE and AMEX for the First Five
Trading Days 1963-1979

Trading Day	Average Daily Return Difference (percent)
1	3.20%
2	1.68
3	1.25
4	1.14
5	0.89
Five-day total	8.16%

large returns during the first trading week of the year. Further-more, because small firm stocks tend to be thinly traded and generally held by individual investors rather than institutions that generally don't engage in tax loss selling, their prices are more depressed by tax loss selling than large firm stocks possessing a substantial degree of liquidity and widely held by institutional investors.

This tax loss selling hypothesis was rigorously tested by Professor Marc Reinganum. He found that return differences during January tended to favor small firm stocks which fell in price during the previous year. Those small firm stocks least likely to be sold for tax reasons (the prior year's winners) also exhibited large January returns. Thus, the tax loss selling hypothesis does not fully explain the large abnormal returns generated by small firm stocks during the month of January.

Another possible explanation for the existence of the January effect is that most firms make preliminary announcements regarding the year's earnings during January. Because small firms are less widely followed by professional analysts, the preliminary announcements made by managers of small firms do not spread throughout the investment community as fast as the preliminary announcements by large firms. Thus, small firm stocks tend to gradually rise as investors locate, process, and react to favorable earnings announcements from small firms.

Although the existence of the January effect has been confirmed by numerous other researchers whose studies are listed in the bibliography, research conducted by Josef Lakonishok and Seymour Smidt indicate that the January effect actually begins in late December. Their study of firm size and returns around the end of the year covered the period January 1, 1970, through December 31, 1981, and focused on stocks listed on either the NYSE or the AMEX. They classified companies into deciles based on the dollar value of trading during the previous October and November. Because small firm stocks generally exhibit a much lower dollar volume of trading during a given period than do large firm stocks, their classification of firms based on high and low trading volume was highly similar to portfolios constructed on the basis of market value of equity.

Table 8-4 presents the annualized daily rates of return around the turn of the year for the two extreme deciles—the stocks with the highest and lowest dollar volume of trading during the previous October and November. The annualized returns are presented for days −5 to 4; day −1 is the last trading day in December and day 1 is the first trading day in January. Daily returns reflect the difference between the closing price on the previous day and the closing price for the following day in question. I annualized the returns by multiplying the average daily returns by 252 (the number of trading days during a year). The results of this study are consistent with other studies. The returns of small company stocks around the turn of the year are absolutely high and are also substantially higher than the

TABLE 8-4
Stock Returns around the End of the Year (Annualized Daily Rates of Return)

	Trading Day								
Stocks	−5	−4	−3	−2	−1	1	2	3	4
Low volume	1.23	0.05	0.71	0.30	5.37	8.42	6.70	5.77	3.86
High volume	1.21	1.76	0.58	0.05	1.54	0.25	1.41	0.83	0.55

returns from the stocks of large firms. The abnormally large returns for small firm stocks appear to begin during the last day of December (an annualized return of nearly 5.4 percent). The cumulative rate of return for the stocks of the smallest companies over a five-day period from the beginning of the last trading day in December to the end of the fourth trading day in January was about 10 percent versus a 2 percent rate for the stocks of the largest companies.

This study illustrated that the average rates of return for both small and large firm stocks are exceptionally high at year-end. However, small company stocks had larger year-end returns than large company stocks. For example, when the researchers measured rates of return from the closing price on the next to last trading day of the old year to the fifth trading day of the new year, they found that "the rates are 1.9 percent for the largest size decile and 16.4 percent for the smallest. Annualized, these rates of return would equal 166 percent for the largest companies and over 40,000 percent for the smallest."[1]

Data contained in *Stocks, Bonds, Bills, and Inflation: 1992 Yearbook,* illustrates the extent and pervasiveness of the small firm "January effect." As Table 8-5 shows, the returns generated by the stocks of small firms during the month of January greatly exceed the returns from the larger stocks contained in the S&P Index during the last 67 years. Since 1926, the total return from small firm stocks in January averaged 7.3 percent. The average return for these stocks during the remaining 11 months was 0.84 percent per month. S&P Index stocks returned an average of 1.38 percent during the 67 Januarys since 1926 and provided an average of 0.93 percent per month during the remainder of the year. Thus, while it appears that all stocks tend to perform better in January, small firm stocks provide the real bonanza. Furthermore, only ten times during the last 67 years has the S&P Index (larger stocks) outperformed small firm stocks during the month of January.

---

[1] J. Lakonishok and S. Smidt, "Trading Bargains in Small Firms at Year-End," *The Journal of Portfolio Management* (Spring 1986), p. 28.

TABLE 8-5
Total Returns during January: Small Firm Stocks versus Large
Firm Stocks

Period	Small Firm Stocks (percent)	S&P 500 Index (percent)	Difference Favoring Small Firm Stocks (percent)
1926–1939	9.55%	1.79%	7.76%
1940–1992	6.14	1.36	4.78
1926–1992	7.29	1.38	5.91

Table 8-6 illustrates the average monthly behavior of total returns for large and small firm common stocks over the period 1926–91. The small stock premium represents the average monthly return advantage exhibited by small firm stocks over large firm stocks during each month. The small firm return advantage during January is about five times that experienced during any other month. Furthermore, the return differential during January has continued to be pervasive. During the 67-year period for which the average returns were computed, small firm stocks outperformed the S&P Index slightly more than 84 percent of the time.

Over the past 67 years, small firm common stock returns have averaged about 18 percent per year. If this average return was equally distributed throughout the year, small firm stocks would return about an average of 1.5 percent per month. As can be seen from the data in Table 8-5, small firm common stocks perform best during January and have returned an average of nearly 7.3 percent during this month since 1926. Furthermore, small firm stocks have outperformed large firm stocks during January a large percentage of the time. Thus, small firm stock investors must consider actions taken around January very carefully.

Of course, one possible use of the information presented here would be to develop a small firm stock trading strategy calling for the purchase of small firm stocks during late December and their liquidation during early February. Even though small firm stock returns are exceptionally great during January, transaction costs would erode most, if not all, of the excess

TABLE 8-6

Monthly Returns 1926–1991: Small Firm Stocks versus Large Firm Stocks

Asset Class	Average Return In Percent											
	Jan	Feb	Mar	Apr	May	Jun	Jul	Aug	Sep	Oct	Nov	Dec
Small stocks	6.82%	1.81%	0.35%	1.25%	0.41%	1.03%	2.42%	1.79%	-0.82%	-1.08%	1.13%	0.93%
Common stocks	1.65	0.57	0.45	1.33	0.45	1.37	2.12	1.89	-1.00	0.10	1.29	1.73
Small stock premium	5.02	1.21	-0.22	-0.21	-0.18	-0.44	0.25	-0.24	0.03	-1.29	-0.20	-0.84
Number of times premium was positive (in 66 years)	56	38	33	31	29	27	33	33	33	25	30	30

Source: *Stocks, Bonds, Bills, and Inflation: 1992 Yearbook™*, Ibbotson Associates, Chicago (annually updates work by Roger G. Ibbotson and Rex A. Sinquefield). Used with permission.

return potential of this short-run trading strategy. However, knowledge of the January effect can be used by long-term investors to great advantage. In the normal course of managing an overall investment portfolio, investors must make adjustments in their stock holdings due to the need for additional cash or the need to invest additional capital. Thus, investors who hold common stocks of smaller firms can benefit over the long run by scheduling additional purchases during early December and by postponing scheduled December liquidations until late January or early February. Thus, purchases and sales of small firm stocks which would have been made anyway can be scheduled to obtain the maximum benefit of the January effect. In any event, definite long-run gains accrue to those small firm investors who tend to remain in the market during late December and most of the month of January.

DAY OF THE WEEK EFFECT

Several recently published academic studies present conclusive evidence that common stock returns, on average, exhibit a pronounced day-of-the-week effect. According to these studies, investors can enhance their long-run investment returns by buying and selling common stocks on particular days of the week.

Kenneth French, a professor of management at the University of Rochester, conducted the first comprehensive study of day-of-the-week stock returns.[2] French computed the daily returns of the S&P Index for the 6,024 trading days over the period 1953–77. He selected the year 1953 as the initial data collection year because it was the first year that the NYSE abandoned Saturday trading. Returns included both price appreciation and cash dividend payments. Professor French sought to examine the nature of the process by which stock returns are generated. He hypothesized that if stock returns are

---

[2] K. R. French, "Stock Returns and the Weekend Effect," *Journal of Financial Economics,* no. 8 (1980), pp. 55–69.

generated in trading time, that is, only when stock exchanges are open for business, the average rate of return for each day of the week should be the same. On the other hand, if returns are generated continuously in calendar time, the average returns on Monday would exceed the average returns for the other days of the week because Monday's trading activity would represent the uninitiated actions of traders for Saturday and Sunday when stock exchanges are closed, as well as Monday's trading actions.

Professor French was somewhat startled to find that neither hypothesis proved to be correct. In fact, he found that stocks turned in their worst performance on Monday. Over the period 1953–77, the average stock price return on Monday was −0.17 percent, while the average return for each of the remaining days of the week was greater than zero. Over the 25 years studied, the average return on Mondays was negative during 20 years, while Tuesday, with the next largest number of negative returns, had only nine. These findings were later confirmed in an independent study conducted by Professors Michael Gibbons and Patrick Hess.[3]

A later study by Professors Donald Keim and R. F. Stambaugh extended the time period studied to 1928–83, included OTC stocks as well as NYSE firms, and examined the day-of-the-week returns from the stocks of companies of varying sizes.[4] In all cases, the data in this comprehensive study exhibited a weekend effect that is at least as strong as that reported in the previous two studies. In addition, they found the Monday return behavior exists in the OTC market and for all firms regardless of size.

Table 8-7 summarizes the results of these three studies. As can be seen, all three studies (even though conducted over different time periods) indicate that Monday is the bluest day of the week—at least for common stock investors. Furthermore, the standard deviation of stock returns (a measure of return

---

[3] M. R. Gibbons and P. Hess, "Day of the Week Effects and Asset Returns," *Journal of Business* 54, no. 4 (1981), pp. 579–96.

[4] D. B. Keim and R. F. Stambaugh, "A Further Investigation of the Weekend Effect in Stock Returns," *Journal of Finance* 37, no. 3 (1984), pp. 883–89.

variability) indicates that Monday is also the day of greatest trading turbulence. (Monday, October 19, 1987, was in fact the blackest and bluest day in Wall Street's history.) Common stock returns, for example, are nearly 50 percent more variable on Mondays than they are on Fridays, the day of the week with the greatest return conformity.

Why Monday stock returns lag the returns generated on other days of the week is open to conjecture. However, one hypothesis is that corporations systematically release bad news to the investing public after the market has closed on Fridays to allow the investment community time to digest these morsels over the weekend. However, Professor French found that during the second half of 1968, when the NYSE was closed each Wednesday, the average return on Thursday was −0.14 percent. This suggests that negative stock market returns can be expected whenever the market is closed on a regular basis. Furthermore, in an efficient market, investors would come to expect the release of unfavorable information on weekends and would discount stock prices by an appropriate amount throughout the week. That is, efficient market theory dictates that the systematic negative returns experienced on Mondays would be eliminated by rational information processing investors. According to

TABLE 8-7
Day-of-the-Week Stock Return Percentages

Day	Gibbons/Hess		French		Keim/Stambaugh	
	Average Returns	Standard Deviation	Average Returns	Standard Deviation	Average Returns	Standard Deviation
Monday	−0.13%	0.67%	−0.17%	0.84%	−0.19%	1.22%
Tuesday	0.00	0.55	0.02	0.73	0.05	1.09
Wednesday	0.10	0.64	0.10	0.74	0.09	1.18
Thursday	0.03	0.48	0.04	0.69	0.05	1.09
Friday	0.08	0.48	0.09	0.66	0.06	1.13
Saturday	—	—	—	—	0.15	1.01
Monday-Friday difference	0.21%		0.26%		0.34%*	

* Difference between Monday and Saturday returns prior to 1958.

the efficient market theory, the average stock return for each day of the week should be nearly identical.

These studies are of interest to students of stock market theory, but what relevance do they possess for the individual investor? If investors could stay out of the stock market on Mondays, the average annual rate of return obtainable from investment in the S&P Index could be increased by 8.5 percent annually. That's a lot! Compare this to the compound annual rate of return of the S&P Index over the period 1926–86 (12.0 percent), and you can see that investors could increase their annual returns by more than two thirds by avoiding the stock market on Mondays. This, of course, is an impossible result because it requires that investors sell their stock holdings late in the trading day each Friday and repurchase these shares late in the day on Monday. This trading action and the resultant brokerage costs would more than wipe out the enhancement in return.

The presence of a pronounced day-of-the-week effect can be used by investors to improve their long-run investment returns. The fact that, on average, Monday stock returns are negative and lower than the returns on Friday suggests that individuals could increase their expected portfolio returns by altering the timing of trades which would have been made anyway. That is, purchases planned for Thursday or Friday should be delayed until Monday afternoon, and sales planned for Monday should be rescheduled for the preceding or following Friday.

For example, suppose that, on average, you turned over your portfolio once each year. If purchases are made late Monday when stock prices are down an average of 0.17 percent and sales are made late Friday when stock prices are up 0.08 percent, this investment strategy could increase your portfolio return by an average of 0.25 percent annually over the long run. On the surface, this incremental improvement in annual portfolio return appears minute, but when compounded over many years, it can lead to a significant improvement in wealth. For investors who turn over their portfolios once each year, the extra 0.25 percent return generated by following the Monday-purchase-Friday-sell strategy increases the value of a portfolio by 5.1 percent after 20 years and nearly 11 percent after 40 years.

INTRAMONTH COMMON STOCK RETURNS

A relatively recent study of stock market returns has uncovered a strong intramonthly return pattern. Professor Robert Ariel of the City University of New York has found that over the 19-year period from 1963 to 1981, stocks appear to earn positive average returns only around the beginning and during the first half of the calendar month and earn zero average returns during the second half of the month.[5] More startling is the fact that all of the stock market's cumulative advance during this 19-year period can be accounted for by price changes during the first half of the month. So, if you're asking "Where's the beef?" just look in the first half of the month.

Figure 8-1 illustrates the intramonth daily trading pattern for an index composed of all NYSE and AMEX stocks. The average daily price change during each of the first nine trading days of the month, plus the last trading day of the previous month, are greater than zero while only two of the last nine trading days of the month, excluding the last trading day, produce average price gains.

Over the 19-year period covered by this study, the average return for the first nine trading days of the month was 0.83 percent while the average return over the last nine days was −0.18 percent (see Table 8-8). Furthermore, the first half of the month produced higher average investment returns than the second half of the month two thirds of the time. The 19-year cumulative impact of these return differences is spectacular. During the period, stock prices appreciated by 340 percent. However, the return from investing in stocks during only the first half of the month was a whopping 565 percent! (The cumulative return from investing in only the second half of every month was −34 percent.)

Of course, individual investors could not have reaped these returns by trading in and out of the stock market during each

---

[5] R. A. Ariel, "Monthly Market Patterns," *AAII Journal* 9, no. 1 (1987), pp. 8–11. (The article is an excerpt from Dr. Ariel's dissertation, "Some Features of Stock Market Returns.")

FIGURE 8–1
Average Returns before and after the Start of the Month

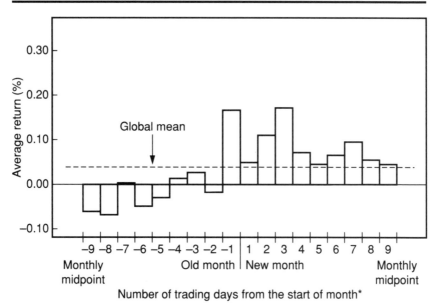

* Nine rather than 10 or more days were selected for presentation to prevent overlap between day-10 and day-10 of the following month in that a significant minority of months have fewer than 20 trading days. The global mean is estimated from the returns to all trading days in this 19-year period.

half of the month. Again, brokerage commissions and existing bid-ask spreads on common stocks would have more than eroded any profit potential of such an active trading strategy. However, this study suggests that investors who trade common stocks over an investment lifetime may add to their investment returns by scheduling their purchases just before the last trading day of the month and scheduling their sales toward the end of the ninth trading day of the month.

For example, investors who turn their portfolios over about once every year could increase their annual portfolio returns by about 0.5 percent per year by employing this trading strategy (the 1 percent difference between intramonth returns divided by two). Although this doesn't appear to be a very large incremental return, over an investment lifetime the same investors would

TABLE 8-8
Cumulative Returns during the First and Last Halves of the Month

	Entire Period 1963 to 1981	Four Subperiods			
		1963 to 1966	1967 to 1971	1972 to 1976	1977 to 1981
Average return: first nine days	0.826%	0.969%	0.866%	0.546%	0.950%
Average return: last nine days	−0.182	−0.290	−0.177	−0.094	−0.188
Frequency of higher first-half returns*	66	79	63	62	62

* The percentage of times the first half of a trading month had a higher return than the last half of that same trading month.

increase their aggregate investment wealth by significant amounts. Over a 20-year period, an additional 0.5 percent annual return would increase investment wealth by more than 10 percent. Over a 40-year period, a 0.5 percent annual incremental return would increase investment wealth by more than 20 percent. Furthermore, those investors who tend to sell at the end of the month and buy during the middle of the month could improve annual investment returns by a full 1 percent by reversing the timing of purchases and sales. These investors could increase their investment wealth more than 21 percent after 20 years and more than 47 percent after 40 years.

Although the persistence of a strong intramonth return pattern defies explanation, the intramonth effect appears to be another quirk in the stock market. As an investor, you can use it to your advantage. Remember, the stock market is more efficient than most investors believe. In an efficient market, it is difficult to earn abnormally large investment returns without incurring large investment risks. However, by exploiting the pockets of inefficiency in the market, you can accumulate small percentages of additional investment return. These percentages, when aggregated, can enhance your investment wealth by a significant amount.

THE PREHOLIDAY EFFECT

In a very recent study of daily trading patterns and investment returns, Professor Robert Ariel found that on trading days before holidays when the stock market is closed, stocks advance with disproportionate frequency and have average returns that are about 14 times those of the average return for the remaining trading days.[6] The holidays studied were New Year's Day, Presidents' Day, Good Friday, Memorial Day, Independence Day, Labor Day, Thanksgiving, and Christmas.

Professor Ariel first computed the daily returns for 5,020 trading days over the 20-year period from 1963 to 1983. He then

---

[6]_____. "Holiday Market Patterns," *AAII Journal* 9, no. 5 (1987), pp. 8–11.

FIGURE 8–2
Returns around Holidays

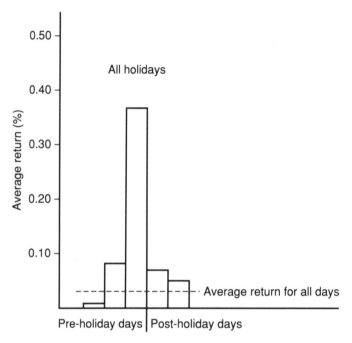

Pre-holiday days | Post-holiday days

Source: Robert Ariel, "Holiday Market Patterns," *AAII Journal,* May 1987, p. 9. Reprinted by permission, American Association of Individual Investors, 625 N. Michigan, Chicago, Illinois.

divided daily returns into two subsets: the trading days prior to holidays (160 days) and all other days (4,860). Then, he obtained an average return for each subset. As Figure 8-2 shows, common stocks appear to provide greater-than-average returns during the two days preceding and the two days following these eight holidays, with the largest average daily return occurring during the trading day immediately preceding the holiday. The average return for this one day exceeded the average for all days by a factor of 10, and it exceeded the average for all trading days that were not preholiday trading days by a factor of 14!

Table 8-9 details the magnitude of these anomalous preholiday returns. On a cumulative basis, total investment return over all 5,020 trading days amounted to 427 percent. However, during the 160 preholiday trading days, the cumulative investment return amounted to nearly 79 percent. That is, 3 percent

TABLE 8-9
Holiday Return Patterns: 1963-1982

	Average Returns	
	Average Returns	Variability
Preholiday trading	0.365%	0.609%
Non-preholiday trading	0.026	0.783
All holiday days	0.036	0.780

	Cumulative Returns	
	All Trading Days	Preholiday Trading Days
Number of days	5,020	160
Cumulative return	427.2%	78.6%

	Individual Holidays	
	Average Returns	Number of Advances
New Year's Day	0.437%	17
President's Day	0.027	11
Good Friday	0.272	14
Memorial Day	0.510	15
July Fourth	0.223	13
Labor Day	0.607	18
Thanksgiving	0.460	18
Christmas	0.383	14

Source: Robert Ariel, "Holiday Market Patterns," *AAII Journal,* May 1987, pp. 10-11. Reprinted by permission, American Association of Individual Investors, 625 N. Michigan, Chicago, Illinois.

of the trading days during this 20-year period accounted for nearly 35 percent of the stock market's total return. In addition, an analysis of the variability of investment returns during the day preceding a holiday indicated that returns during these days are less volatile than the average trading day. Thus, during preholiday trading days, the stock market yields greater returns and lower risk.

Investment returns from these two subsets represent two distinct categories. If preholiday days were merely random draws from the total number of days studied, one would expect the frequency of positive return days would equal the frequency of positive return days for all trading days. But that does not appear to be the case. Preholiday trading days produced positive investment returns 75 percent of the time compared with 54 percent for all trading days.

As noted earlier, other studies of daily stock market returns indicate that Fridays provide the greatest returns while Mondays provide the poorest. Thus, because many holidays fall on Monday, the trading day prior to that holiday is always a Friday. The holiday effect may be nothing more than an enhanced weekend effect. However, when this thesis was examined by Professor Ariel, he found that "little of the measured high preholiday average return is derived from a disproportionate number of preholidays that occur on a Friday."

Why does the holiday effect exist? Apparently no one knows. Could it be that in anticipation of a holiday, investors' moods become so overly joyous that they bid up stock prices? I doubt it, as trading volume tends to shrink during preholiday trading days because many institutional investors leave their trading desks early and head for the Hamptons. I suspect that a greater-than-normal percentage of preholiday trading volume is attributable to individual investors.

Even though all securities bought during a particular trading day must, by definition, equal the number sold, I suspect that many of the preholiday returns can be explained by the actions of floor traders and others who, at times, maintain relatively large short positions. Because stock market closings extend the time period between trading days, such investors must hold their short positions a bit longer during holidays and, thus, are exposed to greater risks. Many of these traders tend to close out their short positions before holidays—and in fact before weekends—to reduce their risk exposure. It may be that a flurry of short covering before holidays tends to buoy up stock prices.

Whatever the reason for the holiday effect, you can use your knowledge of its existence profitably. Of course, although quite large in a relative sense, the returns are too small to yield aftercost profits from jumping in and out of the market around holidays. But you may want to time buy and sell decisions with the holiday pattern in mind. For example, if you are considering the purchase of a stock, you may want to commit your money several days before a holiday, just before the returns begin to rise, rather than making purchases immediately following the holiday. Or, if you are considering the sale of a stock, you may want to do so after a holiday, following the price run-up, rather than just before. Again, while the profitability of following this strategy may not be great, over time, these small bits of additional investment return add up. An old adage states: "Watch your pennies and the dollars will follow." To restate: Watch the small fractions of investment return readily available in a highly efficient market, and the large returns, over time, will follow.

THE LOW PRICE-EARNINGS RATIO EFFECT

Simply stated, the low P-E ratio effect is the apparent ability of low P-E stocks to outperform high P-E stocks of similar risk. The rationale is simple: Low P-E stocks are better buys than high P-E stocks. For example, suppose that you have the opportunity to purchase shares in one of two companies. Both companies are expected to earn $1 per share each and every year in the future. However, one company's stock currently sells for $10 per share while the stocks of the other cost $5 per share. The investor who pays $10 for $1 of future earnings earns a return of 10 percent. On the other hand, the astute investor who pays only $5 per share for a continual earnings stream of $1 per share earns 20 percent on the investment. Thus, it is no secret why portfolios of low P-E ratio stocks provide greater investment returns than do portfolios of high P-E ratio stocks.

Actually, it's not that simple. As was explained in Chapter 5, P-E ratios reported in the press are computed by taking last year's per share earnings and dividing them by today's price. However, since common stock buyers receive a claim against next year's earnings and not last year's, the relevant valuation measure is today's price divided by next year's anticipated per share earnings. Thus, a firm that earned $1 per share last year and whose stock is currently priced at $10 (giving it a reported P-E ratio of 10), may be less of a bargain than the shares of another firm that earned $0.50 per share last year and whose shares are currently priced at $8, giving it a reported P-E ratio of 16. Suppose, for example, that the earnings of the first firm are expected to fall from $1 to $0.50 while those of the other firm are expected to rise from $0.50 to $1. On an expected earnings basis, the first firm is currently selling at a price expected earnings multiple of 20 while the second is priced at only 8 times expected earnings.

An ample body of research indicates that, all other things being equal, portfolios containing lower P-E ratio stocks do, in fact, yield superior investment returns. Ben Graham, the father of modern securities analysis and an advocate of buying out-of-favor or low P-E stocks, states:

> If we assume that it is the habit of the market to overvalue common stocks which have been showing excellent growth or are glamorous for some other reason, it is logical to expect that it will undervalue—relatively, at least—companies that are out of favor because of unsatisfactory developments of a temporary nature. This may be set down as a fundamental law of the stock market.[7]

As documentation of this fact, Graham offers the results of a study conducted by one of his students, H. G. Schneider. Published in the June 1951 issue of *The Journal of Finance*, the study covered the years 1917 through 1950. For each year, Schneider constructed a portfolio of the 10 stocks in the Dow Jones Industrial Average with the lowest P-E multipliers and compared that portfolio's performance with a portfolio containing the 10 issues with the highest P-E multipliers. For nearly every period examined, the low P-E portfolio provided greater rates of return than the high P-E portfolio after five years. Even though this study is far from scientific, it does lend some credence to the low price-earnings ratio/high return hypothesis.

Sanjoy Basu conducted the first detailed scientific study of P-E ratios and investment performance.[8] Professor Basu found a

---

[7] Ben Graham, *The Intelligent Investor* (New York: Harper & Row, 1973), p. 79.

[8] S. Basu, "Investment Performance of Common Stocks in Relation to Their Price-Earnings Ratios: A Test of the Efficient Market Hypothesis," *Journal of Finance,* (June 1977), pp. 663–83.

very pronounced P-E ratio effect even after adjusting portfolios for risk, transaction costs, and personal taxes. His study examined the P-E effect on investment return for over 1,400 industrial stocks traded on the NYSE between September 1956 and August 1971. Beginning with 1956, he computed the P-E ratio of every sample security by dividing the market value of the common stock as of December 31 by reported annual earnings (before extraordinary items) available for common stockholders. Then he ranked these P-E ratios from high to low and formed five portfolios. He assumed that these P-E portfolios were purchased on the following April 1. Thus, even though the P-E portfolios were formed using year-end earnings, he assumed that these earnings would not be reported to investors until three months later. Thus, Basu's theoretical portfolio construction procedure could very easily be duplicated by investors purchasing actual securities. Next he computed the monthly return on each of these portfolios for the next 12 months assuming an equal initial investment in each of the respective securities. The process was repeated each year from 1956 to 1971. The performance results appear in Table 8-10.

Over the period studied, the market portfolio (M) returned 12.1 percent annually. On the other hand, the portfolio consisting of the highest P-E stocks (A) returned 9.3 percent while the portfolio consisting of the lowest P-E stocks (E) returned 16.3 percent annually. Although the return differential between the

TABLE 8-10
Performance of Portfolios with Varying Price-Earnings Ratios: 1956-1971

	P-E Portfolios					
	A	*B*	*C*	*D*	*E*	*M*
Median P-E ratio	38.5	19.1	15.0	12.8	9.8	15.1
Average annual rate of return	9.3%	9.3%	11.7%	13.6%	16.3%	12.1%
Beta	1.11	1.04	0.97	0.94	0.99	1.01
Alpha	−3.3	−2.8	0.2	2.3	4.7	0.3

Source: S. Basu, "Investment Performance of Common Stocks in Relation to Their Price-Earnings Ratios: A Test of the Efficient Market Hypothesis," *Journal of Finance*, June 1977, p. 667.

lowest and highest P-E stocks amounted to 7.0 percent per year, some of the difference can be accounted for by differences in investment risk. The high P-E portfolio possessed a beta of 1.11, while the low P-E portfolio possessed a beta of 0.99. However, when Basu adjusted the returns for their risk differences, a significant return differential favoring low P-E stocks still remained. The two lowest P-E portfolios, D and E, earned about 2 percent and 4.5 percent more annually than that implied by their level of risk; the two highest P-E portfolios earned 2.5 to 3 percent less than that implied by their level of risk (see alpha). Professor Basu also found that excess returns are available to investors even after accounting for transaction costs and taxes. By investing in portfolio E and reallocating investment dollars each year to the lowest P-E stocks, investors could have earned returns after costs and taxes amounting to 2 to 3.5 percent per year more than the associated random portfolios of equivalent risk.

Even though the Basu study of P-E ratios and investment performance was indeed comprehensive, other researchers pointed out a few critical flaws. First, later research indicated the presence of what we now call the small firm effect: that small firm stock returns exceed the returns dictated by their risk. Second, small firm return research indicated a high degree of correlation between firm size and P-E ratio—the larger the firm, typically the higher the P-E ratio. This correlation is not too surprising because, given two firms with an identical number of shares outstanding and identical per share earnings, the firm with the highest P-E multiplier is the larger firm. For example, suppose that two firms each have 10 million shares outstanding and per share earnings of $1. Both firms, thus, have $10 million in current earnings. If one firm sells at 20 times earnings, its market capitalization is $200 million. On the other hand, if the other firm sells for 8 times earnings, its market capitalization is only $80 million.

Third, the Basu study suffered from statistical bias introduced by computing beta over a short period of time and including stocks infrequently traded. Both of these biases tend to understate investment risk and, thus, overstate excess investment returns. Finally, by aggregating companies from all industries into one sample, the Basu study failed to identify any industry effects on the P-E ratio performance results.

A later study conducted by John Peavy and David Goodman controlled for all of these alleged biases.[9] To control for the firm size bias, they studied only those firms whose equity capitalization exceeded $100 million. Thus, their P-E study excluded small firm stocks. They also made adjustments in their beta measures and eliminated any stock with a monthly trading volume less than 10,000 shares. Finally, they eliminated potential industry bias by analyzing stocks by industry classification. A summary of their results appears in Table 8-11.

The data in Table 8-11 indicates that after the elimination of statistical and selection biases, low P-E ratio portfolios still significantly outperform high P-E ratio portfolios. The portfolio containing the lowest average P-E ratio stocks (portfolio 1) produced the highest rates of return across each industry, while the portfolio containing the highest P-E stocks produced the lowest rates of return. The return differentials between the highest and lowest P-E stocks ranged from 7 percent per quarter for the high-risk electronics industry stocks to 4.8 percent per quarter for the low-risk food industry stocks. On an annual basis, the P-E effect leads to differential returns from 11 to over 30 percent.

In a later study, Sanjoy Basu explored the notion that small firm stocks account for much of the excess returns attributed to the P-E ratio effect. The results of this study confirmed the P-E ratio effect demonstrated in his first study. Basu's second study also indicated that although small firm returns exceed those of large firms, the size effect virtually disappears when returns are controlled for differences in risk and P-E ratios. However, he found that the P-E effect was not entirely independent of firm size.

The finding of an interrelationship between market value and P-E ratios has caused considerable debate as to which effect really is at work. This is no trivial question because the answer

---

[9] J. W. Peavy and D. A. Goodman, "The Significance of P-Es for Portfolio Returns," *Journal of Portfolio Management,* Winter 1983, pp. 43–47.

TABLE 8-11
Price-Earnings Ratios and Portfolio Performance: 1970-1980

Industry	P-E Portfolios					
	1	2	3	4	5	Industry Average
Electronics						
Average P-E ratio	7.1	10.3	13.4	17.4	25.5	14.7
Average quarterly return	9.2	5.5	5.1	3.0	2.2	5.1
Average beta	1.2	1.1	1.1	1.2	1.3	1.2
Paper/container						
Average P-E ratio	6.7	8.5	10.2	12.4	20.2	11.6
Average quarterly return	5.4	3.4	4.0	2.4	0.9	3.4
Average beta	1.0	1.0	1.0	1.0	1.0	1.0
Food						
Average P-E ratio	7.2	9.5	11.1	12.8	16.8	11.5
Average quarterly return	5.5	3.8	2.7	0.8	0.7	3.0
Average beta	0.9	0.9	0.9	0.9	0.9	0.9

Source: J. Peavy and D. Goodman, "The Significance of P-Es for Portfolio Returns," *Journal of Portfolio Management*, Winter, 1983, p. 46. This copyrighted material is reprinted with permission from The Journal of Portfolio Management, 488 Madison Avenue, NY, NY, 10022.

indicates how investors seeking abnormally large investment returns should select assets for their common stock portfolios. To one camp, the dominant variable is firm size; to another, it is P-E ratio.

Professors Thomas Cook and Michael Rozeff asked and answered the pertinent question in a study entitled, "Size and Earnings/Price Ratio Anomalies: One Effect or Two?"[10] Using data restricted to NYSE-listed stocks over the period from 1964 to 1981, they tested the interaction effects of both variables on portfolio performance. Although their statistical techniques were rather complicated, their conclusions were straightforward. Their results strongly indicated that both factors have an independent influence on stock returns. That is, both are

---

[10] T. J. Cook and M. S. Rozeff, "Size and Earnings/Price Ratio Anomalies: One Effect or Two?" *Journal of Financial and Quantitative Analysis* (December 1984), pp. 449–66.

important in stock selection. Investors seeking the highest returns for a given level of risk should select small equity capitalization firms that also possess relatively low P-E ratios.

Goodman and Peavy illustrated the additive value of both the P-E effect and the firm size effect, especially for very small firms. They employed a rigorous control procedure to test for the independence of the two effects.[11] Initially, they grouped all observations for the entire study period into equal quintiles based solely on P-E ratios. Then they divided each P-E quintile into subquintiles based on ascending size. This procedure resulted in a complete control for the P-E effect and allowed observation of the size effect alone. Their results appear in Table 8-12.

Although a strong firm size effect was not evident after controlling for P-E ratio, the lowest P-E quintile portfolio exhibited a strong size effect. The smallest market value subquintile within the PE1 group yielded a 5.08 percent quarterly excess return, the highest for any of the 25 portfolios and considerably higher than the 2.7 percent average excess return for the overall PE1 quintile. Thus, a very strong additive excess return effect apparently existed within the lowest P-E, smallest size portfolio.

---

[11] D. Goodman and J. Peavy, "The Interaction of Firm Size and Price-Earnings Ratio on Portfolio Performance," *Financial Analysts Journal*, January-February 1986, pp. 9–12.

TABLE 8–12
Average Quarterly Excess Returns by Firm Size, P-E Controlled Firm Size

P-E Ratio	FS1 (smallest)	FS2	FS3	FS4	FS5 (largest)
PE1 (lowest)	5.08	3.81	2.86	−0.40	2.29
PE2	2.52	2.25	1.82	0.89	0.07
PE3	−0.93	−0.01	0.46	−0.42	−1.45
PE4	−0.65	−1.36	−2.26	−1.08	−1.73
PE5 (highest)	−2.61	−2.89	−1.39	−2.63	−2.60

Source: D. Goodman and J. Peavy, "The Interaction of Firm Size and Price-Earnings Ratio on Portfolio Performance," *Financial Analysts Journal*, January-February 1986, p. 10.

To me, the evidence appears to support both a P-E ratio effect and a firm size effect. Thus, when selecting common stocks, either large or small, investors should seek to include the stocks of well-positioned companies whose shares are selling at relatively low P-E multiples. (In Chapter 9, I indicate how to evaluate the relative attractiveness of common stocks with varying P-E ratios.) However, when selecting small firm common stocks, the additive nature of the P-E ratio and firm size effects should not be ignored. As the evidence here suggests, investors who select small firm emerging growth stocks should select among those with relatively low P-E ratios.

CONCLUSION

Is the stock market truly efficient? Recent research appears to indicate that it is not as efficient as once thought. January, it turns out, provides investors with greater rewards than does any other month. In a truly efficient market, investors would anticipate the excess January returns and add to their common stock portfolios during December. Such actions would eventually lead to an end of the excess January returns as they would eventually become spread evenly over the remaining 11 months of the year. But, this has not occurred.[12]

The discovery of several unique return patterns during particular days of the week also indicates that the stock market is not perfectly efficient. On average, investors lose money on Mondays and make money on Fridays; they tend to earn greater-than-average returns a couple of trading days around stock exchange holiday closings; and the first part of the month appears to reward investors more than does the end of the month. In an efficient market, knowledge of these patterns would eventually lead to their destruction.

Finally, a large body of research indicates that small firm

---

[12] The January effect is discussed in detail in Robert Haugen and Josef Lakonishok, *The Incredible January Effect: The Stock Market's Unsolved Mystery* (Homewood, Ill.: Business One Irwin, 1987).

stocks perform better than large firm stocks even after adjusting for the additional risk contained in small firm stock portfolios. In addition, several researchers have documented a low P-E ratio effect (i.e., low P-E ratio stocks beat the pants off high P-E ratio stocks). It also appears that the small firm effect and the low P-E ratio effect are additive. Small firm stocks with low P-E ratios offer the largest investment free lunches.

Although the stock market is less than perfectly efficient, it is not completely inefficient either. Except for a few morsels here and there, investors earn rates of return dictated by the portfolio risk they assume. That is, investors must pay for most of their investment returns by assuming investment risk.

As pointed out in Chapter 2, on a before-cost basis common stocks have provided about 12 percent annually over the last 66 years. Given that the stock market is reasonably efficient, you probably shouldn't expect to earn more than a few percentage points more than this annual rate. Successful investors assume a bit more than average risk and keep their statistical weapons in shape. Their portfolio strategies are built around facts based on solid research rather than myths.

Although the extra rewards in the stock market are few, you should attempt to wring out every bit of free return available. Picking up a quarter percentage point here and a half a percentage point there will add up. Furthermore, the compounding effect of these small excess returns will impact your total wealth by a significant amount over long periods of time. For example, an investor who begins with $10,000 and who earns the 12 percent stock market average will have $299,590 after 30 years. The investor who earns two percentage points more annually (14 percent) through proper portfolio management will exit the investment arena with more than $509,500 after 30 years. That's an increase in wealth of more than 70 percent! So, don't let anyone tell you that the attention you are giving your portfolio is a waste of time. Take care of your investment dollars, and you will amass a fortune in the stock market. You won't earn that fortune overnight, but by capitalizing on some of the cracks in an otherwise efficient market, you will end up much farther down the road toward financial independence.

CHAPTER 9

MANAGING A GROWTH STOCK PORTFOLIO: SOME PRELIMINARY CONSIDERATIONS

For years I've been fascinated, and sometimes horrified, by the way many people—even some market pros—choose their investments. They rush in without a well-defined plan and buy some of this and some of that with little thought as to how their portfolios will eventually look. It's similar to people going into a supermarket without grocery lists; by the time they're at the checkout counter their carts are full of odds and ends, but they've missed most of the bargains and forgotten half the things they came for.

Behind every successful endeavor—be it going to the supermarket, starting a business, playing sports, or investing your money—you will find a well-defined plan. In the world of investments, a plan tells you where you're going and how you're going to get there. A good plan guides you toward your goal. Figure 9-1 illustrates the building blocks of such a plan. It leads you through a briarpatch of distractions and temptations. When a stockbroker calls with a hot stock idea, or when excess cash is burning a hole in your pocket, an investment plan saves you from costly mistakes.

Essential as a plan is to your success, you should know that it is not the starting point. The plan must be based on something even more basic; I call that the investment philosophy.

FIGURE 9–1
Building Blocks of a Rewarding Game Plan

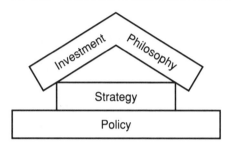

CONSTRUCTING YOUR INVESTMENT PHILOSOPHY

Investment philosophy defines the risks to be taken, the cost to be assumed, and the strategies to be employed as part of a game plan. Naturally, investment philosophy is highly personalized. It must come from within, from knowing who you are, and what you want to accomplish. They say that "if you don't know who you are, the stock market is an expensive place to find out." Thus, the importance of developing a coherent investment philosophy before you get into the game.

Your investment philosophy must be strong enough to support a lifetime of investing. It may change over the years, especially as your ability, inclination to tolerate risk, and need for investment income change. Even though your specific philosophy may evolve over time, it will still be composed of a specific statement of investment policy and a list of action guides.

Investment policy is merely a statement of your desired investment return and the degree of risk you're willing to live with in pursuit of that return. It is the foundation on which you can build your investment strategy. Investment strategy is the process of implementing a set of criteria which you believe will give you an advantage over other investors. That is, by applying investment strategies you attempt to earn excess rates of return. As I noted in Chapter 2, it's these excess returns—even 2 or 3 percent above the market averages—that spell the difference between a tidy nest egg and a modest fortune over time. The way to capture these higher returns is by seeking out undervalued assets or by avoiding overvalued assets.

Strategy implies action; we live in a society that glorifies action. "Actions speak louder than words." "Doing anything is better than doing nothing at all." Remember these platitudes? Since most investors want to feel that they are doing something, they tend to jump into the market without first establishing a solid foundation. They go about implementing investment strategies before first establishing investment policies to guide their actions. Obviously, it's more fun to buy stocks and watch them rise in price than to think through how much risk belongs in your portfolio. But it's not a lot of fun to buy stocks and watch them fall, taking your hard earned cash with them. So a little less excitement at the beginning of your investment program is worth a lot more later on—when you proceed toward your investment goal.

A sound investment philosophy won't guarantee success. However, a lack of a sound investment philosophy almost certainly guarantees failure. Your investment philosophy is similar to insurance. Accidents may happen, but if you're properly insured, they won't destroy you financially.

SETTING INVESTMENT POLICY

As mentioned earlier, investment policy is the specification of the amount of risk that you can accept while pursuing investment return. Of course, it would be great to earn big returns while assuming no risk. Unfortunately, the world is just not built that way. There are very few free lunches! You have to take on some risk. If you want to stalk big returns, you'll have to live with greater risk. This brings us back to the trade-off we discussed in earlier chapters. Figure 9-2 demonstrates the trade-off between investment risk (as measured by portfolio beta, or relative systematic risk) and investment return. Point A describes a riskless asset (perhaps short maturity T-bills). With luck, the return from this asset will equal the rate of inflation, so it's a no-loss portfolio. It's also no-win.

FIGURE 9–2
Trade-Off between Portfolio Return and Risk

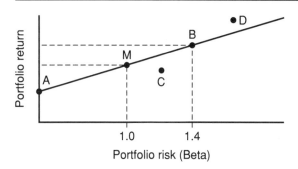

Point M represents the market portfolio, typically the S&P Index whose beta is—by definition—1.0. Historically, its return has averaged about 9 percent above the rate of inflation. A portfolio containing a mix of T-bills and the market portfolio would put you somewhere on the line between A and M: a portfolio with less return than the market portfolio but also less risk. Point B is a high-risk portfolio (beta equals 1.4). It can be formed by holding high-risk securities or by investing in the market portfolio using stock market margin (i.e., borrowing money and investing in S&P Index stocks). Although it contains more than average risk, this portfolio should also produce greater than average returns. Portfolio B is efficiently priced since it lies on the capital market line defined by A and M. It's efficiently priced because the return anticipated corresponds to the amount of risk assumed.

Portfolio C, falling below the upward-sloping line, is not efficiently priced. Its return is not enough to compensate for the risk taken. As such, this portfolio is overpriced. Portfolio D, on the other hand, is underpriced because its return more than compensates for its risk.

In an efficient market, all portfolios fall on the upward-sloping line because, given knowledge of relative under- and over-valuation, investors try to buy portfolio D and sell C. As a result, the price of D increases, lowering its return; the price of C decreases, raising its return. As pointed out in Chapter 5 in an efficient market all assets are fairly priced in terms of risk; therefore, they lie somewhere on the capital market line.

The stock market, though highly efficient, is not perfectly so. The only exceptions to the efficient pricing market mechanism are small equity capitalization firms. Consider Table 9-1. The historical relationships between types of investments have been stable enough to be useful in predicting future return. A large-stock portfolio of average risk (beta equals 1.0) should return 8.8 percent above the annual rate of inflation. A small firm common stock portfolio, which is relatively more risky than the market portfolio (beta of approximately 1.3), should provide an inflation adjusted return of about 12.0 percent annually. These portfolios have, in fact, done better than that by slightly higher than 2 percent annually. That is, portfolios of small firm common stocks provide more return than they are supposed to and are mispriced as is portfolio D in Figure 9-2.

In setting investment policy, you must first indicate the real rate of portfolio return desired. Next, you can use the capital market line to determine the amount of risk which must be taken to obtain the desired portfolio return. Suppose, for example, an investor decides that a 7 percent real rate of return is needed. The combination of large firm common stocks and T-bills that produce this inflation-adjusted return can also produce a portfolio with a beta of about 0.80. (Remember, beta is an index of the responsiveness of a portfolio to changes in the stock market as a whole.) If there is a 10 percent gain in stock market prices, an 0.80 beta portfolio will gain only about 8 percent. On the other hand, a fall in portfolio value is cushioned; if the market drops by 10 percent, the portfolio value falls by only 8 percent. This portfolio contains less than average risk,

TABLE 9-1
Real Returns and Portfolio Risk: 1926-1992

Asset Class	Beta	Average Annual Real Return	Average Excess Return
S&P 500 stocks	1.00	9.2%	0.0%
Small firm stocks	1.30	14.3	2.3
Treasury bills	0.00	0.6	0.6

thus, over the long run, it should also produce less than average investment return.

ESTABLISHING AN INVESTMENT POLICY

The relationship between risk and return for portfolios on the capital market line can be expressed mathematically:

Portfolio return = T-bill return + Beta (Market return −
T-bill return)   (9-1)

On average, the historical market rate of return, which is the return on the S&P Index whose beta is assumed to be 1.00, has exceeded the rate of return on bills by 9.2 percent during the past 67 years. Therefore, this equation can be restated using this historical relationship:

Portfolio return = T-bill return + Beta (9.2%)

or   (9-2)

Portfolio return = T-bill return + Risk premium

In an efficient market, portfolio return equals the annual rate of return on short-term T-bills plus a risk premium equal to approximately 9.2 percent multiplied by the beta of the portfolio. For example, if three-month T-bills are expected to yield approximately 6 percent, the specific capital market line appears in Figure 9-3.

Given a 6 percent expected annual yield on short-term T-bills, the market portfolio (whose beta is 1.00) would be expected to provide a long-run annual rate of return of about 15 percent. A portfolio whose beta is 1.40 would be expected to return about 19 percent annually, while a portfolio whose beta is 0.60 would be expected to return about 11 percent a year. You can determine the expected annual rate of return for any portfolio which lies along this specific capital market line by applying Equation 9-3.

Portfolio return = 6% + Beta (9.2%)   (9-3)

Of course, as short-term interest rates change, so does the

FIGURE 9–3
Contructing the Capital Market Line: An Example

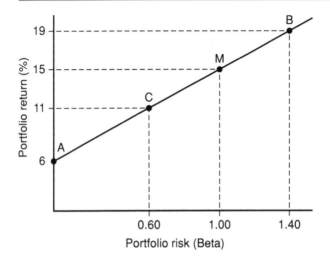

capital market line. Rising interest rates raise the line; falling interest rates lower it. The slope of the capital market line can also change as a result of changing investor risk preferences. For example, if investors were to become more averse to investment risk, then, the slope of the capital market line would become steeper. On the other hand, if investors were to become less averse to risk, the slope of the capital market line would decrease.

The following example illustrates how the capital market line may project the long-run expected annual rate of return for a specific portfolio. Mrs. Smith is somewhat conservative and prefers to hold an overall portfolio with a beta of approximately 0.70. She plans to invest $100,000 in a well-diversified portfolio of large firm common stocks and T-bills.

Suppose that the common stock portion of Mrs. Smith's overall portfolio has a beta of 1.10. This means that she must invest $64,000 in common stocks and $36,000 in short-term money market instruments to produce a portfolio whose overall beta is 0.70. Remember that the overall portfolio beta is a weighted average of the betas of the assets in that portfolio (i.e., 64% × 1.10 plus 36% × 0.00 equals approximately 0.70). Using the capital market line applicable to current market conditions, her expected portfolio return can be determined as follows:

Expected portfolio return = 6% + 0.70 (9.2%) or 12.2%

If Mrs. Smith desires a greater return, she must increase the beta (risk) of her overall portfolio by either investing in more risky common stocks or by reducing her investment in T-bills and increasing her commitment to common stocks.

The point is that expected investment return must be set on the basis of overall portfolio risk. Furthermore, an investor must preestablish the desired level of portfolio risk by having a specific investment policy in mind before undertaking asset selection. Once policy has been set, your investment strategy can be formulated, and asset selection can begin.

Each investor must establish an investment philosophy in accordance with personal needs, desires, and psyche. Although investment philosophies vary greatly from individual to individual, all philosophy statements contain a few common threads. To assist in the formulation of your own investment philosophy, these are my own investment action guides:

1. The common stock portion of the overall investment portfolio will be well diversified and include the common stocks of at least 14 small equity capitalization firms (or a mutual fund that specializes in small firm common stock investments) and at least 10 large firm common stocks (or a mutual fund which specializes in large firm common stock investments).
2. The overall portfolio will contain some liquid assets at all times. Being out of the market means holding 20 percent equities (80 percent cash) while a fully invested position requires holding 20 percent cash.
3. Common stock purchases will be made with a view toward long-term returns. No purchases will be made unless a minimum four-year holding period can be maintained. Although conditions may dictate that some stocks should be sold in less than four years, purchases will be made with the intent of holding on for at least four years.

4. Overall portfolio risk will generally exceed that of the market as a whole. The common stock portion of the overall portfolio should possess a beta of from 1.2 to 1.4.
5. All cash dividends will be reinvested in the shares of common stocks currently held.
6. Every attempt will be made to inject as much new capital into the overall portfolio each year as can be tolerated given current consumption requirements and safety needs.
7. To reduce the negative impact of trading costs and income taxes on total investment return, common stock portfolio turnover should average less than 30 percent annually.
8. Portfolio strategy decisions will be based on scientific fact rather than market folklore or emotionally based hunches or current fads. Implementation of investment strategy will be guided by the following:

   a. Investment preference will be given to firms with at least a three-year earnings history. Firms that have demonstrated they are capable of growing at rapid rates will be given preference.
   b. No attempt will be made to engage in short-run market timing. Increases and decreases in liquid assets will be determined by the real rates of return available on short-term maturity assets. Common stocks will not be sold merely because the market is falling. However, liquidity may be increased by placing newly acquired investment dollars on the sidelines during periods of extremely adverse market movements.
   c. The common stock portion of the overall portfolio will contain from 30 to 50 percent small equity capitalization firms.
   d. Investment preference will be given to firms paying some cash dividends.
   e. Investment preference will be given to common stocks whose P-E ratios are below their respective industry average P-E multiples.

  f. Investment preference will be given to firms with low levels of debt in their capital structures.
  g. Investment preference will be given to those firms financing a significant portion of their growth with internally generated cash.
  h. Investment preference will be given to firms whose shares of stock are not widely held by institutions.
  i. Investment preference will be given to firms with a significant degree of management ownership.

Although these action guides do not guarantee investment success, when consistently followed they provide insurance against many of the disasters that befall the undisciplined investor who has not developed and maintained a well-thought-out plan. If you have not yet established your plan of action, do it now. Write it down and refer to it each and every time you modify your investment portfolio. All portfolio adjustments should agree with the requirements of your investment philosophy. Remember, consistency in investment action can and will improve investment results over the long run.

INVESTING IN EMERGING GROWTH COMPANIES

When it comes to different approaches to investing in the stock market, there is no shortage of ideas. Some investors maintain portfolios of out-of-favor or low P-E ratio stocks. Others look for turnaround situations. Quite a few purchase penny stocks, or accumulate only newly issued shares. Still others endeavor to time the market or invest only in the shares of seasoned high-dividend-yielding corporations.

Some approaches come and go with the market cycle. In the 1960s, the fad was to trade in the common stocks of so-called conglomerates, which grew by gobbling up companies in return for their own shares. By trading paper for income-producing assets, most of these companies multiplied their sales tenfold or more in a few years.

As sales growth soared, so did the earnings per share and

P-E multiples of these firms—and so did the returns for those investors who got into the game early.

As the bubble expanded, institutional investors, too, became mesmerized. The rush to once-in-a-lifetime investments by young institutional money managers—"gunslingers" they were called, because of their bravado with other people's money —drove the P-E ratios of common stocks into the stratosphere.

Then a few people began to notice that these stocks were flying high on nothing but air, and the sell-off began. The resulting stock market crash rivaled that of 1929. The across-the-board stock price drops were not as great as in 1929, but there were about 30 times as many investors in the stock market in the 1970s as there were 50 years earlier. Thus, many more people were personally affected by the market sell-off during the early 1970s.

In the early 1980s the stock market was dominated by emerging growth company strategists. At first, they invested in computer and computer-related firms. Then the popular favorite became biotechnology. Shortly thereafter, the hot stocks were from any small firm with a technology base. As the bull market expanded and the new issues market heated up, investors scrambled to get aboard any new company with a novel idea.

A virtual investment boom occurred in the small emerging growth company segment of the market. Price-earnings ratios of emerging growth companies exploded as institutional money managers acquired shares of firms in this coveted group. In addition, investors established a number of investment pools to invest specifically in this market segment. For example, by 1992, there were more than 100 mutual funds whose statement of investment objectives contained the phrases "small firm" or "emerging growth." Of these, 80 percent commenced operations in the 1980s. With all of this attention, some investors have begun to wonder whether this approach to investing in common stocks has a solid foundation or is merely another investment fad. Furthermore, many investors have begun to wonder if the small firm effect can continue to exist. According to efficient market theory, exploitation of excess return opportunities by a large number of investors should result in more efficiently priced assets. Due to the increase in demand, prices rise and rates of return fall to the point where investment return is solely dependent on investment risk. Now that most institutional money managers are aware of the small firm effect, won't their entry into this market segment hasten the demise of this free lunch? What's your answer?

I answer with a no, and here are the reasons why. First, a small firm emerging growth strategy is not a fad. It is not an investment bubble destined to burst. Growth company stocks will continue to reward investors handsomely when they buy right and hold on for long-run appreciation. Second, the notion that excess returns will be squeezed from small firm stocks now that we know such returns exist is unfounded. As pointed out earlier, most institutional investors cannot effectively exploit the small firm segment of the stock market. You need only examine the portfolios of so-called small firm mutual funds to see the proof. Of the 25 mutual funds officially committed to investing in small firms, less than a handful invest in firms whose equity capitalization is less than $150 million. That leaves a vast market segment of more than 2,000 publicly held small companies almost entirely to individual investors. These same individual investors possess limited access to information and limited financial resources. And that is why the small firm effect can be successfully exploited for years to come.

Let me repeat: To capture the handsome returns these stocks offer, you must buy right and hold on. Buying right means accumulating shares at reasonable earnings multiples. Holding on means that investors must be willing to live with price volatility for at least three to five years, and be willing to accumulate additional shares on price declines. That takes a lot of grit, and most people don't have it.

THE DEFINITION OF A GROWTH FIRM

A growth firm is one whose sales, earnings, dividends, and stock price are expected to grow at a faster than normal rate. A normal growth rate is defined by the growth rate of the U.S.

economy. Since the mid-1940s the U.S. gross national product has grown at a 9 percent compound annual rate. During this period, the earnings and dividends of stocks in the Standard & Poor's 500 Index have grown by approximately 7 percent per year. The annual inflation rate over this same period has averaged around 4 percent. Thus, a normal annual rate of corporate growth averages between 3 and 5 percent in real terms.

Today, expectations are that the long-run rate of inflation will average between 3 and 5 percent annually. So a growth firm is expected to grow at a rate in excess of 10 percent per year over an extended period of time. Although there are no upper bounds on supernormal growth for such firms, you have to recognize the fact that a firm cannot grow at a faster rate than the overall economy forever. Trees don't grow to the sky and growth companies cannot outpace the economy forever. If you pursue a small stock strategy, you must recognize this fact.

CORPORATE GROWTH: AN INDUSTRY PERSPECTIVE

To understand how and why a firm's rate of growth changes over time requires an understanding of the life cycle of an industry. Figure 9-4 graphically illustrates a typical industry life cycle. The cycle generally begins with the invention of a new product or service. Because no market for this product or service has previously existed, user demand for the industry's output is nearly insatiable. Attracted by intense product demand, numerous firms enter the industry. Because many of these firms are new and there is nearly unlimited demand for their products, they possess a healthy need for additional capital. Cash dividend payments are generally nonexistent for these firms and sales growth rates in excess of 100 percent per year are common.

In young industries, however, management expertise is low, competition is high, and many firms struggle just to get beyond their break-even points. Investment risk is extremely high. During this embryonic stage of the industry life cycle (which I call the innovation stage), the casualty rate for newly organized

FIGURE 9–4
The Industrial Life Cycle

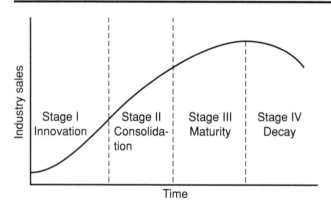

firms is monumental. The common stocks of those few firms which have managed some degree of profitability tend to sport atmospheric P-E ratios.

The second stage of an industry life cycle is the consolidation stage. It is marked by a significant reduction in the number of firms in the industry. Many firms are not able to maintain quality output and are forced out of business. Other firms, with acceptable product innovations but inferior production capabilities, or an inability to raise capital to expand output, are acquired by stronger firms in the industry. Annual sales growth slows to a more moderate rate (between 15 to 40 percent). At the same time, the level of management expertise and the firm's production and distribution efficiency increases.

The industry's surviving firms are still growing at a rapid pace, and their need for new capital remains high. As a result, they retain most of their earnings for reinvestment. Payout ratios—the proportion of earnings paid out in cash dividends—may average 10 to 30 percent. Many firms engage in secondary common stock offerings to raise additional capital. Investment risk remains moderately high during this stage of development. However, due to the existence of high growth prospects, the P-E ratios of such firms are also relatively high and commonly range from 20 to 40 times expected per share earnings.

During the third stage of the industrial life cycle, the maturity stage, the industry is dominated by only a few very large and seasoned firms. Since much of the product demand is replacement demand, sales and earnings growth slow to a rate paralleling the growth rate of the overall economy. The need for new capital diminishes and firms pay out a higher percentage of their earnings in cash dividends. Payout ratios of 50 percent or more are common. As would be expected, P-E ratios fall considerably and most firms sell at a multiple of from 5 to 15 times next year's estimated per share earnings. Investment risk is moderately low and institutional shareholders tend to dominate the trading in the shares of mature companies.

The fourth stage of the industry life cycle is the decay stage. Like people, most firms try to avoid it. During this stage, demand for output declines and firms begin to liquidate their production facilities. Firms with capable management try to acquire firms in stage II of the industrial life cycle, thus attempting to replace their dated product lines and avoiding industrial decay.

When investing in growth firms, I strongly suggest that investors wait until the industry has moved from stage I to stage II of its life cycle. Although large returns can be earned by investing in firms located in the innovation stage of the cycle, corporate mortality rates and investment risks are too high to justify the potential rewards. This is especially true of those investors who cannot afford to widely diversify their growth stock holdings.

On the other hand, investing in firms that reside in the consolidation stage of the industrial life cycle can provide handsome returns with far less risk. Investment in growth firms at this stage of their lives can provide investment returns that average approximately 15 to 20 percent per year. Investing at this stage means paying higher than average P-E multiples (from 10 to 30 times estimated EPS) and sacrificing some current dividend yield. Furthermore, these firms are still relatively small and have not as yet gained a large following among institutional investors. Many firms at this point have less than 15 percent of their outstanding common shares held by institutions.

HOW MUCH SHOULD YOU PAY FOR A GROWTH STOCK?

As indicated in the previous section, growth companies possess widely varying P-E multiples during the various stages of their lives. In the earlier and more rapid growth years, firms tend to carry lofty P-E multiples. As growth slows, P-E multiples tend to fall. This observation leads to the question: How much should an investor pay for corporate growth?

Some investors look for investment bargains among the low P-E multiple common stocks. Frequently, however, these low P-E ratio firms turn out to be anything but a bargain. Remember that corporate earnings can and do grow over time. Thus, bargain hunters who only invest in companies with very low P-E ratios often overlook real bargain issues which may sport slightly higher P-E ratios. To see why, consider the following example:

Suppose that firms A and B report per share earnings of $1 during 1986. Also suppose that these firms possess equivalent risk and that the common stock of firm A is currently priced at $8 (i.e., the stock is trading at a multiple of eight times last year's per share earnings). Firm B, on the other hand, is trading at $10 per share and thus carries a multiple of 10 times the previous year's earnings. Suppose that over the next five years firm A grows at a 10 percent compound annual rate while firm B grows by 20 percent each year. Furthermore, suppose that after five years the future growth rates of both firms are equal; at this time both firms sell at a multiple of eight times the then current earnings. Future per share earnings for both firms appear in Table 9-2.

After five years of growth at 10 percent annually, the per share earnings of firm A become $1.60, while the earnings of firm B, growing at a 20 percent annual rate, become $2.49. If the shares of both firms are priced at eight times current earnings in 1997, the shares of firm A would be worth $12.80 (8 × $1.60) while the shares of firm B would sell for $19.92 (8 × $2.49). Over this five-year period, an investor would have earned a 60 percent return from investment in firm A's common stock while an investment in the common stock of firm B would

TABLE 9-2
Future Corporate Earnings and Corporate Growth

	EPS	
Year	Firm A	Firm B
1992	$1.00	$1.00
1993	1.10	1.20
1994	1.21	1.44
1995	1.32	1.73
1996	1.45	2.07
1997	1.60	2.49

have returned nearly 100 percent. This is true even though the P-E ratio of firm B falls from 10 to 8 times earnings at the end of the period.

As it turns out, the shares of firm B, which initially possessed a higher P-E multiple than those of firm A, represented the real investment bargain. If, on the other hand, an investor had paid $15 to acquire the shares of firm B back in 1992, that is paid 15 times current earnings, total investment return over the five-year period would have been slightly less than 50 percent. Thus, firm A, with a P-E multiple of eight times current earnings, would have been the better buy.

A common stock's P-E multiple is a function of several variables including the risk of investment, future income payments (the firm's dividend growth rate), and the rate of return on alternative investments. The greater the investment risk, the lower the P-E multiple; the greater the rate of corporate growth, the greater the P-E ratio. For efficiently priced growth stocks, the investor's rate of return is a function of current dividend yield and future growth. For example, an investor purchases a growth stock with a current yield of 3 percent whose earnings and dividends are expected to grow at a 15 percent annual rate. If the investor paid a fair price, he or she should receive an 18 percent annual rate of return if these expectations are borne out.

Growth company investors should require a greater than average return on their investments due to the presence of greater investment risk. How much more than the 11 percent historical average return for average risk common stocks is open to conjecture. However, when examining the nature of investment risk and the long-run rates of return obtained by successful growth stock portfolio managers, it becomes apparent that a long-run annual compound rate of return between 15 and 20 percent is generally sufficient compensation for the risks taken. And rates of return within this range are indeed obtainable. Even though we would all like to earn annual rates of return of 30 or 40 percent or more on our investments, it is impossible to obtain returns of this magnitude consistently over the life of a long-run investment program. (This was explained in Chapter 2.) Thus, in the following valuation model I have settled on an 18 percent annual rate of return as the desired investment goal of growth stock investors.

Table 9-3 contains a listing of the maximum P-E multiples which yield an 18 percent annual rate of return on investment in the common stocks of firms with varying projected growth rates and dividend yields. The P-E multiples result from assuming that the indicated firm growth rates will persist for 12 years. I then assumed that at the end of the 12-year period the growth rates of these firms would approximate that of the U.S. economy. The shares of these common stocks would then be priced at 10 times current earnings, or the average P-E multiple of the market over the past 50 years.

TABLE 9-3
**Maximum P-E Ratios Providing an 18 Percent Compound Annual Rate
of Investment Return for Various Combinations of Current Yield
and Earnings Growth**

	Estimated Earnings Growth Percentages					
Current Dividend Yield (percent)	5	10	15	20	25	30
0	3	4	7	12	20	32
1	3	5	8	14	22	35
2	3	5	9	15	24	39
3	3	6	10	17	27	44
4	4	7	11	19	30	49
5	4	7	12	21	34	54
6	5	8	14	23	37	60
7	5	9	15	26	42	67
8	6	10	17	29	46	74

Using these assumptions, I projected earnings per share and stock prices 12 years into the future. Then I discounted these prices, along with any cash dividend payments, to the present using an 18 percent discount rate and obtained the P-E multiple by dividing the result by the assumed current per share earnings.

For example, if the earnings per share of a nondividend paying firm are currently $1, earnings per share will become $8.92 after 12 years of compound growth at the annual rate of 20 percent. If growth then slows to a rate equivalent to that of the average common stock, the P-E multiple at that time would be approximately 10 times current earnings and share price at that time would be $89.20 (10 × $8.92). The present worth of this amount received 12 years in the future, when discounted back at the required 18 percent rate of return, becomes $12.20. Dividing this amount by current per share earnings of $1 provides a P-E multiple of approximately 12. Thus, an investor who pays no more than 12.2 times current earnings to obtain shares in this firm earns a compound annual rate of return of 18 percent on the investment.

A 12-year time span is assumed to be the supernormal growth period. This, of course, is an arbitrary assumption because some firms grow at faster than normal rates for longer periods of time. For example, IBM grew at a 20 percent compound annual rate for nearly 30 years before its growth moderated. Any firm with an equity capitalization of $100 million will become a billion dollar company after 13 years of growth at a 20 percent annual rate. Because large firms find it much more difficult to grow at supernormal rates than smaller firms do, it is exceptional to find a billion dollar company growing at a supernormal rate. There are very few IBMs in this world. Furthermore, since the goal of this exercise is to value growth stocks at reasonable P-E multiples, a set of conservative assumptions is warranted. Finally, most investors who accumulate shares of growth firms generally err on the optimistic side when making projections of future growth. Thus, when these optimistic projections are tempered with conservatively determined maximum P-E multiples resulting from the assumption of a short supernormal growth period, a more realistic assessment of investment value results.

To obtain an estimate of the P-E multiple for a particular growth firm using the data in Table 9-3, first estimate the long-run growth prospects of the firm and obtain its current dividend yield. Locate these values on the chart and find the point at which the appropriate row and column intersect. The value at this point of intersection represents the maximum P-E multiple which should be paid to obtain common shares of the firm and still have a reasonable chance of obtaining an 18 percent compound annual rate of return. This P-E multiple is applicable to next year's per share earnings estimate. For example, a firm with expected growth of 25 percent per year (and currently retaining all earnings and paying no cash dividends) should return investors 18 percent per year if they pay no more than 20 times next year's estimated earnings. If this firm is currently providing a 2 percent dividend yield, the maximum P-E that will still provide an 18 percent annual rate of return is 24 times next year's estimated earnings. On the other hand, high-yielding common stocks with a current yield of 8 percent and expected growth prospects of 10 percent per year will return 18 percent annually if an investor pays no more than 10 times next year's estimated per share earnings.

This presentation has focused on the valuation of growth stocks. However, successful investors couple stock valuation with proper portfolio management techniques. Investors who have paid reasonable prices for growth stocks have enhanced their chances for success. Such chances can be further enhanced by applying portfolio management techniques applicable to growth stock portfolios. One must know how and when to take profits and when to accumulate additional shares of firms purchased at an earlier date. Furthermore, proper portfolio diversification and a long-run orientation are requisites for investment success. We discuss these issues in detail shortly.

HOW DO FIRMS GROW?

Small firm managers choose from four basic growth strategies. The choice makes a difference in whether a small firm becomes successful and grows large enough so that its shares become fully priced. Take for example, Friendly Freddy, with stars in his eyes, a desire to become a multimillionaire, and founder of Friendly Freddy's Frozen Frosties—an ice cream parlor. After a very successful first year, Freddy turned his attention toward corporate growth.

First Freddy thought he might expand by increasing the size of his existing store. Soon he realized that sales growth would be limited by the number of potential customers who lived near enough to come in. He decided this probably wasn't the way to go—people just wouldn't drive an hour or two to the store no matter how good the ice cream was. He next considered expansion by fission—dividing his initial outlet into two identical stores. He could incorporate again and open a second store, which his wife Freda would operate. Each outlet would then operate separately and draw on different groups of customers.

This was better than the first strategy; however, he realized that it also was limited. So Freddy thought about a chain of ice cream parlors, with centralized management to supervise and provide resources to each location. His ideas were getting better, but Freddy found some flaws in this strategy, too. A chain would expand sales volume, but it would be just a multiple repetition of the single store. The corporate entity would not be changing much from its original form.

Finally, with the help of a friend with a new MBA from a well-known business school, Freddy decided to implement a much more complex strategy, one that required the corporate entity to take on different shapes. Freddy decided to increase the number of outlets and, at the same time, expand the product line to full-course meals. Now Freddy had gone beyond the ice cream industry into the broader fast-food industry. He would then acquire (1) a food distributor to provide products to his stores, (2) a small transportation company to get the products to his stores, and (3) a real estate firm to acquire, develop, and manage the sites for his stores.

At some point all of today's large corporations have chosen a complex growth program. The strategy is riskier than simply doing the same thing over and over again, but the rewards are greater—for both the investor and the corporation.

THE ANATOMY OF A GROWTH COMPANY

My investment advisory newsletter, *Investment Horizons,* helps individual investors capture the small firm effect. To do this, we seek out small equity capitalization firms with the potential to grow successfully over time. One firm remained on our recommendation list for nearly three years, as many do; during that time it grew from a small single-product firm into a multidimensional corporation. Along the way it rewarded its stockholders handsomely. It provides an interesting case study.

We first recommended buying Mayflower Group on April 29, 1983, when it had an equity capitalization of about $42 million. Over the next three years, Mayflower's sales grew from $314 million to $619 million, and its equity capitalization rose to $227 million. An investor who bought in April 1983 and held for three years earned nearly 250 percent on the original investment. An analysis of the company's growth strategy and financial results give valuable insights into the small firm effect and how it can be exploited.

To better understand how an actual company grows, I have included a summary of Mayflower Group's growth strategy and financial results. Figure 9-5 lists the major events that shaped the company over those three years. For the first 54 years of its corporate life, management had been quite content to grow simply by increasing its truck transportation business. In 1981, however, the company embarked on an ambitious and successful program of diversification. Mayflower management redirected the company into a risky, but successful strategy of growth. The result was an increasing level of sales, profits, and dividends to shareholders.

Figure 9-6 shows what happened with Mayflower stock while the major changes occurred. Table 9-4 shows how an investor's wealth would have increased along with the company's. A Mayflower shareholder who invested $1,637.50 in 100 shares of the company's stock in April 1983 would have obtained a total of $294.50 in cash dividends. These cash dividends increased 400 percent over the three years. The shareholder would have ended up with 180 shares, thanks to

FIGURE 9–5
Mayflower Group: A Corporate History

General Background

The Company was founded in 1927 and prior to 1981, its only significant business activity was its truck transportation business. Mayflower was incorporated in 1973 and became a publicly held firm in 1976. Its common shares were traded over-the-counter from May 1976 until November 1981 when its stock was listed on the American Stock Exchange. Through acquistions, the company entered the appliance and home entertainment products business in 1981, and entered the business of wholesale distribution of prerecorded videocassette tapes in 1982. The company entered the contract school bus transportation business with the acquisition of R. W. Harmon in 1984, and expanded its operations with the acquisition of three additional companies in the fall of 1985.

Significant Events since Initial Recommendation April 29, 1983

April 1983	Initially recommended as a buy.
May 1983	Completed an offering of 1,075,000 shares of common stock at $17.
November 1983	Increased quarterly dividend from $0.15 to $0.175.
August 1984	Increased quarterly dividend from $0.175 to $0.20.
September 1984	Declared a 20 percent stock dividend thereby increasing the quarterly dividend by 20 percent.
October 1984	Agreed to acquire R. W. Harmon & Sons, Inc. for $9 million in notes and $15 million in cash. Harmon is a Kansas City company that sells school buses and offers school bus transportation services. Company stated its intent to file with the SEC an offering of 700,000 common shares.
November 1984	Company issued 685,000 common shares at $21.
April 1985	Announced a 3–2 stock split payable in June 1985. Company also announced its regular quarterly dividend of $0.20 on the postsplit shares. This amounted to a dividend increase of 50 percent.
August 1985	Placed on hold list due to large equity capitalization.
September-December 1985	Acquired all of the outstanding shares of three corporations in the school bus contract services area for a total of $6.4 million.
March 1986	Announced a public offering of $25 million of convertible bonds due 2006 with a conversion price of $32.50 per share.
April 1986	Changed name from Mayflower Corp. to Mayflower Group to more adequately describe the diverse nature of the company.
May 1986	A $28 per share tender offer was made for Mayflower Group by Laidlaw Transportation. The offer was subsequently increased to $29.50 per share. *Investment Horizons'* sale recommendation given in early May due to pending tender offer made by Laidlaw.

FIGURE 9–6
Mayflower Group Stock Price History

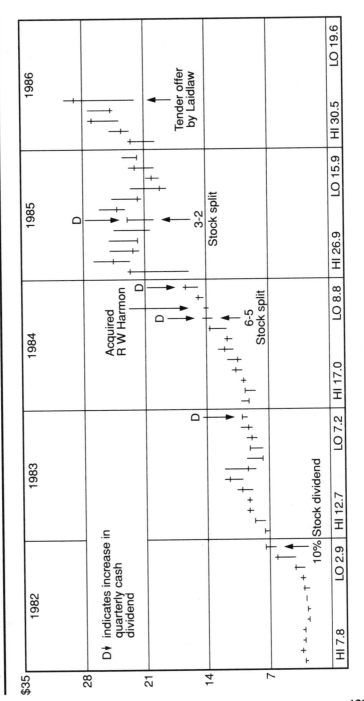

TABLE 9-4

Mayflower Group Investors' Return during Three-Year Holding Period

Payment Period	Actual Cash Dividend/ Share	Actual Number of Shares Held	Total Cash Dividend Received	Market Value of Shares Held
Initial Purchase of 100 Shares April 1983 at $16.375/Share				$1,637
Q II 1983	$0.15	100	$15.00	2,100
Q III	0.15	100	15.00	1,600
Q IV	0.175	100	17.50	1,750
Q I 1984	0.175	100	17.50	1,837
Q II	0.175	100	17.50	1,975
Q III	0.20	100	20.00	2,150
Shares Held Increased from 100 to 120 due to 20% Stock Dividend				
Q IV	0.20	120	24.00	2,010
Q I 1985	0.20	120	24.00	2,505
Shares Held Increased from 120 to 180 due to 3-2 Stock Split				
Q II	0.20	180	36.00	2,760
Q III	0.20	180	36.00	3,735
Q IV	0.20	180	36.00	4,117
Q I 1986	0.20	180	36.00	4,725
Sale of 180 Shares at $29.50				$5,310
Total cash dividends $294.50				

stock dividends and stock splits, and would have been able to sell those shares for $5,310 in 1986.

Table 9-5 compares the financial profile of Mayflower in April 1983 with its profile three years later when I made a sell recommendation. The size of the firm more than doubled during these years of supernormal growth. The P-E multiple also increased as the larger investment community recognized Mayflower's growth prospects. Finally, the number of shares increased due to stock offerings and stock splits; as a result, institutional ownership of the stock climbed from 6 to 47 institutional shareholders, who collectively held a third of the outstanding shares.

Increasing institutional interest is one way that a growing

TABLE 9-5
Mayflower Group: The Transition from a Small to a Large Company

	April 1983	May 1986
Revenues	$341 million	$620 million
Total assets	$ 82 million	$257 million
Equity capitalization	$ 42 million	$227 million
Employees	1,236	2,485
Shares outstanding	2.6 million	7.7 million
Shareholders of record	1,212	1,536
Insider holdings (percent)	8.5%	8.0%
Institutional holdings (number)	6	47
Institutional holdings (percent)	9%	33%
Book value per share	$11.83*	$11.34
Share price	$16.38*	$29.50
Dividend yield	3.6%	3.0%
Price-earnings ratio	9 x	18 x

*Does not reflect stock split and stock dividend. Adjusted book value was $6.37 and adjusted share price was $9.10 for April 1983.

firm's stock achieves full value in the marketplace. In the case of Mayflower, a suitor squeezed the last drop of undervaluation out by making a tender offer for all the outstanding shares of common stock.[1] As we'll see later, takeovers are frequently last act in a growth stock's performance.

I'm not suggesting that all small equity capitalization companies will reward you as well as Mayflower rewarded its investors, but the case of Mayflower does illustrate how significant returns can be earned from similar companies. The Mayflower scenario also illustrates the importance of patience. A small firm has to be given time to carry out its growth strategy. Furious short-term trading in small equity capitalization stocks may occasionally be profitable for the fast buck artist, but the slow bucks accumulated by long-term investors tend to build a larger pile over an investment lifetime.

---

[1] Mayflower was able to successfully block the unfriendly takeover attempt and eventually went private in a management-sponsored leveraged buyout. Shareholders received $31.50 per share in cash.

CHAPTER 10

MANAGING A SMALL FIRM GROWTH STOCK PORTFOLIO: THE FINER POINTS

In the last chapter I outlined a procedure for determining the reasonableness of emerging growth stock prices. As important as proper stock selection is, it alone is not enough to guarantee investment success. Frequently, growth stock investors are less than successful, even though they apply proper stock selection techniques. That is, although they select good solid companies, they either pay too much for stock or they mismanage their growth stock portfolio.

Several years ago a friend—and an astute investor—gave me a list of some 30 stocks he had purchased during the 1980s. Over half were among the top performers of the decade. He asked me to guess how successful his investments had been. I responded that, depending on the amount of money initially invested, he must have made a bundle. I was surprised to learn that he had barely broken even. It seems that he either sold too soon or held his stocks too long. He sold potentially big winners after a 20 or 30 percent advance. Others initially doubled and tripled in price but he sold them only after they moved to much lower ground; he even sold some at a loss. My friend concluded that knowing what to buy and when was not a guarantee of investment success. Sadly, I had to agree.

Contrary to popular belief, the most important element of a successful investment program is not stock selection—as many investors believe—but proper portfolio management, something very few individual investors practice. Furthermore, proper portfolio management techniques can and do differ for different investment strategies. The characteristics of the investments held dictate the proper portfolio management techniques. A growth stock investment strategy, for example, requires knowledge of what to buy, an estimate of reasonable value, and a thorough understanding of the behavior of growth stock returns.

RISK MANAGEMENT

Growth stock investing is risky business. However, the investor can control a great deal of the risk. One method of controlling risk is to take a proper orientation to investment holding periods. Over the short run (a week, a month, or even a year) the prices of growth stocks can rise and fall dramatically. Most small company growth stocks have betas far greater than the market average of 1.00. Furthermore, the average level of unsystematic, or company-specific risk, for a small firm is twice that of a large firm. Thus, stock price volatility for these companies, when considered individually, is generally much greater than is indicated by betas.

The extreme price volatility of growth company stocks has led many investors into short-run, technically based trading strategies. This, of course, is a grievous error because most of the price volatility they hope to cash in on is related to company-specific factors or unsystematic risk rather than to stock market factors, systematic or beta risk. The systematic or market risk component of total risk is much more predictable than nonmarket risk; therefore, stocks containing large components of nonmarket risk are highly unsuitable vehicles to use in a short-run trading strategy that relies on the prediction of overall stock market prices. Thus, growth stock investors must assume a long-term holding strategy to control investment risk. Furthermore, the characteristics of the industrial life cycle (see Chapter 9) make it imperative that growth company investors allow sufficient time for the firm to realize its growth potential. My advice is to never invest in a growth stock if you intend to hold on for less than four years. This does not mean that all growth stocks are held for four years or more. It means that, in the absence of unusual circumstances, you intend to hold the investment for at least four years.

A second method of controlling growth stock investment risk is portfolio diversification. With large company common stocks, you can eliminate nearly 90 percent of company-specific risk by holding a portfolio of 10 to 15 stocks of firms in unrelated industries. However, gaining the optimal benefits of diversification for small growth company stocks requires a portfolio of from 15 to 30 stocks in unrelated industries. If you hold less than 15 you are taking far too much risk given the potential returns. Furthermore, because an optimally diversified small company growth stock portfolio contains more risk than one composed of large company stocks, the growth stock investor must couple portfolio diversification with time diversification. Time diversification requires injecting new capital into the portfolio, or withdrawing cash, gradually over time.

WHEN TO BUY GROWTH COMPANY STOCKS

If you're just beginning to assemble a small firm growth stock portfolio, now is the time to buy. By now I mean anytime—today, tomorrow, or next month. However, remember the concept of time diversification. Make small purchases of the shares of numerous companies and add to your individual commitments gradually over time until the value of your total portfolio meets your dollar target.

For example, suppose that you want to invest a total of $30,000 in small firm stocks. Rather than commit this entire amount to a portfolio of at least 15 small firms now, consider investing about $15,000 (approximately $1,000 per company) now and adding the remaining $15,000 gradually over the next 12 to 24 months. This may require odd lot purchases that increase transaction costs a bit. If it does, think of the additional costs as risk insurance paid to gain both asset and time diversification.

For individuals who have already established a growth stock portfolio, injections of new capital can expand the number of securities held or increase the commitment to issues currently held. In either case, the rule of time diversification applies. Furthermore, growth stock investors should increase their current holdings when the share prices of sound companies drop due to glitches in corporate growth (notably a temporary softening of earnings accompanied by strength in sales) or during periods when stock prices in general are falling.

In the case of a corporate earnings glitch, share price often tumbles due to selling by technical traders, who are short-term trend followers. Sales made by these traders frequently depress stock prices far below investment value for short periods of time. However, as long as these firms maintain the good fundamentals that lead to future earnings growth, you should view stock price declines as excellent opportunities to accumulate additional shares. Think of these as good investments that have just gone on sale.

In the case of a general stock market decline, remember that the prices of the stocks of good companies go down with the bad—at least temporarily. The lessons of the great bear markets of 1969–70 and 1973–74 must be remembered in this regard. During these periods, stock prices in general fell by an average of 50 percent. However, many companies increased per share earnings during each period, only to see their share prices falter along with the rest of the market. (Remember, all stocks contain some degree of systematic risk; thus, stock market trends affect them no matter what.) Rather than panic and sell out at these times, growth stock investors with well-diversified portfolios should increase their holdings of those companies whose growth fundamentals remain intact.

The maintenance of a diversified portfolio makes such purchases easier to take emotionally. Someone holding the shares of only one or two companies must continually worry about permanent capital losses if share prices were to fall and never rebound. However, well-diversified investors know that although a few companies may not be able to survive prolonged periods of recession or excessively high interest rates, others prosper and increase total portfolio value over time. For example, if you had bought the S&P Index the day before the 1969–70 bear market began and had held on, your portfolio would have returned to the black in 22 months. If you had held on to that position until the end of 1992 (and had reinvested all cash dividends), the value of your portfolio would have increased by 1,053 percent, even though the initial purchase was made at a most inopportune time.

For a great many individuals, investing is anything but a happy experience. When stock prices are rising, those who are heavily invested worry that they won't be able to get out before the onset of the next bear market. Those who are sitting on bundles of cash worry that the market will leave them behind before they can get on the bandwagon. When stock prices have fallen, these cash rich investors worry that stock prices will continue to deteriorate. Thus, it makes no difference what direction stock prices take—unhappiness abounds.

Investors are most unhappy during periods of steep stock price declines—just when they should be overjoyed! Bear markets represent tremendous opportunities because so many quality stocks are put on sale at bargain prices. Even so, most investors respond negatively to lower prices. One of the crazy things about the stock market is that it's the only business in the world where lower prices for the product actually drive away customers. The same people who bargain hunt for cars and toilet paper, who never tire of telling friends about their latest great deal, are usually the same people who wring their hands during stock market slumps. You should welcome periods of price decline. Think of them as big clearance sales. The only time you should want stock prices to be high is on the day you plan to terminate your investment program and sell out.

Of course, to take advantage of these great buying opportunities, you're going to need cash. Thus, good portfolio management requires you to have some cash on hand at all times. Consistent with your risk tolerance level, you should determine the minimum percentage of the overall portfolio to be held in cash. I suggest that this minimum never be less than 10 percent of the portfolio's overall value. Except in extreme circumstances, a fully invested posture means holding at least 20 percent of investment funds in money market instruments. Proper portfolio management requires the development and implementation of a sound cash management plan. Remember, even if you do not plan to make periodic injections of new capital into your growth stock portfolio, cash is generated from dividends and from stock sales made for a variety of reasons. This cash, of course, should be periodically reinvested in stocks.

WHEN SHOULD YOU TAKE PROFITS?

Ideally, the answer is never. The ideal company grows and grows, the stock continues to appreciate at supernormal rates, and investment wealth continues to pile up. Common stock sales do not have to be made to qualify as profits. A stock purchased initially for $10 which increases in price to $40 represents a profit of $30 for every share purchased regardless of whether or not the stock is sold. If the stock is sold, the profit already obtained is realized. For most investors, this means that income taxes must be paid on the gain. Thus, the sale reduces actual profits and investor wealth. Furthermore, since cash received from stock sales must eventually be reinvested, commission charges reduce investment wealth even further. Thus, investors should not be tempted to sell merely for the sake of selling. In fact, a leading inhibitor of long-run portfolio performance is the tendency to sell too soon. As the old adage says, "If it ain't broke, don't fix it." This is good advice for growth stock investors. If you don't need the cash for other purposes, and if the company continues to possess fundamentally sound growth prospects, don't sell the stock.

However, as we explained in the last chapter, even a well-managed company cannot grow at a supernormal rate forever. Thus, you should sell growth company stocks when corporate size becomes a hindrance to future supernormal growth. Although no exact size threshold should automatically signal a sale, companies with equity capitalizations of over $500 million generally find it most difficult to grow at supernormal rates. Size does not necessarily preclude a company from being a good investment; however, it does signal the end of its classification as a true growth company.

Of course, it also makes good investment sense to sell out when the health of a company deteriorates to the point where it is incurable. Remember that the company's stock was purchased for its growth potential. As long as that potential exists, hang on. The loss of a large customer, excessive competition in the industry, and myriad other factors may reduce sales and earnings temporarily. But as long as the company maintains sufficient resources—a positive, internally generated cash flow being one of the most important—these temporary problems will probably be overcome and supernormal growth resumed. On the other hand, analysis of the firm's financial condition indicates that when growth potential cannot be realized share holdings should be sold. Most likely, such sales will result in investment losses. Fortunately, portfolio diversification softens the blow. Even though losses in individual investments periodically occur, highly diversified growth stock portfolios generally offset such losses with gains from other securities. The result is a gain in overall portfolio value and investment wealth.

Another good time to sell is when large institutional investors begin to dominate trading in a growth company's shares. In general, when institutional shareholders own more than 50 percent of the company's common shares, and when trading in large blocks becomes excessive (more than half of the total shares traded week after week), it's time for you to head for the exit. Yes, there are numerous exceptions to this rule, but I have found that individual investors earn much higher returns when they compete with other individual investors rather than institutional investors.

Frequently, small firm stock investors are forced to sell out when a company is acquired. Indications are that about 5 percent of the nationally listed small growth companies are acquired by other firms during any given year. At least that has been the case over the last 10 years. If this average continues to hold, the investor who maintains a 30-stock small firm portfolio would lose an average of three issues every two years due to acquisition. Thus, small firm investors are frequently forced to sell some of their holdings. Of course, cash received from such sales must be reinvested in additional issues to maintain the desired degree of portfolio diversification.

Even investors who take a buy-and-hold approach to small firm common stocks must continually engage in active portfolio management. Remember that cash dividend payments represent capital returns and hence a return of profits. These profits can be very substantial over the long run. In fact, a growth stock held over a several-year period will most likely return the entire amount of the initial investment in dividends. I have discovered many small growth firms have been increasing their dividends each year over periods as long as 25 years. It's imperative that these dividends be reinvested in additional small firm shares.

When investors think of stocks with impressive dividend growth records, their thoughts typically rush to such well-known names as IBM or AT&T. Although many small capitalization stocks also sport impressive records of dividend growth, these issues are usually given a quick brush-off by investors who view them solely as a source of capital appreciation—ignoring their dividend yields. Even a modest 1 or 2 percent dividend yield over time can substantially boost investment results.

Another reason for selling is to take advantage of even better opportunities. If you find that limited investment capital is continually forcing you to pass up potentially profitable investments, consider selling some of your current holdings and redeploy your investment capital. For example, one investor recently asked for advice about a stock that he had held for approximately three years. Initially he purchased 100 shares and now held 250 shares due to stock splits and stock dividends. On examination of his investment returns, I found that if he sold one half of his current holdings he would more than recoup his initial investment. The original investment, now returned, could be redeployed while he still maintained an investment position in the original company.

As I have pointed out, there are many valid reasons for selling small firm stocks. Whenever you're tempted to sell, always ask yourself what you would do if you owned the entire company. If you wouldn't sell if you were the sole owner, don't be tempted to sell merely because you own a few hundred shares. View your investment just as you would if you were a full partner in the business. In fact, I strongly suggest not even making the purchase in the first place if you would not want to be a partner with the existing management team. Ask yourself:

"Is this the kind of company in which I want to be a major owner?"

HOLDING PERIOD AND INVESTMENT RISK

I have continually pointed out that small firm investors must manage their portfolios with a view toward the long run. My advice has been to buy in and hold on. One reason for doing so is to give your growth company selections time to realize their growth potential. Another reason is to reduce the trading costs and taxes that eat into your net investment returns. Even though these are compelling reasons to assume a long-term investment horizon, one more very important benefit accrues to long-term holders of small equity capitalization firms—risk reduction.

According to traditional risk measures, the extra return that goes along with small firm investing is in part due to greater risks. In a recent study of the returns of small and large firm common stocks over the period 1926–92, for example, researchers found that the annual standard deviation of return for a portfolio of S&P 500 stocks was 21 percent versus 36 percent for a portfolio of small firm common stocks.

If you're not in tune with this statistical jargon, these figures mean that on an annual basis, the prices of small capitalization firms rise by about 50 percent more than S&P stocks in bull markets and fall by about 50 percent more than large company stocks in bear markets. So in the short run, small firm common stock portfolios give you a more thrilling ride—one that's 50 percent more risky than large firm stock portfolios.

In the long run, however, variability of return does not provide an adequate index of investment risk. For example, suppose that one investment alternative promises to return 6 percent per year with perfect certainty while another alternative promises to deliver a return of either 6 or 10 percent with each potential outcome possessing a 50 percent probability. Under the traditional definition of risk, the second alternative would be considered more risky than the first because its standard deviation of return is 2 percent while the standard deviation of the first alternative is zero. However, I question whether this is truly the case; under no circumstances will the taker of the second alternative be worse off. The real risk is that the higher return will not be achieved. In general, when there is only a very small probability that one investment will be valued less than a second at some future point in time, I don't consider that first investment to be much more risky than the second. In other words, short-term variability of portfolio return alone does not adequately paint the correct picture of investment risk.

Consider, for example, the case of a small firm portfolio relative to a large firm portfolio. If both portfolios formed today were compared on the basis of variability of return over the next year, there is no doubt that the small firm stock portfolio would be riskier. If over 10 years the small firm portfolio grows at the average annual compound rate of 15 percent, while the large firm portfolio grows only 10 percent, the value of $1,000 invested in the small firm portfolio would be $4,036. The same amount invested in a large firm portfolio would be $2,593. Now, assuming a decline in the stock market, the small firm stock portfolio must fall by $1,443 or by 35.7 percent more than the fall in the value of the large firm stock portfolio before small firm common stock investors would be worse off in portfolio value. Furthermore, the longer the holding period, the greater must be the decrease in small firm stock prices before they fall below the value of the larger firms. For example, $1,000 invested in small firm stocks back in 1926 would have become $1,847,629 by the end of 1991. On the other hand, the same amount invested in a large firm stock portfolio would have grown to only $675,592. That means that after holding on for 66 years, the small firm stock investor would have to experience a decline in portfolio value of 63.5 percent more than the decline in the large firm portfolio to be worse off. Thus, for long-term holding periods, investors must change their view of relative investment risk. The definition of risk as potential single-period (annual) return variability is not a valid risk measure for long-term investors.

This is exactly the position taken in a recent research report presented by three Northwestern University professors—Robert Machol, Eugene M. Lerner, and Pochara Theerathorn. They state that the risk associated with portfolios possessing high standard deviations of returns disappears over time. Furthermore, they concluded that long-term investors can virtually ignore risk, at least according to the classical (standard deviation) definition of risk.

How long is long-term? An investment strategy which contains a long-run investment holding period is definitely preferable to any strategy based on short-run trading tactics. However, as one astute market player once observed, "In the long run, we are all dead." Again, the Northwestern researchers constructed and maintained several hypothetical common stock portfolios over the period from June 1973 through December 1981. One group of portfolios consisted of only small equity capitalization stocks; the other group consisted of portfolios containing stocks in the S&P Index. They found it took only 45 months, on average, before the small stock portfolios could be considered less risky than the large stock portfolios. Less risky was defined in relative portfolio value variation at the end of the period. That is, on average, after 45 months the probability that the value of a small stock portfolio would be less than the value of the large stock portfolio was less than 5 percent (1 chance in 20).

For small firm stock investors, the long run turns out to be relatively short—less than four years! Conditions in the future may not mirror those in the past, but I don't believe this will be the case. A portfolio turnover rate of less than 25 percent or a planning horizon of four years should be sufficient to mitigate the risk of small stock portfolios. When viewed in this light, it becomes readily apparent that all investors, whether young or old, who can afford to maintain a widely diversified portfolio of common stocks should include some small equity capitalization firms. For long-term investors, the result should be greater investment returns and more substantial terminal portfolio values without the accompaniment of larger amounts of risk. In fact, risk may be less than you would be exposed to with large capitalization firms—especially if you accept a contemporary definition of portfolio risk.

MONITORING YOUR INVESTMENT HOLDING PERIOD

I am always surprised how very few people can accurately describe their investment portfolios. Most know which stocks and bonds they're holding and which issues were liquidated in the recent past. But when I ask about the current yield of their portfolios, which rate of return they've earned over the last year, or their portfolio turnover rate, I am greeted by puzzled looks and sometimes red faces. Remember that investment action should only be taken within the framework of a sound plan. Investment control requires that plans be set, actions be monitored and measured, and results be compared to the initial plan. If results are not in conformance with the initial plan, plans must be monitored or corrective action taken.

The management of a small firm stock portfolio requires patience. Stocks must be held for an average of at least four years to reap the benefits of extra investment return without the assumption of extra investment risk. You must continually monitor your trading activities to ensure taking a long-term posture. To estimate your average investment holding period you must first determine your portfolio's turnover ratio. This ratio is obtained by dividing the lesser of your annual security purchases or sales by the average value of your portfolio. For example, suppose that last year your stock purchases totaled $50,000, your stock sales totaled $30,000, and that the average value of your portfolio was $90,000. (To obtain the average value of your portfolio, total the monthly valuations and divide by 12.) Since the value of stocks sold was less than the value of those purchased, divide $30,000 by $90,000. That yields a ratio of 0.33. In other words, you "turned over" one third of your portfolio last year. To obtain an estimate of your average annual holding period, divide 1.00 by the value of this ratio. In this example, 1.00/0.33 equals 3.0, a three-year average holding period.

Admittedly, this might be a difficult task the first time through. If you have difficulty obtaining the needed data inputs, you need to improve your record-keeping procedures. Old income tax returns may provide sufficient data for this exercise if you cannot locate your brokerage confirmation slips. Repeat this exercise at least once each year. Compare your recent average holding period with that of the past. Look for trends toward more rapid portfolio turnover. Be sure to compare your average holding period with your initial plan or statement of investment philosophy. Correct any deviations between actions and plans. I am sure that you will find this exercise informative. It will most certainly pay off in increased investment returns over an investment lifetime.

THE OVERALL INVESTMENT PORTFOLIO: CASE STUDIES

During the years that I have published *Investment Horizons,* I have received many letters from subscribers who want to take advantage of the small firm effect but are not sure of the extent to which they should include small firms in their overall stock and bond portfolios. The answer to these questions concerning portfolio composition is: "It depends." Portfolio composition should reflect the desires and needs of each individual investor. Some investors prefer high current yields and must, therefore, assume lower risks. Some prefer a mix of current income and capital appreciation; they are willing and able to assume moderate investment risks. Others prefer an aggressive portfolio with low amounts of current income and large capital appreciation potential; they are willing to assume above-average investment risk.

Individuals must assess their own income needs, their ability and inclination to assume risk, and their tax situation before getting their feet wet. Because each individual has different needs and desires, it is difficult to make blanket recommendations. However, to give nonprofessional investors some direction, I have created several hypothetical investors with differing income, lifestyle, and tax situations. In the following pages I outline a portfolio for each hypothetical investor and give the reasons why I recommend these portfolios.

These illustrations serve two purposes. First, they highlight the key factors to consider when planning the composition of a stock and bond portfolio. This study provides a basis for self-assessment and should assist in personal financial planning. Second, because the four hypothetical investors cover a wide spectrum of risk-return needs and desires, you should find a scenario close to your own situation. Use this recommended strategy as the starting point for personal portfolio construction. The recommended portfolio composition is only a first approximation; it is meant to be tailored to specific investors' requirements. This exercise can be of great benefit as a guide to portfolio construction. Because we are all different, no one should follow any blanket investment recommendation blindly.

With this caution in mind, let's begin. My first hypothetical investor is Alice Able, age 29. Currently a marketing analyst for a large corporation in the Midwest, Able is a fast track employee who should climb the corporate management ladder at a steady pace. She is single, currently earns $25,000 a year, and is eligible to join the company's pension plan within two years. She has approximately $20,000 available for investment and has $20,000 in other assets, primarily a small amount of equity in her recently purchased condominium apartment.

Recommended investment portfolio:

Money market mutual fund	$ 4,000	20%
Small firm mutual fund	16,000	80
Total assets	$20,000	100%

Comments:

Able can most likely assume higher than average investment risk due to her youth and future income prospects. Being young, she can look to the distant future for investment rewards; this suggests a focus on assets with potential long-term capital appreciation. Thus, Able appears to be ideally suited to invest in a portfolio of small equity capitalization stocks. However, Able possesses too few assets for direct investment in common stocks. Remember, investors can reduce their risk through portfolio diversification only when holding at least 10 different common stocks. At an average share price of $20, Able would have to invest at least $20,000 in small firm common stocks to obtain even a modest degree of diversification. Thus, Able should invest in a mutual fund which invests in small

equity capitalization firms rather than attempt direct investment in such companies at this time. Eventually, due to
injections of new capital and capital appreciation of her mutual
fund portfolio, Able could begin to shift from indirect to direct
investment. A relatively high beta fund (greater than 1.20) is
consistent with her ability to assume greater than average risks.
The recommended investment in a money market mutual fund,
or money market bank account, is for liquidity purposes. This
should allow Able to maintain her equity investment and to
avoid a forced sale due to unforeseen cash needs. Thus, she has
obtained some assurance of being in the stock market over the
long run.

Ben Brown, age 40, is married and has one child 10 years
old. Brown is an attorney in private practice and has a gross
annual income of $70,000. He has recently begun a company
pension program and contributes 15 percent of his gross income
to the plan. His wife Betty is not currently employed. Brown has
$90,000 available for stock and bond investments. The family
possesses other assets of approximately $60,000, including
equity in a home, two cars, a boat, and a one-acre lakefront lot
on which they hope to build someday.

Recommended investment portfolio:

Money market mutual fund	$18,000	20%
Large firm common stocks	27,000	30
Small firm common stocks	45,000	50
Total assets	$90,000	100%

Comments:

Brown's income and age suggest that the investment portfolio should be oriented toward capital appreciation. He can
assume larger than average risks on his equity investments but
should maintain a degree of liquidity to take advantage of
additional opportunities should they arise. In addition, the
recommended money fund position should be sufficient to meet
most unexpected needs for cash, thus protecting him against
premature liquidation of the common stock portion of the
portfolio. Although the income from the money market mutual

fund is fully taxable, he possesses sufficient income tax deductions to offset this additional taxable income. The small firm common stock portion of the overall portfolio should contain from 15 to 20 different stock issues which currently pay little or no cash dividends and possess relatively high betas (1.10–1.40). I suggest investing the large firm common stock portion of the overall portfolio in one or two equity mutual funds. These funds should possess capital appreciation objectives and betas greater than 1.00. If direct investment in large firm stocks is preferred to investment in a mutual fund, this portion of Brown's portfolio should contain from 12 to 15 different common stock issues (drawn from different industries). Stocks should be selected on the basis of their prospects for growth. Stocks with relatively high dividend yields should be avoided. It is somewhat doubtful, however, that a 12-stock portfolio could be constructed without the use of odd lot purchases. The result of this investment strategy is a portfolio whose equity portion contains greater than average risk (an average beta of approximately 1.20) and provides only a modest amount of current income. The beta of the overall portfolio is approximately 1.00, but due to investment in aggressive growth common stocks should outpace the rate of inflation by a significant amount over the long run. In addition, I strongly recommend that Brown personally manage his pension fund assets. This can be easily done by investing contributions in mutual funds. The funds selected should possess capital appreciation investment objectives and thus will contain greater than average investment risk. However, due to the tax shelter aspects of income earned in a pension program, Brown should consider equity mutual funds with a history of paying income distributions. These distributions must be automatically reinvested by the fund.

Calvin Crisp, age 57, holds an upper level management position with a consumer products firm. His annual gross income is $75,000 and he has nearly $200,000 available for stock and bond investment. His wife Corie has resumed her teaching career after raising two children and earns approximately $30,000 a year. She has regularly contributed to a teachers' pension program, and Calvin has been under a company pension program for 20 years. Calvin and Corie Crisp's other assets include equity in their home, a Florida vacation condominium and some tax-advantaged investments (primarily oil and gas limited partnerships). These assets total $200,000 (net).

Recommended investment portfolio:

Tax-exempt bond funds	$ 70,000	35%
Large firm common stocks	60,000	30
Small firm common stocks	70,000	35
Total assets	$200,000	100%

Comments:

This family's investment program should include assets oriented toward capital appreciation and those somewhat sheltered from taxes. Given their ages, income, and level of total assets, the Crisps can assume a moderate degree of risk in their investment portfolio. Thus, the recommended portfolio is tilted somewhat toward common stocks (65 percent of total financial assets). The portion of the portfolio devoted to investment in large firm common stocks should be diversified among 15 different issues with approximately an equal dollar amount invested in each. The large firm stocks selected should possess moderate betas (from 1.00 to 1.20) and relatively low current dividend yields. The Crisps should keep the taxable returns from this segment of the portfolio to a minimum and take a moderately aggressive posture to increase real wealth over the long run. The $70,000 invested in tax-exempt bonds, provided that maturities are kept to two years or less, will provide a degree of needed liquidity as well as offset some of the risk assumed in the equity portion of the overall portfolio. They can use the current income provided by this portion of the portfolio to accumulate additional shares of common stocks on price dips. They should invest the small firm common stock portion of the portfolio in approximately 20 different common stock issues. Because the Crisps are nearing retirement age, I suggest less concentration of investment in individual small firms. Spreading investment dollars among many firms reduces the possibility of capital losses due to firm failure. The Crisps should spread additional capital committed to small firm stocks among an even larger number of firms, perhaps 40 different issues. The common stocks they choose for the small firm portfolio segment should possess low to modest current dividend yields and moderate betas (from 0.90 to 1.20). The equity portion of their portfolio will possess a beta of approximately 1.10, and the beta of their entire portfolio will be less than 0.80. Overall, this is only a modestly aggressive portfolio; it should protect against loss of purchasing power while at the same time giving the Crisps only a modest degree of risk exposure.

Donald Downes, age 65, recently retired. His wife Dora, age 62, has terminated her employment so that she and her husband have time to travel. The Downes' total annual pension income from all sources is $36,000. They have $400,000 available for stock and bond investment. They own their own home and possess other assets totaling $300,000. The Downes need additional income to support their intended lifestyle; yet as young retirees, they want to protect their investment portfolio and income against erosion in value due to the effects of inflation.

Recommended investment portfolio:

Bond and money funds	$150,000	38%
Large firm common stocks	150,000	38
Small firm common stocks	100,000	24
Total assets	$400,000	100%

Comments:

The Downes' overall portfolio should not only stress income and safety but also provide an inflation hedge. An annual rate of inflation averaging 3 percent doubles consumer prices after approximately 24 years. The bond and money fund portion of the overall portfolio should provide income necessary to supplement current consumption needs. However, I suggest that the maturity of this portion of the portfolio be kept relatively short. Bonds should not possess maturities greater than five years (one-to-three-year maturities are preferable); they should invest some portion of this portfolio segment in a money market fund or insured money market bank account. Because the yields on short-term bonds and money market funds move in step with rising interest rates, they provide some protection against the erosion of portfolio value due to rising interest rates.

The large and small firm common stock portion of the overall portfolio should provide an offset against inflation and increase in real value over the long run. As young retirees, Don and Dora Downes should still be concerned about long-run portfolio performance. Although retired persons attempt to maximize current income by investing heavily in long-term bonds of all types, I believe this to be faulty investment strategy. They can obtain both the required degree of safety and sufficient current income from a portfolio containing money market assets, short-term bonds, and the right kind of common stocks. The large firm common stock portion of the overall investment portfolio should contain at least 15 different issues. These issues should have a history of paying from 40 to 60 percent of earnings out in cash dividends and possess high current yields from 4 to 8 percent given the current market environment. Also, these stocks should possess low betas (0.70 to 1.00). The small firm stock portion of the equity portfolio should contain at least 25 different issues. These issues should also possess low betas and relatively high current yields. The Downes' overall portfolio beta should be approximately 0.60. It is somewhat conservative, yet possesses capital appreciation potential.

As you have probably noticed, all of the recommended portfolios consisted of a combination of money market assets or very short-term maturity bond funds, common stocks of large firms, and the common stocks of smaller firms. I recommend that investors avoid investment in long-term bonds no matter how attractive their current yields appear. The record speaks loudly to the dismal real returns of long-term bonds. Over the past 50 years, they have provided investment returns significantly below those provided by common stocks. Furthermore, as was seen in the 1970s and 1980s, the market values of long-term bond portfolios can take tremendous beatings. Finance researchers and practitioners are becoming aware that the process of rolling over one-year bonds or investment in money market instruments provides greater returns at far less risk than do investments in long-term bonds. As one disgruntled bond investor put it: "Sell bonds on good news—and also on bad news."

Also apparent in these recommendations is my belief that investors of every stripe—aggressive and conservative, young and old—should hold a portion of their assets in a diversified portfolio of the common stocks of smaller equity capitalization firms. For the investor highly averse to risk, this portion of the portfolio should be approximately 10 to 20 percent of the overall portfolio. For the more aggressive investor, the small firm common stock portion could be as great as 80 percent. Finally, I recommend a combination of investment in both large firm and small firm common stocks for nearly all investors. This recommendation is made on the belief that common stock investment risk can be reduced by combining equities of small and large firms. Because of their relatively low correlation of returns with one another, this mixture produces a decrease in overall volatility of the portfolio.

Figure 10-1 illustrates the various percentages of assets

FIGURE 10–1
Summary of Recomended Investment Portfolios

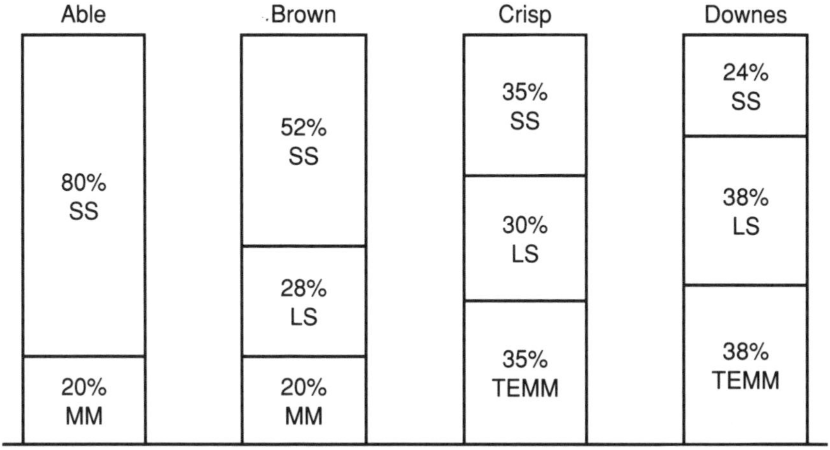

Able	Brown	Crisp	Downes
			24% SS
	52% SS	35% SS	
80% SS			38% LS
	28% LS	30% LS	
			38% TEMM
20% MM	20% MM	35% TEMM	

MM-Money market mutual funds
TEMM-Tax exempt money market
mutual funds

LS-Common stock of large firms
SS-Common stock of small firms

held by our four hypothetical investors. Able does not need current income and can afford to assume relatively high investment risks. Brown wants to assume slightly less risk than Able and is willing to accept a little more current return. Crisp is willing to assume modest investment risk and desires some capital appreciation. Downes needs a high current yield and will sleep better with a low level of investment risk. Collectively, they form a spectrum of investor objectives and risk sensitivities into which most people would fit.

If you don't find yourself in this diagram, don't be surprised. We are all different. Still, you can use these hypothetical portfolios as the cloth from which to cut and tailor your own. To do this, identify the two hypothetical investors whose personal characteristics most closely approximate your own. Look at their portfolios in Figure 10-1, and interpolate between them as appropriate. The various percentages recommended for each segment of these portfolios should provide the upper and lower boundaries for each segment of your portfolio. Simply modify these percentages according to your own needs and desires.

Of course, the recommendations given here are made for only the financial asset portion of the overall personal portfolio. Most people have nonfinancial assets—precious metals, jewelery, or real estate—which are not a part of this discussion. Even with this limitation, hopefully this analysis will, give you some guidance in managing your own investment portfolio.

CHAPTER 11

USING MUTUAL FUNDS TO CAPTURE THE SMALL FIRM EFFECT

A mutual fund is a corporation chartered to conduct business as an investment company. As such, its sole business and reason for existing is to invest in a pool of financial assets. In general, investment companies are corporations that obtain money by selling their own stock. The proceeds of such sales are invested in a variety of securities issued by government entities or corporations. Thus, any income received by investment company shareholders results from income produced by the investment company's portfolio of stocks or bonds. Furthermore, the price of an investment company's shares is related to the market value of the securities in the company's investment portfolio.

Open-end mutual funds are perhaps the most well-known investment companies. Fund shareholders elect a board of directors who in turn hire an investment advisory firm to manage the firm's investment portfolio. Open-end funds are aptly named because the number of shares outstanding continually changes. New investors purchase shares of the fund from a salesperson for load funds or directly from the fund for no-load funds. When such purchases are made, the fund issues new shares priced at the fund's net asset value per share for no-load funds or at the per share net asset value plus a sales commission for load funds. Individuals wishing to terminate their fund share holdings sell them directly to the fund at a price equal to the per share net asset value of the fund. Shares sold to the fund are then canceled. Each day funds determine their per share net asset value by taking the total market value of the fund's portfolio of assets less any outstanding liabilities divided by the number of fund shares outstanding at the end of the day.

Mutual fund shareholders thus participate in common stock and bond investment indirectly. That is, fund management makes purchases and sales in the shareholders' behalf. Any income earned on these investments is passed along to shareholders. The fund is considered a conduit by the IRS and thus pays no taxes on income earned and distributed to shareholders. Shareholders, on the other hand, are taxed the same as if they had earned income from direct investment in stocks or bonds.

THE BENEFITS OF MUTUAL FUND INVESTING

The greatest benefit of investing in common stocks via mutual funds is the risk reduction obtained by holding a widely diversified portfolio. First, mutual funds eliminate the risk of permanent, catastrophic loss. Second, diversified portfolios of common stocks contain much less price volatility than do individual stocks. The prices of risky assets, such as individual common stocks, are highly volatile—they can rise and fall by significant amounts in a short period of time. Some stocks fall in price, never to rise again. But stock prices, when taken in aggregate (e.g., the S&P 500 Index) have always moved to higher ground— even after significant drops over prolonged periods of time.

Analysts measure investment risk by the volatility of investment return. The greater the volatility, the greater the investment risk. Modern investment theory tells us that the risk of a single investment consists of two components: systematic (market-related) risk and unsystematic (company-specific) risk. We also know that the average common stock contains 30 percent market risk and 70 percent company-specific risk. That is, 30 percent of the variability in the price of a single stock is related to the ups and downs in the stock market while 70 percent of the variation is related to specific company factors. This is an extremely important point because proper portfolio diversification eliminates all company-specific risk without sacrificing one bit of portfolio investment return. And that's what mutual funds can do for you.

A second benefit of mutual fund investment is simplified record-keeping. Anyone who has held 40 or 50 common stocks in a portfolio at a given point in time knows the trouble caused by scores of dividend checks which must be cashed and reinvested in additional shares. Keeping track of cash dividend payments, stock splits, interest payments, purchase and sale prices, and brokerage commissions and fees is demanding work.

With mutual fund investments, management receives and reinvests dividends and interest payments from its investments and ultimately pays out this investment income to fund shareholders in a single check. Also, fund investors, through automatic distribution reinvestment plans, can instantly reinvest fund distributions in additional fund shares and thus gain the full advantage of compound growth. Finally, each mutual fund shareholder is sent an annual report indicating the returns earned and transactions made during the year. This report is especially convenient at tax time.

A third benefit of mutual fund investment is that investors obtain a high degree of liquidity by investing this way. That is, it is easy to become fully invested in a diversified portfolio of common stocks (or bonds) in a short time. Rather than placing buy or sell orders for the 20 to 50 stocks in an individually managed portfolio, a fund investor can get in or out of the market with a single buy or sell order. Many money market mutual funds offer a telephone switching service allowing investors to make a 180 degree turn in investment posture from stocks to cash.

The fourth advantage of fund investment is the presence of low-cost professional management. For a management fee of as little as 0.5 percent, investors obtain full-time management governed by a strict investment strategy as outlined in the fund's prospectus. Thus, to some degree, the investment portfolio is managed by rationality rather than by emotion. Fund managers must stick to the investment objectives outlined in the prospectus and are not free to follow the investment fad of the day.

These professional investment managers work on behalf of

shareholders. The fund's advisor or manager determines the specific issues to be purchased, the timing of such purchases, and the proportions of various assets held by the fund. Investors who cannot afford to hire professional analysts or portfolio managers to guide them obtain such guidance at a modest cost through mutual fund investments because the management fees charged are divided on a pro rata basis. In addition, the fund management bears the cost of data collection, information processing, and portfolio tracking. Thus, mutual fund shareholders can avail themselves of modern investment management technology at minimal cost.

THE SMALL FIRM EFFECT REVISITED

Up until about a dozen years ago, almost all academics and more than a few professional investors subscribed to the notion that the U.S. stock market was highly efficient. That is, securities are generally priced to yield returns based solely on the amount of nondiversifiable risk that they contain. In a truly efficient market, there can be no bargains: Some investors cannot obtain an advantage over other investors by purchasing undervalued assets or selling those that are overvalued. All assets are—in theory—fairly priced. In this efficient market, portfolio managers must establish the level of portfolio risk they choose to live with and then buy and hold a randomly selected portfolio of assets with the desired risk/return characteristics. It's a no-brainer. Efficient market disbelievers like to tell the story of three efficient market academics on a field trip to Wall Street (the real world). At the famous corner of Wall Street and Broad they spot a $100 bill lying on the sidewalk. Since these efficient market theoreticians know that there can be no undisclosed values or so-called free lunches in an efficient market, the professors reason that the $100 bill cannot really be there. So they continue their stroll, leaving the $100 bill behind. A bag lady spots it and eats well for the next week.

With the publication of research on the risk/return relationship of the stocks of small firms by Rolf Banz in 1978, a few cracks in the walls of the so-called efficient market hypothesis began to appear. Banz discovered that a widely diversified portfolio of small firm common stocks consistently produced rates of return larger than could be accounted for by portfolio risk.

Small firm common stock returns above those necessary to compensate for the investment risk that is assumed clearly violate the efficient market hypothesis. And if such excess returns did exist, one would reason that, once discovered by a number of market players, subsequent trading actions should cause the prices of small firm stocks to nearly instantaneously adjust upward until the excess returns disappeared. However, the small firm effect continues to persist even though its existence is known by a great number of individual and professional investors.

How big is this investment free lunch? Small firm common stock investors can earn from 0.2 to 0.5 percent per month more than they should earn given the level of risk that they assume. Small firm stocks have persistently rewarded their investors with superior investment returns. For example, over the last 20 years small firm common stock investors' wealth would have grown by 1,526 percent, while that of large firm common stock investors would have expanded by only 948 percent. That's a large difference!

Admittedly, the ride has been bumpy for small stock investors. Although small firm stocks have outpaced those of larger firm common stocks over the long run, they have not produced superior rates of return during each and every year. In fact, from 1984 through 1990, the return of the large-cap dominated S&P 500 Index exceeded that of small-cap stocks during six of the seven years. During that period, the S&P 500 Index returned a total of 241 percent versus a total of only 20 percent for small-cap stocks.

SMALL FIRM RETURNS: A RATIONALE

The reason why small firm common stocks produce excess risk adjusted rates of return is still open to conjecture. Whatever the reason, it's surely not because the firms are small. Instead, size must be a proxy for one or more true factors highly related to firm size.

The most plausible explanation appears to be that a lack of information about small firms causes investors to lavish their attentions and investment dollars on larger firms. (See Chapter 6 for a more complete explanation.) Smaller firms receive infinitely less attention from professional stock analysts and institutional investors (who rely heavily on the advice of professional stock analysts). Because supply and demand determine share price, the lack of demand for small firm stocks causes their prices to be less than they otherwise would be given their fundamental earnings and growth prospects. Thus, the stocks of small firms are more likely to be underpriced (relative to their risk) than are the stocks of large firms, which may even be overpriced due to the extreme attention they receive from institutional investors.

Why, then, don't institutional investors tap into the small firm market segment and extract the extra return that these firms provide? Although institutional investors would like to enter this segment of the market, transaction costs generally prohibit them from doing so. A recent study of institutional trading costs by Thomas Loeb, a vice president of Wells Fargo Investment Advisors, vividly illustrates the trading barrier that all but prohibits institutional investment in small equity capitalization firms. Institutional investors aren't like us; they don't buy stocks in 100- to 300-share lots. With assets running into the billions of dollars, these institutions possess too much money to make anything but 10,000- to 100,000-share transactions. This is no problem when they wheel and deal with the IBMs and AT&Ts—firms with tens or hundreds of million shares outstanding. When they enter the thin markets of small firm stocks, however, they are like giants trodding through a small village. They shake up the whole place and seriously disturb share pricing. When institutional investors buy and sell large blocks of stock, they must offer market makers a price concession to affect a timely trade. The result is a widening of the so-called dealer's bid-ask spread. For common stocks of firms with equity capitalizations between $25 million and $100 million, Loeb found the average bid-ask spread for a 100 share trade to be 2.32 percent. An institutional trader who is interested in making a $1 million trade would find the bid-ask spread widening to an average of 17 percent—or 34 percent for a round-trip. In a nutshell, the stock has to go up 34 percent for the institution to break even! On the other hand, the same round-trip trade in the common stock of a firm whose equity capitalization exceeds $500 million produces an average trading cost of 4 percent. It is of little wonder, then, that institutional investors generally avoid firms with equity capitalizations less than $100 million. Trading costs are just too high in this market segment. Instead, institutional investors conduct the bulk of their business in the shares of the giants of corporate America.

THE BEST WAY TO INVEST IN SMALL FIRM STOCKS

Given that small firm stocks and their excess investment returns are readily available to individual investors, it is surprising to me that so few individuals make a concerted effort to capture them. Of course, investing in small firms may entail more work. First, investors must do their own homework because most of the recommendations made by stockbrokers are based on the research of their firm's analysts who concentrate their attention on the large capitalization stocks that institutions can buy.

Second, investors in small firms must hold a more widely diversified portfolio. My firm's research shows that it takes at least 14 different small firm stock issues (and upwards of 50) to provide the same degree of risk reduction as is obtainable by holding as few as 10 large firm common stocks. Thus, the capital requirements may be too steep for many individuals who want to hold a diversified portfolio.

Finally, small firm stock investors must possess a lot of one very rare commodity—patience. Small firms are generally growth-oriented firms. They pay very little in current dividends, choosing instead to reinvest most of their earnings in future growth. It often takes several years for the strategies of these small firms to materialize and be recognized in higher stock prices. Even though individual investors are not subject to the same pressures for short-term results as are institutional money managers, most people do not have the patience to wait five or more years for small firms to produce results.

Thus, limited time, scant financial resources, and investor temperament often preclude individuals from investing in small firm stocks directly. For these individuals, mutual funds may provide the appropriate entry into this market segment.

MUTUAL FUNDS AND THE SMALL FIRM EFFECT

These days more than 100 open-end mutual funds include the phrases "small firm" or "emerging growth" in their statement of investment objectives. These funds attempt to capture the small firm effect by concentrating their investments in small firms with the potential to grow at a faster rate than the economy as a whole. Of course, because mutual funds are themselves institutional investors, one might logically ask whether or not this is a paradox. That is, if the most likely reason for the existence of the small firm effect is the lack of institutional investor interest, can small firm mutual funds really deliver the goods?

The answer to this question is: maybe. There is no doubt in my mind that some recently organized small firm funds have no intention of capturing the full small firm effect. Instead, they are attempting to capture investor dollars by advertising themselves as something they are not. For example, I recently examined a new fund's prospectus which stated that it would attempt to capture the small firm effect by investing only in those companies with equity capitalizations below $500 million dollars. Because academic research indicates that small firms are generally those with equity capitalizations below $120 million, it is doubtful that this fund's management can be successful in producing excess risk-adjusted investment returns.

Although this fund may be an exception, the truth is that most of the mutual funds investing in small firms must operate in the second tier of the market—the stocks of firms that are no longer very small. Because of limited liquidity and excessive transaction costs, most small firm funds invest in firms with equity capitalizations between $200 million and $1 billion. Thus, even those funds with legitimate intentions cannot deliver the full amount of the small firm effect. Indications are, however, that they may capture a portion of the effect. These funds cannot deliver a free lunch, yet they may at least offer an hors d'oeuvre. Thus, the best way to capture the small firm effect in its entirety is to invest in small firms directly, if you can.

MUTUAL FUND PERFORMANCE AND MARKET CAPITALIZATION

Only recently has the performance of mutual funds that invest in small firm common stocks come under research scrutiny. A recent study examined the risk-adjusted net return performance of mutual funds grouped according to the size of the companies they invest in.[1] Researchers categorized the investment returns over the period 1975–83 for 254 mutual funds as aggressive growth, growth, or income and growth. Next, they determined the weighted average market capitalization of each fund's common stock investment. Then they split the 254 funds into three groups. The small equity capitalization group consisted of 50 funds with the smallest company holdings. The medium equity capitalization group consisted of the next 154 smallest funds, and the large equity capitalization group contained the funds with the largest holdings.

Researchers obtained the average monthly returns for these three fund groups for 6 three-year intervals. Then they obtained risk-adjusted investment returns for each group for each three-year interval. To find risk-adjusted excess returns (called *alpha*) they applied a statistical technique called *ordinary least squares regression analysis*.

------

[1] Gerald P. Madden, Kenneth P. Nunn, Jr., and Alan Wiemann, "Mutual Fund Performance and Market Capitalization," *Financial Analysts Journal,* July–August 1986, pp. 67–70.

TABLE 11–1
Excess Investment Return (Alpha) and Size of Fund Holdings

Period Ending	Equity Capitalization Funds (percent)		
	Smallest	Medium	Largest
June 1978	9.2%	5.4%	1.2%
June 1979	12.5	7.4	2.3
June 1980	12.2	6.4	2.4
June 1981	5.9	3.8	0.9
June 1982	5.3	4.9	1.2
June 1983	5.5	4.6	0.4
Average	8.4%	5.4%	1.4%

Source: Gerald P. Madden et al., "Mutual Fund Performance and Market Capitalization," *Financial Analysts Journal*, July–August 1986, p. 68.

Table 11–1 illustrates the average alphas for various three-year periods for each fund group. The group of funds which held the shares of the smallest equity capitalization firms produced the greatest alphas for all periods. Remember, the greater the value of alpha, the greater the investment returns. The alpha for the small company fund group averaged 8.4 percent. That's 8.4 percent more each year than they should have, given the riskiness of their portfolios. On the other hand, the average alpha of the funds investing in large company common stocks was 1.4 percent. Thus, while mutual funds, on average, provided excess risk-adjusted investment returns, small company funds yielded the largest investment free lunch.

SMALL FIRM MUTUAL FUND SELECTION

For investors who can't invest directly, the mutual fund route is better than avoiding the small-cap segment of the market completely. But these investors must apply a set of rigid screens when selecting such funds.

First and foremost, small-cap funds must concentrate their investments in firms that are truly small. (Remember, the strict definition of a small-cap firm is one with a market value of equity below $120 million.) Although more than 100 mutual funds "claim" to invest in small-cap stocks, less than a handful allocate the bulk of their assets to these stocks. Instead, most invest in the mid-cap sector of the market (i.e., companies with equity caps ranging from $150 million to $500 million). Thus, I suggest that you investigate before you invest in these funds. One of the best mutual fund data sources is *Morningstar Mutual Funds,* a subscription service located in Chicago (1-800-876-5005). This service provides a wealth of mutual fund statistics for more than 1,200 publicly available funds. Included in these statistics is the median market-cap of its portfolio of stocks. If the median market-cap for a particular fund is below $120 million, more than half of its investments are small-cap stocks.

Second, since it takes time for small firms to grow, select only those funds whose investment managers have exhibited patience. Look for those funds with average annual turnover ratios of less than 40 percent. The reciprocal of the turnover ratio indicates a fund's average holding period. For example, a fund with a 40 percent turnover ratio is holding on to its investments for an average of two and one half years (1.0/0.40 = 2.5). When evaluating small firm funds, the lower the average turnover ratio, the better I like it.

Third, look at the total amount of money that the fund has under management. Funds with an extremely high level of total assets may find it very difficult to operate in the small firm market sector. For example, a fund with $1 billion in total assets must either diversify across at least 1,000 different small firm stock issues or concentrate its investments in larger firms to avoid the large transaction costs that accompany large block trades. On the other hand, a fund with $100 million or less in total assets can easily diversify across 100 or less small firm stocks without experiencing significantly large transaction costs. When evaluating a fund on the basis of total assets, look for funds with less than $300 to $400 million under management. The smaller the amount of total assets, the better I like the fund.

Fourth, look for funds whose long-term performance is better than average for the group of small firm funds. Although superior past performance is no guarantee of above-average future performance, investing in small firms is a tricky business for institutional investors. Many fund managers are not used to operating in the small firm market sector; as a result they may experience larger transaction costs than they should. Furthermore, large investment commitments are easier to make when a large block of stock is offered for sale. Sometimes the seller has unique insights into future corporate events. Thus, when buying small firm stocks in blocks, some fund managers get picked off by sellers who are making the offer in anticipation of impending bad news. Therefore, when making small firm fund recommendations, I place a great deal of attention on the capabilities of fund management.

SMALL-CAP FUNDS

Table 11-2, at the end of this chapter, contains a list of mutual funds that use the phrase "small-cap" or "emerging growth" in the description of their investment objectives contained in their prospectuses. To assist in fund evaluation, I have included a few descriptive items and a summary of each fund's financial characteristics. Telephone numbers have been included so that you may easily obtain a fund prospectus, annual report, latest quarterly report, and statement of additional information. Since financial statistics can change quickly, these documents should be examined before making an initial investment. Excluded from this list are small-cap funds that have closed their doors to new investors.

Of the 71 small-cap funds contained in this list, note that 57 began operations after the publication of Rolf Banz's work on the "small firm effect." Note, also, that the vast majority of these funds' portfolios possess median equity-caps far above the $120 million small-cap threshold. Furthermore, it appears that many of these small-cap portfolio managers are quick to pull the trigger on their investments. Two dozen of these funds have portfolio turnover ratios in excess of 100 percent (i.e., average equity holding periods of less than one year).

TABLE 11-2
Small Firm Mutual Funds

Fund Name	Year Begun	Portfolio Manager	Sales Fee	Total Assets ($ mill)	Median Market Cap ($ mill)	Portfolio Turnover %	Expense Ratio %	Beta	Telephone
Advantage Special	1986	Robert L. Thomas	4.00%	$7	$354	29%	2.88%	1.16	800-243-8115
Alger Small Capitalization	1986	David Alger	(1)	136	520	171	2.20	1.37	800-992-3863
American Capital Emerging Growth	1970	Gary Lewis	5.75	308	993	69	1.14	1.37	800-421-5666 816-471-5200
Babson Enterprise II	1991	James/Schliemann	NL	7	521	—	1.49	—	800-422-2766 212-759-7700
Baron Asset	1987	Ron Baron	NL	42	335	104	1.60	1.21	800-992-2766 617-426-3750
Colonial Small Stock Index	1986	Stephen A. Lanzendorf	5.75	22	84	79	2.06	0.91	800-248-2828 503-222-3606
Columbia Special	1985	Alan J. Folkman et al.	NL	330	516	99	1.19	1.44	800-547-1707
Dean Witter Developing Growth Secs	1983	Robert Kimtis	5.00	138	167	88	1.88	—	212-392-2550 800-869-3863
DFA Small Company	1981	Jeanne C. Sinquefield	NL	635	54	10	.64	0.96	310-395-8005 718-895-1206
Dreyfus New Leaders	1985	Thomas A. Frank	(2)	200	290	108	1.29	0.97	800-645-6561 914-694-2020
Evergreen Fund	1971	Stephen A. Lieber	NL	726	1,105	35	1.14	1.14	800-235-0064 914-694-2020
Evergreen Limited Market	1983	Robin D. Kelly	NL	57	68	55	1.25	0.80	800-235-0064 518-234-7543
FAM Value	1987	Putnam/Van Buren	NL	21	171	14	1.49	0.72	800-932-3271

Fund Name	Year Begun	Portfolio Manager	Sales Fee	Total Assets ($ mill)	Median Market Cap ($ mill)	Portfolio Turnover %	Expense Ratio %	Beta	Telephone
Fasciano Fund	1987	Michael F. Fasciano	NL	$10	$359	29%	1.70%	0.85	312-444-6050 800-848-6050
Fidelity Emerging Growth	1990	Larry Bowman	3.00	511	1,658	558	1.12	—	800-544-8888
Fidelity Low-Priced Stock	1989	Joel Tillinghast	(3)	850	96	82	1.20	—	800-544-8888
Fidelity OTC	1984	Alan Radlo	3.00	1,032	377	245	1.17	0.97	800-544-8888 303-394-4404
Founders Discovery	1989	Michael Haines et al.	NL	55	170	134	1.97	—	800-525-2440 303-394-4404
Founders Frontier	1987	Michael Haines et al.	NL	106	616	171	1.84	1.23	800-525-2440 310-473-0225
FPA Capital	1968	Robert Rodriquez	6.50	100	377	13	1.08	1.49	800-982-4372
Gabelli Small-Cap Growth	1991	Mario J. Gabelli	NL	89	228	—	2.08	—	914-921-5100 800-422-3554
GIT Special Growth	1983	Richard Carney	NL	55	273	24	1.39	0.82	703-528-6550 800-336-3063
Gradison-McDonald Opportunity Value	1983	William Leugers	NL	47	310	64	1.49	0.94	513-579-5700 800-869-5999
John Hancock Special Equities	1985	Michael P. DiCarlo	4.50	33	646	163	2.14	1.40	800-225-5291 617-338-3400
Hartwell Emerging Growth	1968	John M. Hartwell	4.75	143	641	137	1.56	1.60	800-343-2898 414-347-7276
Heartland Value	1984	Nasgovitz/Denison	4.50	35	40	79	1.80	0.91	800-432-7856

Fund Name	Year Begun	Portfolio Manager	Sales Fee	Total Assets ($ mill)	Median Market Cap ($ mill)	Portfolio Turnover %	Expense Ratio %	Beta	Telephone
IDS									
Discovery	1981	Ray E. Hirsch	5.00	$273	$951	90%	1.04%	1.22	612-671-3733
Kemper Small									800-328-8300
Capitalization Equity	1969	C. Beth Cotner	5.75	303	1,019	126	1.27	1.22	312-781-1121
Lazard									800-621-1048
Special Equity	1986	Dana Smith	NL	131	163	19	1.72	0.68	212-632-6000
Legg Mason									800-228-0203
Special Investment	1985	William H. Miller III	NL	205	504	57	2.10	0.89	301-539-3400
Loomis Sayles									800-822-5544
Small-Cap	1991	Dillon/Friedman	NL	23	224	142	1.50	—	617-482-2450
Lord Abbett									800-633-3330
Developing Growth	1973	John A. Gibbons	5.75	130	443	13	1.14	1.31	212-848-1800
Meridian Fund	1984	Richard F. Aster, Jr.	NL	18	573	61	1.74	1.10	800-874-3733
									415-461-6237
Merrill Lynch									800-446-6662
Special Value A	1978	Dennis Slattman	6.50	53	168	99	1.55	1.03	609-282-2800
MFS									800-637-3863
Emerging Growth	1981	Donald F. Pitcher, Jr.	5.75	234	367	114	1.43	1.45	617-954-5000
MFS Lifetime									800-225-2606
Emerging Growth	1986	John W. Ballen	(4)	255	602	112	2.28	1.65	617-954-5000
Morgan Stanley									800-225-2606
Emerging Growth	1989	Dennis Sherva	NL	74	489	2	1.25	—	800-548-7786
Neuberger & Berman									212-476-8800
Genesis	1988	Stephen A. Milman	NL	69	290	23	2.00	1.03	800-877-9700
Nicholas II	1983	Albert O. Nicholas	NL	623	490	15	0.64	0.88	414-272-6133

Fund Name	Year Begun	Portfolio Manager	Sales Fee	Total Assets ($ mill)	Median Market Cap ($ mill)	Portfolio Turnover %	Expense Ratio %	Beta	Telephone
Oberweis Emerging Growth	1987	James Oberweis	NL	$32	$95	114%	2.01%	1.40	708-897-7100
Oppenheimer Discovery	1986	Jay W. Tracey, III	5.75	261	352	158	1.34	1.23	800-323-6166 303-671-3200
Parkstone Small Capitalization	1988	Roger H. Stamper et al.	4.50	180	252	95	1.19	1.26	800-525-7048 614-899-4668
PBHG Growth	1985	Gary Pilgrim	4.75	6	351	115	1.52	1.51	800-451-8377 713-750-8000
Pennsylvania Mutual	1962	Royce/Ebright	(2)	924	242	35	0.91	0.75	800-262-6631 212-355-7311
Perritt Capital Growth	1988	Gerald W. Perritt	NL	8	72	37	2.50	0.78	800-221-4268 312-649-6940
Pioneer Three	1982	Robert W. Benson	5.75	759	394	5	0.74	0.97	800-338-1579 617-742-7825
T. Rowe Price New Horizons	1960	John H. Laporte	NL	1,198	633	33	0.96	1.32	800-225-6292 301-547-2308
T. Rowe Price Over-the-Counter Securities	1956	Greg McCrickard	NL	220	122	31	1.34	0.96	800-638-5660 301-547-2306
T. Rowe Price Small-Cap Value	1988	Preston Athey	NL	157	92	31	1.25	0.76	800-638-5660 301-547-2306
Prudential Growth Opportunity B	1980	Richard P. Fetch	(1)	162	378	111	2.16	0.93	800-638-5660 800-225-1852
Putnam OTC Emerging Growth	1982	Richard Jodka	5.75	253	345	67	1.39	1.39	617-292-1000 800-225-1581
Robertson Stephens Emerging Growth	1987	Robert C. Czepiel	NL	197	265	112	1.37	1.36	415-781-9700 800-766-3863

Fund Name	Year Begun	Portfolio Manager	Sales Fee	Total Assets ($ mill)	Median Market Cap ($ mill)	Portfolio Turnover %	Expense Ratio %	Beta	Telephone
Royce Value	1982	Royce/Ebright	2.50	$165	$227	22%	1.81%	0.76	212-355-7311
Rushmore OTC Index Plus	1985	Daniel O'Connor et al.	NL	21	3,136	443	0.90	1.45	800-221-4268 301-657-1500
Scudder Development	1971	Moran/McKay	NL	693	525	54	1.30	1.42	800-343-3355 617-439-4640
Selected Special Shares	1939	Jim Smith	NL	50	688	74	1.39	0.92	800-225-2470 800-426-6562
Shadow Stock	1987	Schliemann/Whitridge	NL	25	73	23	1.26	0.79	816-471-5200 800-422-2766
Shearson Special Equities	1982	George V. Novello	(1)	62	654	379	2.32	1.18	212-464-8068 800-451-2010
Sit "New Beginning" Growth	1981	Douglas C. Jones	NL	241	1,304	25	0.83	1.25	612-332-3223 800-332-5580
Skyline Special Equities	1987	Bill Dutton	NL	56	232	120	1.53	1.05	312-670-6035 800-458-5222
Southeastern Small-Cap	1988	Mason Hawkins	NL	58	125	65	1.42	0.69	901-761-2474 800-445-9469
Twentieth Century Giftrust Investors	1983	James Stower et al.	NL	71	236	136	1.00	1.71	816-531-5575 800-345-2021
Twentieth Century Ultra Investors	1981	James Stower et al.	NL	3,757	1,095	39	1.00	1.57	816-531-5575 800-345-2021
Twentieth Century Vista Investors	1983	James Stower et al.	NL	777	889	84	1.00	1.62	816-531-5575 800-345-2021
United New Concepts	1983	Mark G. Seferovich	8.50	148	545	74	1.23	1.22	913-236-2000 800-366-5465

Fund Name	Year Begun	Portfolio Manager	Sales Fee	Total Assets ($ mill)	Median Market Cap ($ mill)	Portfolio Turnover %	Expense Ratio %	Beta	Telephone
Vanguard Explorer	1967	Wisneski/Granahan	NL	$458	$170	47%	0.65%	1.15	215-669-1000 800-662-7447
Vanguard Index Extended Market	1987	George V. Sauter	NL	446	953	10	0.21	1.05	215-669-1000 800-662-7447
Vanguard Small Capitalization Stock	1960	George V. Sauter	NL	192	227	6	0.20	1.13	215-669-1000 800-662-7447
Warburg, Pincus Emerging Growth	1988	Elizabeth Dater	NL	91	351	94	1.25	1.15	212-878-0600 800-888-6878
Winthrop Focus Aggressive Growth	1967	Haubold/Engle	(5)	34	377	169	1.85	0.97	212-504-4000 800-225-8011
WPG Growth	1986	Melville Straus	NL	159	370	103	0.95	1.30	212-908-9582 800-223-3332

(1) 5% Redemption
(2) 1% Redemption
(3) 1.5% Redemption
(4) 6% Redemption
(5) 4% Redemption

Source: Morningstar, Inc., 53 W. Jackson Blvd., Chicago, IL 60604, 800-876-5005. Although gathered from reliable sources, data accuracy and completeness cannot be guaranteed. Morningstar assumes no responsibility for any incorrect information.

Although all of these funds have the potential to produce handsome short-term returns, for many that potential comes from the assumption of highly aggressive strategies and higher-than-average risks. Remember, if you want to capture the bulk of the small firm effect, you must invest in true small-cap stocks and have the patience to hold your investments for long-term capital appreciation. Thus, when selecting a small-cap fund you must seek one that has adopted this strategy as well.

During the last three years, more than a dozen small-cap funds have become closed to new investors. These funds have chosen to do so because their popularity with investors attracted so much new money that it was becoming more difficult to concentrate the funds' portfolios in the true small-cap sector of the market. Conversations with small-cap portfolio managers indicate that those who prefer to invest in small-cap stocks exclusively begin to experience problems when fund assets exceed $200 to $300 million.

Small-cap funds tend to fall into three distinct groups: aggressive growth, value growth, and index funds. Aggressive growth small-cap funds place a premium on a company's growth rate. Many of these aggressive funds will invest in a company only if it is capable of growing at better than 20 percent annually. As you might expect, these funds' portfolios are packed with stocks that are selling at extremely high price-earnings multiples. As a result, their share prices tend to be extremely volatile. They are capable of producing substantial returns during a bull market but are also liable to crash during a bear market. These funds are appropriate investments only for aggressive investors who can afford to assume substantial risks. Value funds tend to invest in the stocks of small-cap firms that sell at modest multiples of revenues, earnings, and book values. These funds are far less volatile than aggressive growth funds, on both the upside and the downside. Index funds attempt to duplicate the return of the small firm segment of the market in general either by replicating a small firm stock index, such as the Russell 2000 Index, or by investing in the entire universe of small firm stocks. The risk and return of these funds tends to fall between that of value growth and aggressive growth funds.

WELL-POSITIONED SMALL-CAP MUTUAL FUNDS

This section describes the investment objectives and investment strategies of seven mutual funds that invest a significant portion of their assets in true small firm stocks. Each fund, near year-end 1992, had at least 50 percent of its common stock investments concentrated in companies with equity capitalization below $200 million. In addition, these funds possess below-average portfolio turnover ratios and modest management expense ratios. All appear to be well positioned to capture the small firm effect and are worth further scrutiny.

Babson Shadow Stock

Although actively managed by Peter Schliemann (the portfolio manager of the highly successful Babson Enterprise Fund, which is now closed to new investors), the fund looks more like a passively managed small-cap, neglected-firm index fund. At last glance it held nearly 400 small-cap stocks. When making individual stock selections, management seeks companies with equity-caps between $20 million and $110 million and those that have had annual net profits of at least $1 million for the last three years. In addition, investments are limited to companies that have relatively little professional-analyst following and those whose shares are priced above $5.

DFA Small Company Portfolio

This is a small-cap index fund that invests in all companies with market-caps between $10 million and $120 million. Its portfolio consists of approximately 1,900 small-cap stocks weighted by their relative market values (i.e., larger companies are assigned a larger allocation of fund assets). The portfolio is revised four times annually, at which time management sells the stocks of companies whose equity-caps have appreciated above $350 million and invests in the stocks of companies that have recently fallen within its target equity-cap range. With a $50,000 minimum initial investment requirement, its shares are marketed primarily to pension funds and other institutional investors.

Evergreen Limited Market Fund

This fund generally invests in small, little-known, or special-situation companies, for which there is relatively little analyst following. When making individual stock selections, portfolio manager Robin Kelly emphasizes low price-earnings multiples. As a result, the fund possesses less volatility than the typical small-cap fund. Once closed to new investors, the fund reopened its doors in late 1992. Should the recent small-cap stock rally continue, this fund will most likely close its doors to new shareholders once again.

Heartland Value Fund

This tiny fund produced exceptional returns during both 1991 and 1992. During that period, shares were sold with a 4.50 percent front-end load. Beginning in early 1993, the fund dropped its front-end sales fee and added a 3 percent redemption fee that is reduced to zero for shares held four years or longer. Investors seeking the smallest of small-cap stocks may find this fund their cup of tea. Its $40 million median equity-cap is the lowest of any equity fund. When making individual stock selections, portfolio manager Bill Nasgovitz seeks companies with below-market price-earnings multiples, cash flow greater than earnings, accelerating earnings, a discount to book value, and long-term debt less than 25 percent of total capital.

Perritt Capital Growth Fund

This fund seeks long-term capital appreciation by investing in the common stocks of companies with equity-caps between $10 million and $120 million. When selecting stocks, portfolio manager Gerald Perritt (the author of this book) seeks firms whose shares are not widely held by institutions, those with low price-earnings multiples relative to their growth prospects, those with low levels of long-term debt, and those with a high degree of management share ownership. The fund does not place emphasis on short-term trading profits and its portfolio turnover ratio, under normal circumstances, will not excede 50 percent. As a small-cap value-oriented fund, its share price tends to be less volatile than the typical small-cap fund.

T. Rowe Price Small-Cap Value Fund

As its name suggests, this fund invests in small-cap stocks that sell at reasonable multiples of revenues, earnings, and book values. Although the fund is capable of producing better-than-average returns, its value bent keeps its volatility (on both the upside and downside) below that of most small-cap, emerging growth funds. The key to the fund's recent success has been an emphasis on small companies that have yet to be "discovered" by a large number of Wall Street analysts, coupled with patience to allow growth companies an opportunity to grow, as witnessed by its below-average 30 percent portfolio turnover ratio. Portfolio manager Preston Athey, who has been at the helm for two years, has spent several years managing small-cap portfolios for pension fund clients and is well versed in small-cap stock investing.

Vanguard Explorer

This fund recently assumed the assets of Explorer II and now operates with dual portfolio managers. It seeks long-term growth of capital by investing in common stocks of relatively small, unseasoned, or embryonic companies. In recent years, the fund has held a significant investment position in the stocks of "high tech" companies. Normally, the fund invests at least 80 percent of its assets in common stocks not generally listed on a national securities exchange, but with an established OTC market. Management anticipates that the fund's portfolio turnover ratio will not exceed 75 percent. Because of its emphasis on small, rapidly growing companies, the net asset value of the fund's shares may be expected to have relatively high volatility.

Vanguard Small Company Fund

Formerly the Naess & Thomas Special Fund, this fund changed both its name and investment strategy in 1992. It now seeks to duplicate the performance of the Russell 2000 Index (a commonly cited small-cap market index) by investing in a sample of the 2,000 stocks contained in that index. In late 1992, the fund held about 1,000 stocks, and this number will most likely be expanded as its total assets increase. Indexing has the advantage of boosting total returns by reducing operating expenses as well as maintaining a low portfolio turnover ratio that also reduces transactions costs. This fund, like other Vanguard funds, will not tolerate shareholders who engage in frequent trading.

CHAPTER 12

THE ROAD TO INVESTMENT SUCCESS: IT'S SMOOTHER THAN YOU THINK

The 1980s will long be remembered by stock market players. In late 1982 the stock market began one of the longest sustained advances in memory. From a level of 777, the Dow Jones Industrial Average had risen nearly 2,000 points by mid-1987. At that time, forecasters were predicting that the market would not top out until the DJIA pierced the 4,000 level.

Although this bull market was impressive, it has been topped by other bull markets in both the percentage rise in the DJIA and in duration. Table 12-1 lists eight of the greatest bull markets of this century.[1] The bull markets of 1921–29 and 1949–56 persisted for several months longer than the 1982–87 bull. In addition, both were accompanied by greater percentage increases in the DJIA. To beat the granddaddy of all bull markets, the current bull market would have to persist until the DJIA tops 4,640. Thus, while trees don't grow to the sky and bull markets don't last forever, redwoods grow pretty tall and some bull markets can propel stock prices to great heights before running out of steam.

The 1982–87 bull market was sparked by declining interest rates. It was further advanced by a five–year economic recovery. During its early stages, continued strength of the U.S. dollar attracted foreign investors who could magnify their stock mar-

---

[1] Because there is no exact definition of a bull market, some observers may disagree with the beginning and ending dates that I have chosen.

TABLE 12-1
The Greatest Bull Markets of the 20th Century

Trough		Peak		Percentage Increase	Duration
November	1903	January	1906	144%	27 months
December	1914	November	1919	104	23
August	1921	September	1929	497	96
February	1933	February	1934	121	12
July	1934	March	1937	127	32
April	1942	May	1946	129	49
June	1949	August	1956	222	86
August	1982	October	1987	250	63

ket profits by investing in securities denominated in the world's strongest currency.

On the home front, stocks attracted cash laden pension funds. These institutional investors had been heavy bond buyers in the late 1970s and early 1980s. But the decline in bond yields forced them to seek higher returns elsewhere. With inflation under wraps, real assets such as real estate and precious metals offered little attraction. That left common stocks as the only viable alternative for investing their cash. Furthermore, the rampant inflation of the 1970s had driven the replacement cost of factories and equipment so high that it became cheaper to buy existing facilities than to build new ones. Thus, merger and acquisition activity heightened. Leveraged buyouts (LBOs) became commonplace as investors were able to borrow at relatively low rates, make an acquisition, and sell off a portion of the firm's assets to pay down the loans.

The primary beneficiaries of this frenetic buying action were the large company stocks. Stocks with international reputations attracted foreign investors. Institutional investors, because of their sheer bulk, concentrated their buying on large company stocks. LBO pools also set their sights on large targets where the most substantial dollar profits could be made. Thus, they directed their raids toward billion dollar companies.

On the other hand, individual investors turned to mutual funds. Mutual fund sales broke all records in 1985, 1986, and 1987. Much of this money was concentrated in the bond market.

They liquidated huge amounts of their direct common stock holdings and redeployed it into fixed-income securities. As a result, a two-tier market emerged. The prices of large company stocks, such as those in the DJIA and the S&P 500 Index, soared as a result of institutional buying pressure while the prices of small firm stocks languished under the selling pressure of individual investors.

Table 12-2 lists the total returns of the S&P 500 Index and an index of small firm stocks. Small firm stocks returned more than big firm stocks during every year before 1984; that situation made a 180 degree turn beginning in 1984. Since the bull market began in August 1982, the S&P 500 Index has returned 342 percent versus 183 percent for small firm stocks. Much of the rise in small firm stocks was concentrated in late 1982 and early 1983.

As can be seen in Table 12-2, the last two years have been kind to small firm stock investors when compared to the return of the S&P Index. However, after 50 years of producing a compound annual return of more than 6 percent above that of

TABLE 12-2
Total Returns: Large Firm Stocks versus Small

Year	Small Firm Stocks	S&P 500 Index
1976	54.7%	23.8%
1977	25.4	− 7.2
1978	23.5	6.6
1979	43.5	18.4
1980	39.9	32.4
1981	13.9	− 4.9
1982	28.8	21.4
1983	39.7	22.5
1984	− 6.7	6.3
1985	24.7	32.2
1986	6.9	18.5
1987	19.9	27.5
1988	22.9	16.8
1989	10.2	31.5
1990	−21.6	− 3.2
1991	44.6	30.5
1992	16.5	6.1

their larger brothers, small firm stocks have largely taken a back seat for the past nine years.

Given the fact that the small firm effect has received so much attention in the financial press, many investors have begun to wonder if this crack in the efficient market hypothesis has been mended. (Remember that in an efficient market stock prices are supposed to rapidly adjust to the release of information.) Thus, it is logical to ask if the widespread knowledge of the small firm effect has caused small firm stocks to become more efficiently priced.

I believe the answer to this question to be a resounding no. The relative underperformance of small firm stocks is most likely a short-term phenomenon. First, it is not that small firm common stocks have performed so poorly. Rather, it's that large firm stocks have performed so well. Over the last 66 years, large firm stocks have returned an average of 12 percent per year. During this bull market they have returned nearly twice that amount. Between 1982 and 1987 small firm stocks have returned 17.3 percent annually. That's very close to their historical average. So even though small firm stocks have performed quite well in recent years, their performance pales when compared to large firm stock returns.

Second, small firm stocks returned very high rates during the late 1970s and early 1980s. During the period 1976–82 small firm stocks returned a total of 613 percent versus only 121 percent for the S&P 500 Index. By 1983 small firm stocks had become very pricey. They were selling at P-E multiples far beyond those of most blue chip firms. Thus, we can attribute much of the performance differential favoring large firm stocks to large firm stocks catching up.

By late 1990 the situation had been markedly reversed. Large company stocks were selling at historically high P-E multiples and low dividend yields. In fact, by January 1991 the S&P 500 Index was selling at more than 20 times trailing earnings and providing a scant 2.8 percent dividend yield. On the other hand, small firm stocks were selling at bargain prices. Firms with historical growth rates above 20 percent and P-E multiples below 15 were in abundance. That is, stocks with three times the growth potential of blue chip stocks were selling at a 30 percent discount based on current earnings.

HIT 'EM WHERE THEY AIN'T

With all the attention lavished on large firm stocks by institutional and foreign investors, it is tempting to jump on the bandwagon.

- "Go where the action is."
- "Buy now, sell later—at much higher prices."
- "This bull market is unique."
- "To the venturous go the biggest rewards."

These are but a few bits of ill-founded advice that get passed around when the stock market gets overheated. These bits of wisdom are not get rich quick formulas but prescriptions for disaster. Investors who follow the thundering herd are always trampled when that herd turns and heads in the opposite direction. And every bull market tends to end on the same note. When stocks are obviously overpriced, the majority of investors think that the current bull market will be different from all the rest. This time around, they think, trees will really grow to the sky.

Instead of following crowds, it is much more profitable to buy the stocks nobody wants, hold them for a while, and then sell them when they become the object of cocktail party chatter. As the legendary John Templeton reminds us: "It takes patience, discipline, and courage to buy when others are despondently selling, to sell when others are avidly buying." But if you buy stocks nobody wants, you won't have to pay much for them. If these unloved stocks represent companies with above-average sales and earnings growth, then you will have truly found an investment bargain. And bargains eventually pay off. Go where the institutional investors ain't. By investing in neglected small growth companies, you are able to obtain value at a reasonable price. Remember, small growth companies become larger over time. When they do, analysts begin to pitch them to institutional investors. Then the real fun begins. When institutional investors become so enamored with these little gems that they are willing to pay top dollar, you can accommodate them. Then, everyone is happy: The institutions get the little darlings, and you get big profits.

THE CRASH OF 1987:
SOME LESSONS TO BE LEARNED

October 19, 1987, is a day few investors will ever forget. In six short hours, the Dow Jones Industrial Average plummeted an incredible 508 points. The 22.6 percent decline in the DJIA was nearly twice that sustained October 28, 1929, the day which marked the beginning of the Great Depression. During the October 19 market meltdown, more than 600 million shares of stock changed hands on the New York Stock Exchange. That eclipsed the record 339 million share trading day recorded the previous Friday during which the DJIA sank by 108 points. During these two successive trading days, the DJIA plummeted 616 points and nearly one billion shares of stock changed hands on the NYSE alone.

The market's Monday meltdown erased more than one-half trillion dollars of investor wealth. The sell-off, which began Friday, October 16, reached panic proportions Monday morning. Because of order imbalances, 11 of the 30 stocks in the Dow Jones Industrial Average didn't open for an hour after the exchange's opening bell. By midafternoon the tape was running more than two hours and fifteen minutes late even though the NYSE's automated system can report up to 900 trades per minute. As the market continued to sink, investors unable to meet margin calls were sold out without notice. Mutual funds, whose shareholders began to flee, were forced to dump stocks at any price to raise cash to pay off their redeeming shareholders. Program traders, those who buy puts and sell stocks whenever futures prices fall significantly below existing index prices, added to the selling glut.

Although every time a share of stock is sold one is also

bought, public sell orders greatly outstripped public buy orders. As a result stock exchange specialists and over-the-counter market makers were required to make up the difference. In an attempt to bring buying and selling back into balance, floor specialists halted trading in their assigned stocks. They then opened trading at much lower prices in the hopes of rounding up buyers.

In the over-the-counter market, things were much worse. Some market makers refused to answer their telephones while others set their bid prices at ridiculously low prices. In the thinly traded small firm sector of this market, public buy orders were virtually nonexistent. Thus, sellers were forced to deal directly with market makers who dropped their bids into the basement. As a result, small firm stocks took the largest beatings during the next two trading weeks.

To say that small firm stocks reached bargain basement prices is an understatement. Firms with five and ten year records of 25 percent annual growth in sales and earnings were priced at below eight times current earnings at the height of the panic selling. One could find countless small company stocks which at times were selling below five times current earnings and below their per share book values. Investors with cash and a willingness to swim against the tide could have obtained some of the best buys of the century.

SMALL FIRM STOCKS AFTER THE FALL

Small firm stocks take the largest beating during bear markets because trading in their shares is so thin. Sellers generally must deal directly with market makers who lower bids to decrease the risk exposure which accompanies the buildup of their stock inventories. However, once selling pressure abates, market makers raise their asking prices and unload their inventory at a profit. As a result, small firm stocks show their largest gains in the years following bear markets. Figure 12-1 illustrates the gains in small firm stocks which have followed four of the largest bear markets in this century. During the four years after the great bear market of 1929–1932, the Standard & Poor's Composite Index gained 200 percent while small firm stocks gained nearly 600 percent. During the period following the 1962 bear market, small firm stocks outperformed big company stocks by more than two to one. And after the 1973–74 blowout, small firms stocks outperformed the S&P Composite Index by more than four to one!

FIGURE 12-1
Small Firm Stock Returns and Stock Market Rebounds

Year	S&P Composite Index	Small Firm Stocks
Following the 1929–1932 bear market		
1933	54.0%	142.9%
1934	−1.4	24.2
1935	47.7	40.2
1936	33.9	64.8
Total	200%	597%
Following the 1962 bear market		
1963	22.8%	23.6%
1964	16.5	23.5
1965	12.5	41.8
1966	−10.1	− 7.0
Total	44.6%	101.2%
Following the 1973–1974 bear market		
1975	37.2%	52.8%
1976	23.8	57.4
1977	−7.2	25.4
1978	6.6	23.5
Total	67.8%	272.4%
Following the 1987 market crash		
1988	16.8%	22.9%
1989	31.5	10.2
1990	−3.2	−21.6
1991	30.5	44.6
1992	6.1	13.5
Total	105.8%	74.3%

What should you do in a bear market? The inclination of most individual investors is to sell out at any price. However, the best course of action is actually the reverse. During bear markets, the stocks of financially sound growth-poised companies are priced far below their underlying values. Of course, as stock prices drop so does the value of your investment portfolio and you may feel that it is foolish to throw good money after bad. But if you are a long-term-oriented investor who has built a well-diversified portfolio of quality growth companies, buying during market slumps is more like throwing good money after good. Although the stock market is nearly efficient, during panics the degree of efficiency is greatly reduced. Even though bargains are easily recognized, very few investors have the intestinal fortitude to snap them up. This is especially true of those investors who abandoned sound investment practices during runaway bull markets. These investors include those who assumed more risk than they could tolerate, those who held highly concentrated portfolios, those who bought stocks without assessing their underlying values and those who failed to apply sound cash management techniques. These are the investors who were forced to sell and, thus, created bargain basement buying opportunities.

In this book I have outlined sensible methods for investing in small firm growth stocks. I began with a discussion of investment return. The goal was to enable you to set reasonable investment goals. Those investors who set their goals beyond reasonable expectations were those who suffered the greatest losses during the market's decline. In many cases they were the ones who were sold out after failing to meet margin calls. They were also the ones who bailed out at the height of the selling panic and received the lowest prices for their merchandise.

In previous chapters I pointed out the risks of investing and suggested methods of reducing risk without reducing investment return. I urged investors to assess value before making an investment and presented a few simple methods for assessing value. Finally, several chapters were devoted to proper portfolio management techniques. If followed, these techniques would have reduced both investment losses and the anxiety which accompanies stock market panics.

IS CONVENTIONAL WISDOM
STILL APPLICABLE?

After the crash of 1987, I am sure that many investors found little consolation in the fact that for a half-century small firm common stocks returned an *average* of more than 18 percent per year. After all, averages are just *hypothetical* numbers—a synthetic summary of many independent events. It is very difficult to think in terms of a hypothetical average when the reality of the moment is so far afield. Seeing stock prices drop by more than 25 percent during a single trading week makes it very difficult to think in terms of long-run average investment returns.

Before the stock market's October 1987 meltdown, averages made sense. Back then, many investors were looking ahead at a lifetime of investing and a long-run approach to investing made sense. Back then, many investors knew full well that there would be years marked by exceptional investment gains and even exceptional investment losses. However, back then average returns made sense since investors knew that after many years of investing, their portfolios would provide an average gain determined by the risks they had assumed, investment skill and to some extent luck.

Although the rules of successful investing are no different today than they were before October 1987, I suspect that a number of individuals are beginning to question the wisdom of being a long-run investor. After all, isn't the long run nothing more than a series of short runs strung together? And doesn't success in the long run mean surviving a whole series of short runs?

Perhaps if you had heeded the warnings of those who had been predicting a stock market collapse and headed for the sidelines before October 1987, you would have been many dollars ahead. If you were a technician or market timer, perhaps your models would have signaled the impending collapse in time for you to escape the slaughter. If you hadn't assumed any investment risk, the stock market's crushing blow could have been avoided. Treasury bills were yielding much more than the rate of inflation and if you had opted for this "riskless" portfolio, not only would you have been many dollars ahead, you also would have been spared the agony of seeing your best stock picks head for the bargain basement. Thus, shouldn't you now replace conventional wisdom with more contemporary thinking?

The correct answer to this question is a resounding *no!* While chaotic markets cause investors to question the applicability of conventional wisdom, those who continue to practice it become the eventual investment winners. However, following the market crash, investors were bombarded with advertisements placed by securities hucksters who claimed that those who followed their advice would have come away from the market's dive unharmed. And, as you might have guessed, their prescriptions for investment success violate one or more of the tenets of conventional wisdom. Market timers claimed that nimble feet would have allowed you to dodge this bullet. Goldbugs and perennial bears claimed that by concentrating your portfolio in precious metals you would have cut your losses. The implication is that by following their advice in the future, you will be able to escape future market shocks.

My advice is to ignore wild claims of short-run investment success regardless of the direction of the stock market. Remember, the object of investing is not to obtain the greatest rate of return in the short run. The object is to increase the value of your capital over the long run at a rate of return commensurate with the investment risks you have assumed. Now, more than at any other time, avoid the temptation to jump aboard someone's bandwagon merely because they claim to be in the lead shortly after the parade has begun. The best that anyone can do is to make informed, rational investment decisions. And that means relying on conventional wisdom.

WINNING MADE EASY

Investing is an easy game to play, but a hard game to win. It's not that the prescriptions for winning are so complex. Actually, the reverse is true. The game is hard to win because the requirements for winning are so simple. Similar to the New

Math that humorist Tom Lehrer described as being "so simple
. . . that only a child can do it," the requirements for investment
success are so simple that many people refuse to follow them.
Instead they construct elaborate schemes, employ complex trading strategies, and build incomprehensible portfolios. Instead
of maintaining a steady course, they embrace every fad that
comes along. Thinking "If successful investing were so easy, everyone would be rich," they shun the simple and cleave to the
complex.

There are only three requirements for success in the stock
market:

1. Don't overpay.
2. Invest long term.
3. Manage risk.

There are two payments you make when investing. You pay
other investors for their stocks when you buy. You also pay to
conduct business. Some fail to win the investment game even
though they buy only the stocks of good companies. Their
problem is not stock selection, but paying too much. They read
the glowing reports in the financial press, slickly written
brokerage firm research reports, and they're tantalized when
the stocks they're watching make the most actively traded list.
By then, a large percentage of the profit potential in these
stocks has already been squeezed out. In fact, most of these hot
stocks are selling at such high P-E multiples that the whole
risk-reward relationship is unfavorable.

Other investors pay too much to play the game. Transaction
costs erode profits by a significant amount. Suppose for a
moment that you are an average stock picker who takes average
risks and earns average returns. Historically, that's about 12
percent annually, before transaction costs and taxes. Suppose
further, that to obtain this before-cost return you turn over your
portfolio twice a year (i.e., you maintain an average holding
period of six months). If transaction costs average 4 percent on a
round-trip trade, the net return to you is only 4 percent. To earn
the historical market average return, you must garner a 20
percent return—before transaction costs. Even if you turn over

your portfolio only once each year, you still must earn 16 percent annually just to keep pace with someone who buys and holds the market. Because the stock market is quite efficient, the only way to earn an additional 4 percent year after year is to take greater risks. And the additional risks can lead to substantial losses.

The second prescription for investment success is to invest for the long term. Remember, when you invest in common stock you have become an owner of the company, even though you may only hold a small fraction of the firm's outstanding shares. You should treat that investment the same as though you owned the entire company. My guess is that if you owned the entire company you wouldn't be eager to sell it to the first person who offered you 5 or 10 percent more than you paid for it.

Small growth companies must be given time to reach their growth potentials. Often this means buying and holding for five years or more. Take, for example, a firm capable of growing by 20 percent per year. At this rate, the firm will double its size approximately every three and one-half years. If the firm has a current equity capitalization of $50 million, it will become a $200 million company in seven years. Usually, when companies achieve this size, institutional investors with fat checkbooks begin to acquire their stock. If all goes well, you will have earned an average of 20 percent per year for seven years with a bonus thrown in at the end when the institutions begin their buying binge.

Furthermore, by buying and holding you obtain the added advantage of minimizing transaction costs. If your average holding period is less than three years, you are trading too much.

Buying right and holding long term are the building blocks of successful investing. Risk management is the cement that holds them in place. Before you begin investing, you must determine how much risk you are willing and able to take. You then make only those investments that fit this risk profile.

To be successful you must continue to play the game over the long term. Modest annual returns, when allowed to compound over many years, make a significant contribution to your total wealth. Casino operators have made fortunes by taking a modest cut of every bet laid down. Although many players walk away winners, the operators know that when spread out over thousands of bets, the small percentage favoring the house will ultimately make them the biggest winners in town.

As an investor, you can manage risk in much the same way as a casino operator. The percentages favor common stock investors. The stock market is not a zero-sum game. In a zero-sum game, what one player wins another must lose. Even though some stock prices fall never to rise again, the stock market has always moved to higher ground. Stay in the game and you can't lose. But to stay in the game and let the odds work in your behalf, you must spread your cash among many common stocks—you must diversify your portfolio.

These are the prescriptions for investment success. They are not complicated or fancy. In fact many would consider them boring. But that's not all bad. Over the years I have met many people who would gladly trade their investment losses for a little boredom. Although investing might be exciting and fun, it's supposed to be rewarding. If you practice these three fundamentals, you will have all the fun you can handle when you begin to spend the investment wealth that you have accumulated.

You may never get rich investing in the stock market. But by understanding the rules of the game that you have chosen to play, and by adhering to those rules, you can become a great deal wealthier. Know what return you can expect. Manage risk. Seek out those segments of the market neglected by institutional investors and brokerage firm analysts. Manage your portfolio properly. And above all, invest in small firm common stocks. These are the pathways to investment success. And they are easier to travel than many so-called stock market experts would have you believe.

BIBLIOGRAPHY

Amihud, Y., and H. Mendelson. "Asset Returns and the Bid-Asked Spread." *Journal of Financial Economics,* December 1986, pp. 43–48.

———. "Liquidity and Stock Returns." *Financial Analysts Journal,* May–June 1986, pp. 43–48.

Arbel, Avner. "Generic Stocks: An Old Product in a New Package." *Journal of Portfolio Management,* Summer 1985, pp. 4–13.

———. *How to Beat the Market with High-Performance Generic Stocks.* New York: William Morrow and Company, 1985.

Arbel, Avner; Steven Caravell; and Paul Strebel. "Giraffes, Institutions, and Neglected Firms." *Financial Analysts Journal,* May–June 1983, pp. 57–63.

Arbel, Avner, and Paul Strebel. "Pay Attention to Neglected Firms! (Even When They're Large)." *Journal of Portfolio Management,* Winter 1983, pp. 37–42.

———. "The Neglected and Small Firm Effects." *Financial Review,* November 1982, pp. 201–218.

Arditti, Fred D.; Sirri Ayaydin; Ravi K. Mattu; and Stephen Rigsbee. "Mutual Fund Performance and Market Capitalization." *Financial Analysts Journal,* July–August 1986, pp. 63–66.

Ariel, Robert A. "Holiday Market Patterns." *AAII Journal,* May 1987, pp. 8–11.

———. "Monthly Market Patterns." *AAII Journal,* January 1987, pp. 8–11.

Ball, R., and P. Brown. "An Empirical Evaluation of Accounting Income Numbers." *Journal of Accounting Research,* Autumn 1968, pp. 157–78.

Banz, Rolf W., "Limited Diversification and Market Equilibrium: An Empirical Analysis." Ph.D. dissertation, The University of Chicago, 1978.

———. "The Relationship between Return and Market Value of Common Stocks." *Journal of Financial Economics,* March 1981, pp. 3–18.

Basu, Sanjoy. "Investment Performance of Common Stocks in Relation to Their Price Earnings Ratios: A Test of the Efficient Market Hypothesis." *Journal of Finance,* June 1977, pp. 663–82.

————. "The Relationship between Earnings Yield, Market Value, and Return for NYSE Common Stocks: Further Evidence." *Journal of Financial Economics,* June 1983, pp. 19–46.

Bauman, W. Scott. "Investment Experience with Less Popular Common Stocks." *Financial Analysts Journal,* March–April 1964, pp. 79–81.

————. "The Less Popular versus the Most Popular Stocks." *Financial Analysts Journal,* January–February 1965, pp. 61–69.

Beaver, William. "The Information Content of Annual Earnings Announcements." Empirical Research in Accounting: Selected Studies 1968, supplement to the *Journal of Accounting Research,* 1968, pp. 67–92.

Berges, A.; J. McConnell; and G. Schlarbaum. "The Turn-of-the-Year in Canada." *Journal of Finance,* March 1984, pp. 185–92.

Blume, Marshall E.; and R. F. Stambaugh. "Biases in Computed Returns: An Application to the Size Effect." *Journal of Financial Economics,* November 1983, pp. 387–404.

Brown, Philip; Allan W. Kleindon; and Terry A. Marsh. "New Evidence on the Nature of Size-Related Anomalies in Stock Prices." *Journal of Financial Economics,* June 1983, pp. 33–56.

Brown, Philip; D. B. Keim; A. W. Kleindon; and T. A. Marsh. "Stock Return Seasonalities and the Tax-Loss Selling Hypothesis: Analysis of the Arguments and Australian Evidence." *Journal of Financial Economics,* June 1983, pp. 105–127.

Carleton, Willard T., and Josef Lakonishok. "The Size Anomaly: Does Industry Group Matter?" *Journal of Portfolio Management,* Spring 1986, pp. 36–40.

Chan, K. C.; N. Chen; and D. Hsieh. "An Exploratory Investigation of the Firm Size Effect." *Journal of Financial Economics,* September 1985, pp. 451–71.

Chan, K. C., and R. Stephen Sears. "How Many Small Firms Are Enough?" Carbondale: University of Illinois, Bureau of Economic and Business Research, Working Paper 1013, February 1984.

Constantinides, George M. "Optimal Stock Trading with Personal Taxes: Implications for Prices and the Abnormal January Returns." *Journal of Financial Economics,* March 1984, pp. 65–89.

Cook, Thomas J., and Michael Rozeff. "Size, Dividend Yield, and Co-Skewness Effects on Stock Returns: Some Empirical Tests." Iowa City: University of Iowa, Working Paper Series 82–20, June 1982.

————. "Size and Earnings/Price Ratio Anomalies: One Effect or Two?" *Journal of Financial and Quantitative Analysis,* December 1984, pp. 449–66.

Cross, F. "The Behavior of Stock Prices on Fridays and Mondays." *Financial Analysts Journal*, November–December 1973, pp. 67–69.

Dowen, Richard J., and W. Scott Bauman. "A Test of the Relative Importance of Popularity and P/E Ratio in Determining Abnormal Returns." *Journal of the Midwest Finance Association*, 1984, pp. 34–47.

———. "The Relative Importance of Size, P-E and Neglect." *Journal of Portfolio Management*, Spring 1986, pp. 30–34.

Dubofsky, Dave, and John C. Groth. "Relative Information Accessibility for OTC Stocks and Security Returns." *Proceedings of the Financial Management Association National Meeting*, Atlanta, October 1983.

Dubofsky, David A., and Debra K. Reed. "Successful Strategies: A New Look at Small Firms." *AAII Journal*, October 1986, pp. 11–13.

Dyl, E. A. "Capital Gains Taxation and Year-End Stock Market Behavior." *Journal of Finance*, March 1977, pp. 165–75.

Ehrbar, A. F. "Giant Payoffs from Midget Stocks." *Fortune*, June 1980, pp. 111–14.

Fama, Eugene F. "Efficient Capital Markets: A Review of Theory and Empirical Work." *Journal of Finance*, May 1970, pp. 383–417.

———. "The Behavior of Stock Market Prices." *Journal of Business*, January 1965, pp. 34–105.

———. "Random Walks in Stock Market Prices." *Financial Analysts Journal*, September–October 1965.

Fama, E. F.; L. Fisher; M. Jensen; and R. Roll. "The Adjustment of Stock Prices to New Information." *The International Economic Review*, February 1969, pp. 1–21.

Fama, Eugene F., and Marshall E. Blume. "Filter Rules and Stock Market Trading." *Journal of Business*, January 1966, pp. 226–41.

Foster, G. "Stock Market Reaction to Estimates of Earnings per Share by Company Officials." *Journal of Accounting Research*, Spring 1973, pp. 25–37.

French, K. "Stock Returns and the Weekend Effect." *Journal of Financial Economics*, March 1980, pp. 55–69.

Gibbons, M., and P. Hess. "Day of the Week Effects and Asset Returns." *Journal of Business*, October 1981, pp. 579–96.

Givoly, Dan, and Arie Ovadia. "Year-End Tax-Induced Sales and Stock Market Seasonality." *Journal of Finance*, March 1983, pp. 171–86.

Goodman, David A., and John W. Peavy III. "The Interaction of Firm Size and Price-Earnings Ratio on Portfolio Performance." *Financial Analysts Journal*, January–February 1986, pp. 9–12.

———. "The Risk Universal Nature of the P-E Effect." *Journal of Portfolio Management*, Summer 1985, pp. 14–16.

Haugen, Robert A., and Josef Lakonishok. *The Incredible January Effect: The Stock Market's Unsolved Mystery.* Homewood, Ill.: Dow Jones-Irwin, 1987.

Ibbotson, Roger G. *Stocks, Bonds, Bills, and Inflation: 1992 Yearbook.* Chicago: Ibbotson Associates, 1992.

Ibbotson, Roger G.; Laurence B. Siegel; and Kathryn S. Love. *World Wealth: U.S. and Foreign Market Values and Returns.* Chicago: Ibbotson Associates, 1985.

Jaffe, J., and R. Westerfield. "The Weekend Effect in Common Stock Returns: The International Evidence." *Journal of Finance,* June 1985, pp. 433–54.

James, Christopher, and Robert O. Edmister. "The Relation between Common Stock Returns, Trading Activity, and Market Value." *Journal of Finance,* September 1983, pp. 1075–86.

Jensen, M., and R. Litzenberger. "Quarterly Earnings Reports and Intermediate Stock Price Trends." *Journal of Finance,* March 1970, pp. 143–48.

Kato, K., and J. S. Schallheim. "Seasonal and Size Anomalies in the Japanese Stock Market." *Journal of Financial and Quantitative Analysis,* June 1985, pp. 243–57.

Keane, Simon M. "The Efficient Market Hypothesis on Trial." *Financial Analysts Journal,* March–April 1986, pp. 58–63.

Keim, D. B. "The CAPM and Equity Return Regularities." *Financial Analysts Journal,* May–June 1986, pp. 19–34.

————. "Dividend Yields and Stock Returns: Implications of Abnormal January Returns." *Journal of Financial Economics,* September 1985, pp. 473–89.

————. "Dividend Yields and the January Effect." *Journal of Portfolio Management,* Winter 1986, pp. 54–60.

————. "Size-Related Anomalies and Stock Return Seasonality: Further Empirical Evidence." *Journal of Financial Economics,* June 1983, pp. 13–32.

Keim, D. B., and R. F. Stambough. "A Further Investigation of the Weekend Effect in Stock Prices." *Journal of Finance,* July 1984, pp. 883–89.

Kraus, A., and H. Stoll. "Price Impact on Block Trading on the New York Stock Exchange." *Journal of Finance,* June 1972, pp. 569–88.

Lakonishok, Josef, and M. Levi. "Weekend Effects on Stock Returns: A Note." *Journal of Finance,* June 1982, pp. 883–89.

Lakonishok, Josef, and Alan Shapiro. "Stock Returns, Beta, Variance, and Size: An Empirical Analysis." *Financial Analysts Journal,* July–August 1984, pp. 36–42.

Lakonishok, Josef, and Seymour Smidt. "Trading Bargains in Small Firms at Year-End." *Journal of Portfolio Management,* Spring 1986, pp. 24–29.

Loeb, Thomas F. "Trading Cost: The Critical Link between Investment Information and Results." *Financial Analysts Journal,* May–June 1983, pp. 39–44.

Madden, Gerald P.; Kenneth P. Nunn, Jr.; and Alan Wiemann. "Mutual Fund Performance and Market Capitalization." *Financial Analysts Journal,* July–August 1986, pp. 67–70.

Osborne, M. F. M. "Brownian Motion in the Stock Market." *Operations Research,* March–April 1959, pp. 145–73.

Pari, Robert, and Son-Nan Chen. "A Reexamination of the Small Firm Effect Using Mean Adjusted Returns." *Proceedings of the Financial Management Association National Meeting,* Atlanta, October 1983.

Peavy, John W., and David A. Goodman. "The Significance of P-Es for Portfolio Returns." *Journal of Portfolio Management,* Winter 1983, pp. 43–47.

Perritt, Gerald W. "A Year-End Reward." *Forbes,* 7 December 1992, p. 125.

Perritt, Gerald W. "Capturing the Small Firm Effect." *Forbes,* 4 January 1993, p. 285.

Perritt, Gerald W. "Roses Without Thorns." *Forbes,* 14 September 1992, p. 558.

Pettengil, Glenn N. "Persistent Seasonal Return Patterns." *The Financial Review,* November 1985, pp. 271–86.

Pettit, R. "Dividend Announcements, Security Performances, and Capital Market Efficiency." *Journal of Finance,* December 1972, pp. 993–1007.

Reinganum, Marc R. "A Direct Test of Roll's Conjecture on the Firm Size Effect." *Journal of Finance,* March 1982, pp. 27–35.

———. "Misspecification of Capital Asset Pricing: Empirical Anomalies Based on Earnings Yields and Market Values." *Journal of Financial Economics,* March 1981, pp. 19–46.

———. "Portfolio Strategies Based on Market Capitalization." *Journal of Portfolio Management,* Winter 1983, pp. 29–36.

———. "The Anomalous Stock Market Behavior of Small Firms in January: Empirical Tests for Tax-Selling Effects." *Journal of Financial Economics,* June 1983, pp. 89–104.

Reinganum, Marc R., and Alan C. Shapiro. "Taxes and Stock Return Seasonality: Evidence from the London Stock Exchange." Graduate School of Business, University of Southern California, September 1983.

Roberts, Harry V. "Stock Market 'Patterns' and Financial Analysis: Methodological Suggestions." *Journal of Finance,* March 1959, pp. 1–10.

Rogalski, R. "New Findings Regarding Day of the Week Returns Over Trading and Nontrading Periods: A Note." *Journal of Finance,* December 1984, pp. 1603–1614.

Roll, Richard. "A Possible Explanation of the Small Firm Effect." *Journal of Finance,* September 1981, pp. 879–88.

―――. "Vas Ist Das? The Turn-of-the-Year Effect and the Return Premia of Small Firms." *Journal of Portfolio Management,* Winter 1983, pp. 18–28.

―――. "On Computing Mean Returns and the Small Firm Premium." *Journal of Financial Economics,* June 1983, pp. 371–86.

Rosenberg, B., K. Reid, and Lanstein. "Persuasive Evidence of Market Inefficiency." *Journal of Portfolio Management,* Spring 1985, pp. 9–16.

Rozeff, M. S., and W. R. Kinney, Jr. "Capital Market Seasonality: The Case of Stock Returns." *Journal of Financial Economics,* October 1976, pp. 379–402.

Schultz, Paul. "Transaction Costs and the Small Firm Effect: A Comment." *Journal of Financial Economics,* June 1983, pp. 81–88.

Schwert, William G. "Size and Stock Returns, and Other Empirical Regularities." *Journal of Financial Economics,* June 1983, pp. 3–12.

Stoll, Hans R., and Robert E. Whaley. "Transactions Costs and the Small Firm Effect." *Journal of Financial Economics,* June 1983, pp. 57–80.

INDEX

A

AAA-rated bonds, 78-82
Acquisitions, 245
  and sale of small firm stocks, 206
Aggressive growth small-cap funds, 239
Alger, Fred, 58
Alpha, 95n, 112, 229-30
Amihud, Yakov, 111
Annual average return, on S&P Index, 1953-1992, 15
Arbel, Avner, 106-7, 109
Ariel, Robert, 158, 161-62, 164
Ask price, 111
Athey, Preston, 242
AT&T, 207, 226

B

Babson Enterprise Fund, 240
Babson Shadow Stock, 240
Ball, Roy, 57
Banz, Rolf, 58, 94-95, 97, 121, 143, 224-25, 232
Bar chart, 50
Basu, Sanjoy, 166-69
Bauman, Scott, 105-6
Bear market
  firm size in, 121
  investment strategy for, 252
  lessons of the great, 203
  of 1956-58, 84
  of 1961-62, 84
  of 1966, 84
  of 1968-70, 84

of 1973-74, 22, 84
of 1980-82, 84
of 1987, 84
opportunities offered by, 204
P-E ratio in, 83-84
small firm stocks following, 250-51
start of, 83
stock prices in, 83
Beaver, William, 57
Beta
  definition of, 178
  mathematical relationship between required rate of return and, 73-74
  for measuring risk, 32, 34-39, 82, 100, 201
  in setting investment policy, 177, 179
  and value estimates, 83
Bid-ask spread, 103
  definition of, 111
  and small firm effect, 111-12, 226-27
Bid price, 111
Boesky, Ivan, 52
Bond market, 245-46
Bond yield, and inflation, 84
Brokerage firms, resident technicians at, 54-55
Brown, Philip, 57
Buffet, Warren, 58
Bull market
  firm size in, 121
  of 1921-29, 244
  of 1949-56, 244
  of 1982-87, 244-45, 247